Advance praise for *Spiritual Trusts*

Had the *Spiritual Trust System* been available when my family needed it all those years ago, how different our lives would have been today. This system is clear, concise and motivated by one principle...love. Do it for yourself. Do it for your loved ones. But do it.

Deirdre Felton, M.A.
National Lecturer

This book will not just bless your life now, it is a blessing for future generations. I think everyone should have a *Spiritual Trust* to pass down to their family.

Douglas Weiss, LPC
Author of "Intimacy: A 100 Day Guide to Lasting Relationships"
Executive Director, Heart to Heart Counseling Center

Spiritual Trusts is a practical guide that opened up a whole new world of possibilities for influencing the spiritual lives of my children, grandchildren, and extended family. This is one of the most innovative ideas I have come across in more than 40 years of helping families grow together spiritually.

Jack N. Pape, D.Min., Minister

My perspective of the ability to utilize the power of foresight is forever changed! *Spiritual Trusts* is an exceptional book that shows us how to create and implement a spiritual vision and legacy for our loved ones. *Spiritual Trusts* is a joyous and practical book for families, clergy, and counselors alike.

Steven Earll, MA, MS, LPC, LAC
Author and counselor

In 25 years of working with bereaved people, I've never seen a more creative and spiritually innovative idea than the pioneering concepts that *Spiritual Trusts* offers. I will waste no time in implementing this system as a unique gift to my own loved ones after I'm gone.

Andrea Gambill,
Founder of Bereavement magazine.

Most often we believe our sphere of influence upon family and friends ends at the time of death. The *Spiritual Trust System* opens the door for every believer to extend their influence to generations to come. This outstanding writing presents the incredible possibilities of being a witness beyond the grave.

Pastor Jim Kunes, M.Div.

My Dad died when I was almost four. I never got to know him. I never will. Even though I have worked professionally with children and families for over 20 years, and know all the right "rhetoric" and "treatment modalities" for the grieving...nothing will stop the simple, painful truth that I just wish I could have known my Dad in some way. The pain of that deficit will never be healed or it's space filled. How different my life could have been if he would have been able to implement even a few of the concepts in this book. My wife Becky and I have already started putting this book to practice so our five children will never have to experience the lifetime of aching curiosity
that I have endured.

David Dennis, LPC, LMFT,
Assistant Executive Director, Devereux Foundation, Florida.

These are some of the most authentic ideas you will ever read on leaving a godly inheritance. Applying these concepts into your daily walk will give you peace of mind like you have never experienced.

Pastor Jay Hawpe

This is the best book ever written by anyone.

Mom

Copyright page

Author's note: Many of the specific examples in this book are fictitious and are created from composites of clients who have utilized aspects of this system. In many cases the names and identifying information have been changed to protect confidentiality when deemed necessary.

Edited by Carolyn Acheson
Cover design by Amy Dooley
Interior design by Jamie Dodd

Unless otherwise noted, all scripture quotations are from the
NEW AMERICAN STANDARD BIBLE®, Copyright
©1960,1962,1963,1968,1971,1972,1973,1975,
1977,1995 by The Lockman Foundation. Used by permission.

Scripture quotations marked (NIV) are taken from the
HOLY BIBLE, NEW INTERNATIONAL VERSION®.
NIV®. Copyright©1973, 1978, 1984 by International Bible Society. Used by permission of Zondervan. All rights reserved.

Printed in the United States of America

Copyright© 2001 by Darin Manis and Dr. Milton Smith (All rights reserved.)

No part of this book may be reproduced without written permission except for brief quotations in books and critical reviews. If quotations from this book are used in print, in any form, forward to "Faith Press." For information, write Faith Press, 2330 Pin High Court, Colorado Springs CO, 80907. Or call 1-866-999-5433.

Library of Congress Catalog Card Number: 2002094893
Internationl Standard Book Number: 0-9724288-0-1

Acknowledgements

To my Lord and Savior for saving a wretched soul like me.

To my wife and children who have been my inspiration and encouragers.

To Mark Brown whose support helps make this System possible.

To all of the professionals and clients who have lent their expertise and experiences.

To Dr. Milton "Skip" Smith who has been my friend, partner and contributing author in the creation and implementation of the Spiritual Trust System.

Chapter Overview

Part I - Types of Spiritual Trusts

Chapter One	The Spiritual Trust System: An Overview
Chapter Two	Support Trusts
Chapter Three	Prayer Trusts
Chapter Four	Legacy Trusts
Chapter Five	Stewardship Trusts

Part II - Developing and Implementing Your Spiritual Trusts

Chapter Six	The Four-Step Process
Chapter Seven	Selection
Chapter Eight	Creation
Chapter Nine	Storage
Chapter Ten	Delivery

Appendix A - Trust Directives Forms

Appendix B - Work in Progress Form

Appendix C - Life Questions and Statements

Glossary of Terms

Index

Contents

Foward. . . . .*xiii*

Introduction. . . . .*xvii*

Part One: Types of Spiritual Trusts. 1

1. **The Spiritual Trust System: An Overview**. 3

   Characteristics of Spiritual Trusts   3
   Kinds of Spiritual Trusts   4
      Support Trust   5
      Prayer Trust   6
      Legacy Trust   6
      Stewardship Trust   7
      Developing and Implementing Your Spiritual Trust   7
   A Spiritual Mindset   8

2. **Support Trusts**. 11

   What Is a Support Trust?   12
   Dealing With Death   12
   Experiencing Grief and Bereavement   14
   A Support Trust in Action   16
   How the Family Experiences Death   18
   Phases of Grief   19
   Evaluating Your Family   21
   Spiritual Support Methods   22
      Initial Support   22
      Bereavement Support   38
      Ongoing Support   53
   Double Trouble   61
   Resources for Your Family   62

3. **Prayer Trusts**. 69

   What is a Prayer Trust?   69

Divine Authority to Create a Prayer Trust   70
Meet Mary   71
The "Who" of Prayer Trusts   71
The "What" of Prayer Trusts   72
   Spiritual and Emotional Comfort and Strength   72
   Protection   72
   Salvation   73
   Blessings   74
   All Good Things   75
Prayer Partners   76
   The Micro Method   77
   The Macro Method   78
   Your Prayer Partners Quality and Quantity   79
   Supporting Your Prayer Partners   80
When to Initiate Prayers Through Your Prayer Trust   81
   Initial Prayer Support   81
   Bereavement Prayer Support   83
   Ongoing Prayer Support   86

4. Legacy Trusts.............................91

What is a Legacy Trust?   92
The Moral Need for Your Legacy Trust   93
How Will You be Remembered?   94
Types of Legacy Trusts   95
Your Heritage   96
   LifeStories   98
   A Story of Your Living Parents and Grandparents   105
   LifeTributes   106
Your Messages   108
   Benchmark Deliveries   108
   Legacy Journals   117
   Albums and Scrapbooks   122
   Generational Witnessing   123
Living Your Legacy   125

5. Stewardship Trusts........................127

The Need for Spiritual Stewardship   129
What Does the Bible Say?   130
   Materialism and Consumption   132
   Are You Rich?   133
   An Investment Tip for You From Jesus   134
   Ouch-That Hurts   135
   Giving Patterns   136

        Is God Short on Cash?   *136*
        Saving versus Hoarding   *138*
   Stewardship and Your Family   139
   Spiritual Philanthropy   139
        Your Spiritual Portfolio   *140*
   Spiritual Investments   141
   Giving Through Spiritual Investments   142
   Stewardship Trust Investment Options   143
        The Needs   *144*
        Paths by Which You Can Further the Lord's Work   *148*
        Spiritual Mutual Funds   *151*
   Funding Your Stewardship Trust   151
        Stewardship and Taxes   *152*
        Funding Spiritual Investments During Your Life   *153*
        Funding Spiritual Investments at Death   *155*

Part Two: Developing and Implementing Your Spiritual Trust....................165

6. The Four Step Process.......................167

   A Step at a Time   167
   The Plan   168

7. Step 1: Selection........................171

   Your Recipients   172
   Your Components   173

8. Step 2: Creation.........................177

   The Creation Process   177
     Outline   *178*
     Draft   *178*
     Revise   *180*
     Compose   *180*
     Finalize   *181*
     Ongoing Entries   *182*
   Trust Media Tools   182
     Video   *183*
     Written or Typed Words   *191*
     Images and Photographs   *194*
   Creating Your LifeStory   197

Visual Aids 198
Dealing with Painful Memories 198
Outlining Your Life Chapters 199

9. **Step 3: Storage** 201

Archiving the Trust 202
Digital Preservation 203
Other Preservation Tips 205
Making Copies 212
Store the Trust in an Appropriate Container and Location 213
Using a Trust Box 213
Selecting Appropriate Storage Locations 214
Safety Deposit Box 214
Trust Institutions 216

10. **Step 4: Delivery** 219

Your Trust Directives 219
The Delivery Options 220
Option One: Surprise! 220
Option Two: Pre-Delivery or Personal Delivery 221
Option Three: In-House 222
Option Four: Executor 222
Executor Request Outline 226
Contingency Plans 231
Alternative Executors 231
Alternative Recipients 232
Funding for Your Executor(s) 232
Life Insurance 233
Bank Options 233
Cash 234

Appendix A-Trust Directives 236

Appendix B-Work in Progress Form 252

Appendix C-Life Questions and Statements 254

Glossary of Terms 269

Index 279

Forward

Welcome to a new way of experiencing and deepening your faith — the Spiritual Trust™ System. Through this System you can influence the spiritual existence of your loved ones during your lifetime and long after your life on earth is over. As you follow the Spiritual Trust System, your faith will grow and envelop your family in the spiritual realm, just as financial trusts and life insurance provide for your family in the physical realm. In short, the Spiritual Trust System is an expression of your foresight, faith, and love transcending your life on earth.

One of the first conversations I had about the need for Spiritual Trusts was with my neighbor, confidant, and dear friend. His wife and children have become close to my family over the years, and we have spent many evenings together. One autumn evening Brent and I were on his deck while our wives visited and our children played together inside. He occasionally checked the meat and poultry we were grilling while we watched the magnificent Colorado mountain skyline starting to fade into dusk. Our conversation went something like this:

Me: Brent, what kind of provisions have you made for Shannon and the kids in case of your untimely demise?

Brent: (with a smile) Demise? Do you know something I don't?

Me: Not as far as you know. But seriously, what provisions have you made?

Brent: (after a moment of thought) Well, I have life insurance and a trust to financially provide for my family.

Me: Do you think you're going to die anytime soon?

Brent: No, God willing (as he looked at me strangely).

Me: Why have you made these financial provisions if you don't think you're going to die soon?

Brent: I haven't received any guarantees, and no one knows when it's their day.

Me: Do you think that providing your family with *financial* support is the most important thing you can do for your family right now?

Brent: It's certainly an important responsibility.

Me: (nodding) Do you believe the *spiritual* support you provide your family is more important than your *financial* support?

Brent: Of course it is.

Me: Would you be willing to sell the spiritual well-being of your wife and children for any amount of financial benefit?

Brent: (quickly and firmly) No, of course not!

Me: What kind of arrangements have you made to help support your wife and kids *spiritually* if you die?

Brent: (long pause) …

Me: If financially supporting your family isn't the most important way you support your family in *life*, why is it the *only* kind of support you are arranging for your family in death?

Brent: Because it's the only kind of support I know *how* to provide.

Me: Brent, if something were to happen to you, how do you think Elizabeth [his youngest daughter] will remember you?

Brent: (pause) Well, I hope she'll have memories of me. There are pictures of us, and you know how much I use my video camera.

Me: That's great, but how will she be able to connect with the essence of "Brent?"

Brent: I guess by hearing about me from her mom.

Me: I'm sure she will, but if you die tomorrow, wouldn't you like to be able to talk to her yourself? Tell her about things from your perspective? Wouldn't you want to pass on the insight you've gleaned from your life experiences and share it with her when she turns sixteen, or graduates, or gets married or has children of her own?

Brent: Yeah, but I can't really do that if I'm dead, now can I?

Me: Well Brent, actually you can. You can spiritually and emotionally support your family and continue to communicate with them long after your death by preparing messages now.

If financially supporting your family isn't the most important way you support your family in life, why is it the only kind of support you are arranging for your family in death?

This book was written for those of you, like Brent, who would like to continue to provide emotional and spiritual support to your family after your death, but just don't know how. In addition, if you would like to be intimately remembered by your loved ones years, decades, and even generations after you're not around anymore, this book will show you how.

Grab your Bible and step outside of the box with me for the few hours it takes to read this book. Put on your seat belts and get ready for a ride into the spiritual future of your loved ones.

And God bless you.

Introduction

This book is designed for those who take their spiritual responsibilities seriously during their life and desire to carry on their spiritual objectives after their death. It is a guide that offers powerful concepts, precepts, and tools for changing and influencing spiritual realities — and the means to carry them out.

Anyone can create a Spiritual Trust. You need only the foresight, love, faith, commitment of time, and knowledge to do so. This book will give you the knowledge base to establish your own Spiritual Trusts, which you can expand using your own creativity, imagination, and personal situations and circumstances. Just reading this book can change your perceptions of your spiritual potential. After reading it, I hope you will have the desire and motivation to get started. It's not hard, and most likely you will find it enjoyable and rewarding.

Creating Spiritual Trusts can change your life, and it can change the lives of your loved ones — your family members and future family members, children of God whom you have yet to meet. This System will support your family spiritually in this generation and for generations to follow. But Spiritual Trusts do not just benefit the recipients. You, too, will reap rewards today from what you have set in motion for the future. This book is not just about changing the spiritual realities of tomorrow. It is about living a more spirit-filled life *today*.

The joy and peace that come from establishing Spiritual Trusts are overwhelming. You will experience a peace of mind that providing financial support alone cannot match. To know that an array of spiritually positive things is going to continue to happen long after your death is comforting. To know that you are going to be remembered in a special way by your loved ones and descendants is exhilarating. Implementing this System can bring your faith alive in a unique and fulfilling way.

This book is for mothers, fathers, couples, grandparents and children, the young and old, healthy and sick, men and women — anyone can create a Spiritual Trust, and virtually anyone is a candidate to receive someone's Trust. For married couples, creating Spiritual Trusts together is a great way to learn more about each other. It will likely raise issues that the couple have not discussed with each other before and, in doing so, increase intimacy through the mutual sharing and expression involved in creating and implementing these kinds of Trusts.

Working on Spiritual Trusts as part of a small group — family, friends, or church group — dedicated to the process can be fun and rewarding. Or creating Spiritual Trusts yourself can be an invigorating exploration of your life and being.

If you believe the concepts of the Spiritual Trust System have merit, and want to utilize this System for the benefit of you and your loved ones, *action* will be necessary. Apply the "Noah rule," which simply states that predicting rain doesn't count — building arks does.

The Noah Rule: Predicting rain doesn't count — building arks does.

Many people benefit from reading books that tell or show them how to do things — self-help books. Others are momentarily inspired by books they read but never integrate the truths into their lives. In reading this book, you will be entertained and informed, but above all, I pray that you will be inspired to create your own Spiritual Trusts. Foresight and good intentions alone will not influence the spiritual lives of your spouse, children, grandchildren, and their descendants in the future. The Spiritual Trust System is a call to action. You must actually do something to create your Trusts.

But just remember — Noah built the Ark one plank at a time. As you read this book, evaluate the components and determine which is the most important to do first, given your situation and that of your family. See that component through to completion. Then move to the next.

Part I of this book explains the four key types of Spiritual Trusts you can create: Support Trusts, Prayer Trusts, Legacy Trusts, and Stewardship Trusts. Part II gives you the specific information you need to take action. It covers how to select your Trust components and recipients, how to create Trust components, and how to arrange for the safe storage and future delivery of the Spiritual Trusts you create.

Although the information in this book is sufficient for most people to prepare their own Spiritual Trusts, some may desire additional help. I founded a company called FaithMessages™ to provide this kind of assistance. We have Spiritual Trust Workbooks to walk you through the step-by-step details of creating Spiritual Trusts. These are especially helpful in small groups — which, by the way, can motivate even the worst procrastinator! Or, if you need, consider contacting one of our consultants, who will guide you through any step of the process with which you seek help.

I encourage you to visit our website for additional resources, other helpful information, new ideas and many other examples. You can find us at www.spiritualtrusts.com.

Part I

Types of Spiritual Trusts

Part I of this book explains the four key types of Spiritual Trusts you can create.

- **Support Trust:** Use these powerful precepts to provide for your family in the spiritual and emotional realms in the way that financial trusts and life insurance provide for your family in the physical realm. Your Support Trust establishes "spiritual life insurance" for the benefit of your loved ones.

- **Prayer Trust:** Harness the power of prayer in unique ways. Protect, support and encourage those you love by arranging for prayer partners to continue to pray for your family during significant future milestones even if you are no longer here to do so yourself.

- **Legacy Trust:** Leave a godly inheritance by capturing the essence of who you are, what is important to you, and what you want to tell your family and descendents about your life and faith through a message or series of messages. Learn how to water the spiritual seeds you have planted in life, after your death.

- **Stewardship Trust:** Use spiritual investing principles to convert portions of your temporary financial portfolio—whatever the size—into your eternal spiritual portfolio based upon kingdom currency. Use this Trust to become a spiritual philanthropist.

Spiritual Trusts

These Trusts represent a major planning tool that will change the lives of your loved ones. Not everyone will want to undertake every aspect of the Spiritual Trust System, but you will find many components from which to pick and choose.

ONE

The Spiritual Trust System: An Overview

Although living *today* for Christ is paramount, the Spiritual Trust System is an expansive way of looking at the spiritual life that extends past the self and the present into the hearts of others, even after death.

CHARACTERISTICS OF SPIRITUAL TRUSTS

A Spiritual Trust is an expression of your foresight, faith and love that transcends your life on earth. A Spiritual Trust invests a sum of spiritual wealth that supports your family and others both when you are alive and in the event of your death. The physical manifestation is a collection of deposited messages and directives of future actions.

Spiritual Trusts are tangible, physical trusts for spiritual purposes. They are designed primarily to influence spiritual realities, not physical ones. Thus, the rewards and benefits of Spiritual Trusts are primarily spiritual in nature.

A Spiritual Trust provides for your family in the spiritual and emotional realms in the way that financial or monetary trusts and life insurance provide for your family in the physical realm. This is the avenue by which you can pass on the spiritual insight, wisdom, and knowledge you have accrued throughout your life. It is, in essence, your "spiritual life insurance."

> A Spiritual Trust provides for your family
> in the spiritual and emotional realms
> in the way financial or monetary trusts
> and life insurance provide for your family
> in the physical realm.

Although some components of a Spiritual Trust may be communicated while you are alive, others are held in safekeeping until your passing. Like most financial trusts, you can supplement them whenever you choose. Also, like financial trusts, when you die, the proceeds of the Trust are distributed to your chosen recipients, held for future delivery, or both.

You cannot honestly create Spiritual Trusts without examining your own life. You will find yourself evaluating your convictions and beliefs. Creating a Spiritual Trust is a means of strengthening your own faith by articulating that faith to those whose salvation is important to you. This process will propel you into a deeper spiritual journey full of rewards and personal revelations.

> Creating a Spiritual Trust is a means of
> strengthening your own faith by articulating that
> faith to those whose salvation is important to you.

By concentrating on the principles you advocate in your Spiritual Trusts, you will stay focused on the spiritual realities, both present and future, that are important to you. As you place spiritual principles in your Spiritual Trusts, you recommit your life to those principles.

KINDS OF SPIRITUAL TRUSTS

Although the possible variations of Spiritual Trusts are innumerable, most can be categorized into four primary types: Support Trusts, Prayer Trusts, Legacy Trusts, and Stewardship Trusts. Each component introduced in this chapter is followed by a chapter of its own. You can create a Spiritual Trust in separate components, or you can mix and match aspects of different Trust components into your own, personalized Spiritual Trust customized for you and your family. The components have a symbiotic effect: The power and benefits of each are increased exponentially when they are used in conjunction with each other.

Because every person is at a different point in their spiritual and physical life, your own situation will determine what kinds of Spiritual Trusts you will create and the timing of their creation. Many examples appear throughout this book. Excerpts from existing Spiritual Trusts will show you how others are advancing their spiritual legacies. As you review the highlights of each, imagine the positive impact it can have on *your* family and descendants.

Support Trust

The support precepts in this book are founded on the example of the life and death of Jesus Christ, the ultimate example of one who lived his life with eternity in mind. Jesus spent considerable time preparing those closest to him for his death. He even took extraordinary measures to spiritually and emotionally support those closest to Him *after* his death. We can attempt to be Christlike in living with eternity in mind, and can provide those closest to us with spiritual and emotional support after our death.

Obviously we do not have the power of Jesus to come back from the dead and visit those we love in person as He did. Nevertheless, we do have the power to communicate and share with them through the Spiritual Trust System.

Support Trusts will empower you to:

- Provide emotional and spiritual support to your grieving family after your death through eulogies, byeulogies and other messages. This helps to provide closure and healing benefits while securing your memories into the hearts of others in a special way.

- Help keep members of your family from experiencing a crisis of faith as a consequence of your passing.

- Send messages for special occasions such as your wedding anniversary and your spouse's birthday, as well as each child's birthday, engagement, marriage, first child, and so on.

Spiritual Trusts

Prayer Trust

A Prayer Trust uses foresight to harness the power of prayer for the support, protection, and benefit of your family. You obtain prayer partners who agree to pray for specific prayer requests you have for your family at certain benchmarks or milestones after your death. In short, your Prayer Trust is your "prayer coverage policy" for your loved ones.

Prayer Trusts allow you to:

- Harness the power of prayer in unique ways that will protect and support those you love for years to come.

- Arrange for a multitude of prayer partners to be praying for your family during times of grief and other specific times, long after you are gone.

- Include "reminders" to friends to pray for your family at certain benchmarks in their lives.

Legacy Trust

The Bible is filled with examples of godly men and women whose legacies have impacted billions of people around the world for thousands of years. Although you likely will not have an impact on billions of people, you *can* influence and shape the lives and paths of *your* loved ones and the future members of *your* family.

Legacy Trusts enable you to:

- Leave a Godly inheritance by conveying what is important to your faith and life in a series of written, audio, or video messages capturing the essence of who you are.

- Plant spiritual seeds now by professing and explaining your faith to your family, friends, associates, and nonbelievers. Water the spiritual seeds you have planted during life, after your death.

- Use generational witnessing techniques to witness to your family for generations to come!

Stewardship Trust

Stewardship is discussed in the Bible more than any other subject. Our stewardship of what God has given us is an integral part of our spirituality. A Stewardship Trust is a spiritual application of financial planning. There are two kinds of portfolios, one financial and the other spiritual. Financial portfolios consist of everything we own on earth. A spiritual portfolio consists of "kingdom currency" — rewards, promises, blessings, crowns, and the like — that we receive after we die.

With your Stewardship Trusts you can:

- Convert a portion of your temporary financial portfolio into your eternal spiritual portfolio through spiritual investing and spiritual mutual funds.

- Inject thousands of dollars (and more) into the financial mission of the Lord through the work of churches and ministries.

- Become a prolific spiritual philanthropist no matter what your current financial situation.

Developing and Implementing Your Spiritual Trusts

An integral part of the Spiritual Trust System is the systematic development and implementation of your Spiritual Trusts. This is addressed in Part II and it involves a four-step process. In step one you *select* which Spiritual Trusts you want to create and whom you will create them for. In step two, you *create* your Trusts with a variety of media tool options from pen and paper to voice and video recordings. In step three, you *store* your Trust in ways that assure their preservation until they are delivered to your recipients. In step four, you select a Spiritual Trust executor and prepare your Trust Directives, a written form that explains when, where, and how you want your Trusts delivered. Although this process may sound difficult, most Trusts can be developed and implemented with relative ease. The System really works!

A SPIRITUAL MINDSET

> "For those who are according to the flesh set their minds on the things of the flesh, but those who are according to the Spirit, the things of the Spirit." *Romans 8:5*

A Spiritual Trust is not just a state of mind; it is the physical application of a spiritual mindset. This System deals with issues of life and death from the spiritual perspective. It teaches how Spiritual Trusts can be utilized to unleash the power of God and the protection and wisdom of the Holy Spirit.

In our culture, the topic of death and dying is often taboo. Apart from Jesus, death *is* bleak and final. But to avoid thinking about death is to avoid thinking about the consequences of life. This attitude ignores reality and furthermore is not Biblical. The Spiritual Trust System, in contrast, is based on faith, hope, love, and eternal life. Therefore, I have no qualms about being frank and to the point concerning the issues of life and death, which Chapter 2 deals with in more depth.

As believers, we should not fear for our lives (2 *Corinthians* 5:8). We have within us a power mightier than death. We are saved, our eternal life secured. Our human, physical, fragile bodies will die someday, but our soul will live on. We can use that spiritual knowledge to help our families after we're gone.

As humans, we all know we're going to die at some point. We see the evidence all around us in car wrecks, cancer, heart attacks, murders, war, plane crashes, terrorism, and on and on.

People are constantly dying all around us. I have yet to watch the news and *not* hear of the death of someone who was in the wrong place at the wrong time. I have never seen an obituary page stating, "There are no entries for today." In fact, about 6,000 Americans died this very day. I am willing to bet that most of them didn't know they would be dying today. I am sure most of them thought they were going to be around on this earth longer, if not a lot longer.

A Spiritual Trust is not just a state of mind; it is a physical application of a spiritual mindset.

It is an ironic blessing that the microscopic amount of time we spend on earth will determine were we spend eternity. This short window of time is critical because so much is at stake.

Recall the man in the parable that Jesus relates in *Luke* 16:19–31. This rich man died and was in Hades. He remembered who his brothers were and, furthermore, was deeply concerned about them. He was willing never to see them again if only they would not join him in that place. He wanted to get a message to his family, but of course he could not.

Now try to think of your own family members as he did, after you die, but from paradise, knowing that you had not yet finished sharing your faith with them when you left. Through your Spiritual Trusts, you can have many conversations with your loved ones for many years after your death.

If you have a life-threatening illness or if someone you love does, you likely will find it easier to visualize the impact these Trusts will have on your family. Grasping the power of this System is usually easier for those who do not need a telescope to see the end coming. If you are healthy, you still do not have any guaranteed lease on life.

Embracing the truth that you may die, unpredictably, at any time, keeps things in perspective. It will keep you from taking your family and friends for granted. It will keep you from taking the grace of God for granted. It will keep you focused on the essential and fundamental things in life. It certainly will keep the spark ignited in your prayer life. Living through this perspective, with eternity in mind, is the objective of the Spiritual Trust System.

TWO

Support Trusts

"It ought to be the business of everyday to prepare for our last day."
— Matthew Henry[1]

Life is fragile and uncertain. Some people are more acutely aware of this because of a life-threatening illness. For others, it is a big question that will not be answered until the very day or moment of death. Yet, that time inevitably arrives for everyone. When it does, the burdens and stress on the surviving family are enormous. If you would like to provide spiritual and emotional support to your spouse, children, and grandchildren when your time comes, whether you are healthy or ill, young or old, you are a candidate for a Support Trust. A central aspect of support — prayer — is covered in Chapter 3, Prayer Trusts. Other aspects of support are covered here.

This chapter may be the most difficult of the chapters in this book for you because it deals head-on with the emotions surrounding grief and loss, and most people, including believers, tend to avoid thinking about and facing mortality. We have no reason to avoid the topic. The Bible establishes that through Jesus we have eternal life, and that belief provides the motivation for the Spiritual Trust System.

Support Trusts are designed to be delivered and implemented after death. I deal bluntly with the possibility that you, the reader, will be the first in your immediate family to die. With your Support Trust, you will find comfort in knowing that you have provided far more than just financial support for your family after your death.

Whether your death is anticipated, as the result of a life-threatening illness, or is completely unexpected, your Support Trust will benefit your family tremendously. If you have a life-threatening illness, a Support Trust offers a wonderful opportunity to prepare living messages and other support. If you die unexpectedly, the benefits that your Support Trust provides might be even more crucial because your family members will have had no time to prepare for or adjust to the thought of living life without you. Moreover, you will have had no time to communicate your final thoughts and wishes to them.

WHAT IS A SUPPORT TRUST?

A Support Trust is a means for you to provide emotional and spiritual support for your family in the event of your death. You create your Trust, properly store it, and when you pass away, your chosen executor delivers the Trust contents according to your directions and instructions.

Leaving your family prepared and supported through a Support Trust is a loving act of compassion. It reflects that you are at least as concerned with spiritual support for your family as you are with financial support such as life insurance.

Money is certainly not the most important thing in the world. Would you sell the spiritual well-being of your family for any amount of money? Of course not! If money is not the most important kind of support we provide for our families in life, why would it be the only kind of support we provide at our death?

DEALING WITH DEATH

"Not talking about death won't postpone it an instant. Talking about death won't bring it a moment closer. But it will give us the opportunity to be better prepared for what surely lies ahead."
— Randy Alcorn[2]

If we are to take responsibility for providing spiritual and emotional support after our death, we should take the initiative to discuss death during life. We should teach and affirm our mortality, because it brings the preciousness of life to the surface. In our family discussions, we should not skirt the topic of death, because death is the prerequisite to eternal life. At the same time, we should not dwell on it because this is equally as unhealthy. Living with eternity in mind requires balance.

Death is what makes life precious. This is perhaps the granddaddy of all the ironies of life. Nevertheless, people avoid the one issue *everyone* faces while willingly talking about almost any other issue. To be able to help our family members deal with the inevitability of our death, we must fully grasp the reality of our mortality and deal with it directly.

Dealing with death is difficult. People with life-threatening illnesses have called me to help them arrange certain things they wanted done after they die because their family members would not help; they would not allow themselves to accept the reality of the situation.

A gentleman told me that every time he wanted to let his children know something about his life or certain wishes he would like them to carry out after his death, he would get the same response again and again: "You're not going to die. Stop talking that way." But he *was* going to die. Although he was at peace with it, his family was not. He didn't want to wait until his family finally came to terms with what he and his doctors already knew, and he needed guidance on how to proceed.

One reason we avoid mentioning death is that in modern society death has been largely removed from our daily lives. Family members typically do not die at home as they formerly did. Most often, people die in hospitals or nursing homes. Modern medical technology is a wonderful thing, but it has isolated and even inoculated many of us from the reality of death.

Another reason we avoid mentioning death is that many of us think that if we are good and lead a good life, nothing bad — such as the death of a loved one — will happen to us. If something bad does happen, we feel betrayed, wronged, even cheated. In many cases, death is perceived as unfair. Death, however, pays no attention to age, gender, wealth, color, or "goodness."

Scripture tells us that there is a season for everything. There is life, and there is death. To ignore death robs life of its true value.

> "To everything there is a season,
> And a time for every purpose under heaven:
> A time to be born, and a time to die;
> A time to break down, and a time to build up;
> A time to weep, and a time to laugh;
> A time to mourn, and a time to dance."
>   (*Ecclesiastes* 3: 1–4)

We often concentrate on only one side — the "born, build up, laugh, and dance" side. But there *is* the other side — the side where we "die, break down, weep, and mourn." Creating Support Trusts will help your family members through this other side of life, when they are dealing with the loss of *your* life. It will also make you feel alive as perhaps never before by embracing the fact that although tomorrow may be your last day here, eternity is just around the corner.

EXPERIENCING GRIEF AND BEREAVEMENT

Even people of great faith are not immune from grief. No one escapes the profound sadness surrounding the death of a loved one. When you die, your family likely will cycle through many emotions. Your death probably will be the most devastating experience any member of your family has ever had to handle. Coping with your loss will be a long and difficult process.

Our society has taught us to avoid grief and the church often reflects our culture. When we experience loss, we frequently are expected to grieve quickly and silently so our grief does not affect others. Unfortunately, many times those who grieve are judged as not being spiritually mature or strong. One lady who experienced this told me that the Christian army is the only army in the world that shoots its own wounded. Your Support Trust will help your loved ones get through it.

Creating Support Trusts for your family is compassion in action. When you love someone and see that person in pain, you have compassion. In reading the Bible, have you noticed that whenever Jesus had compassion for someone, He always took action? He didn't feel sorry for the person and then walk away. He acted! A Support Trust is a form of compassionate action.

Creating a Support Trust for your family is compassion in action.

To glimpse what your family members will go through in the event of your death, close your eyes. Take a moment to grasp the totality of it. They will never again be able to talk with you on earth, or hug you, or hear you laugh. Put yourself in your family's shoes. Feel the sense of loss. Now imagine how you would feel if you were to lose one of *them*. Don't push away those feelings that are starting to churn in your stomach and rise to your throat. Embrace your loved one just a bit longer. Now thank God that you still have your loved one.

Can you recall how you feel when a loved one is hurting? When my little girl (I guess she will always be my "little" girl) was learning how to ride her bike, she was riding around in big circles with an air of confidence that had replaced an unsure and nervous look minutes before. She periodically glanced at me proudly with a big smile. During one of these glances, she lost her concentration, and when she tried to correct herself, she overcompensated and crashed hard onto the street. Her helmet and kneepads could not protect her from the force of the blow and the resulting scrapes up and down her arm and leg. She was bleeding — and not just physically; her pride was bleeding as well. I rushed over, quickly picked her up, and assessed her injuries. I tried to soothe her loud and poignant cries.

To see the shocked look on her face and the physical and emotional pain that showed through her tears made me feel sad and helpless. At that moment, I would have done anything I could to comfort her. All parents have gone through similar situations with their children. When you see them in pain, you will do anything you can to help them through it.

Now imagine your children's pain when you pass away. From time to time, I think about what my little girl will go through when I die. The pain my death will cause her (if it is half the pain I would feel in losing her) will be a thousand times more painful than the pain from the bike accident. After 20, 30, or 40 years she may not remember the bike story, but she will remember my death for the rest of her life.

As parents and spouses, we have compassion for our loved ones and we seek to protect them from harm and comfort them through life's little tragedies. With a Support Trust we also can seek to protect them from harm and comfort them through the major tragedy of life — the loss of a loved one.

> "The parent who dies leaves a relationship, a role, and a hole that no one else can fill. The surviving parent cannot be both mother and father. A Support Trust helps fill the gap."
>
> — Steven Earll, MA, MS, LPC, LAC[3]

A SUPPORT TRUST IN ACTION

To provide a perspective on how you can utilize Support Trusts, I'll introduce you to two different families. One has a Support Trust, and the other does not. The first family consists of John, his wife, Susan, a daughter named Lauren, and two sons, RJ and Tyler. The second family consists of Bill, his wife, Mary, and two daughters, Isabella and Shay. John and Bill are good friends. They go to the same church, often followed on Sunday mornings by going out to lunch together with their families. Both are physically healthy and spiritually devout men of faith.

Susan originally created messages for their children in case something were to happen to her before she could witness each of her children's wedding days. After reading these letters, John became motivated to start writing letters himself. Once he started, he kept it up.

John and Bill enjoy going to baseball games. On their way home from a game one day, they were talking about how poorly their team had played and offering their "expert" opinions on how the team could improve. John was driving and Bill was doing most of the critiquing. They didn't know that a pick-up truck coming the opposite way on this two-lane highway was being driven by a man who had spent the last three hours at a bar drinking heavily.

Bill and John at the same time noticed the oncoming truck veering into their lane. John reflexively tightened his grip on the steering wheel and started braking. A quick prayer and a fleeting moment later, they realized they were going to be hit by this truck traveling in excess of 60 miles per hour. It seemed like a million thoughts raced through their minds as the truck hit John's car head on. Both men were killed instantly.

Three hours later, police officers visited John's home and Bill's home. They delivered the bad news to Susan and Mary.

*S*upport *T*rusts

Mary sat down on her living room chair and cried like she had never cried before. She felt as if someone had just ripped her heart out. Susan went into complete and utter shock. She couldn't grasp the reality that her husband had just died.

That night, both women went through a myriad of emotions. They were overwhelmed with disbelief, anxiety, confusion, and the deepest, most profound sense of loss that either one thought she could feel. Neither had felt so alone in her entire life. Both were gripped by overwhelming fear — fear of what their children were about to experience, fear of what life would be like without their husband, fear of the unknown. They wished they could see their husband just one more time and hear his voice. Each wanted to tell her husband how much she loved him.

After hearing the tragic news, the children, too, suffered. Lauren, RJ, and Tyler couldn't believe they never were going to see their daddy again. At this point, it was beyond their grasp even to imagine such a thing. Isabella and Shay wanted their dad back so much it made them physically sick.

Fortunately, John had the foresight to develop a Spiritual Trust System. Bill had heard about this System from John and had pondered the idea of creating a Support Trust for his family. Although he thought it was a good idea, Bill didn't like to think about his mortality and believed it would take too much time to create a Spiritual Trust right now. Bill put it off until it was too late.

These decisions had consequences for their families. John and Bill went into God's presence at the same time and in the same way. They were both men of faith, and both are in heaven. Both of their families will be financially provided for because both John and Bill had adequate life insurance. But that's where the support from Bill stops, while John's family will benefit at the times they will need it the most, from the emotional and spiritual support that John had arranged for them.

In this chapter you will learn what John's family will receive from his Support Trust and how you can use such a Trust to support your family. In this example, John is a man, husband, and father. The example, however, could just as well be that of a women, wife, and mother. I know I would need more support from my wife than she likely would need from me — issues involving children, balancing the checkbook, paying the bills, and the like. Also, I have a selective hearing and memory problem (according to my wife). I would have a hard time imagining my life and functioning in many ways without her.

Fortunately, my wife has created a Support Trust for me, articulating, among other considerations, the practical things I would need to know and think about if she were to die. Wives and mothers often are the glue that holds their family unit together. When this glue is dissolved, the family unit can begin to unravel.

HOW THE FAMILY EXPERIENCES DEATH

To paraphrase Dr. Alan D. Wolfelt: "Mourning is different from grieving. Grief is the internal awareness of pain when we lose someone we love. Mourning is the outward expression of that pain."[4]

After your death, wouldn't it be wonderful if your family could be spared any grief from your loss, could rejoice that you are in heaven, and would not need to mourn your passing. Many who have been through the loss of a loved one would prefer to bypass the grief and bereavement process. John's and Bill's families certainly felt this way. Grieving is significant, however, because it demonstrates our capacity to love. Those of us who have experienced love would not trade it away just to avoid having to deal with grief when we lose a person we love. The magnitude of the grief reflects just how deeply we are able to love and be loved.

Your death will impact your spouse and children physically, emotionally, spiritually, intellectually, socially — every aspect of their lives. Before your death, there was a relationship built upon plans, expectations, experiences, beliefs, hopes, and dreams. After your death, this future is gone and they will have to travel a long and difficult road of grief.

Here is a list of many of the feelings and emotions that accompany the grief and bereavement process. These are some of the feelings and emotions that *your* family members will experience.

Profound sadness	Sense of loss
Isolation	Pain
Exhaustion	Regret
Fear	Shock
Confusion	Loneliness
Guilt	Anxiety
Shame	Disorientation
Despair	Depression
Loss of faith	Disgrace
Bitterness	Resentment
Loss of appetite	Anger toward God
Panic	Denial
Heartache	Rejection
Loss of identity	Irritability
Numbness	Loss of motivation
Sleep disruptions	Physical pain
Weight gain or	Stress
Weight loss	Weeping

To be sure, your family will be really hurting. Any of us would take measures to support our loved ones if they were experiencing even a couple of these emotions during our lifetime. Now you can help them when they will be *deeply* experiencing *many* of these feelings.

PHASES OF GRIEF

> "People who have not lost a loved one often see grief as a very temporary and a fairly rational process that stops soon after the funeral. They don't understand grief's scope or depth."
> — Carol Staudacher[5]

A common misperception of people who have never lost a loved one is that grief is temporary, with the funeral being the primary focal point. In truth, grief and bereavement have no end point, although we can divide the process into three *general* phases of grief that are both broad and overlapping: initial phase, bereavement phase, and rebuilding or ongoing phase. Although each stage has certain characteristics, they may overlap. Also, the grieving person likely will pass through each phase many times.

> "Grief has no clear direction. There is no direct path through the many emotional territories that make up our loss."
>
> — Carol Staudacher[6]

Nevertheless, the following *general* characteristics of each phase should be kept in mind when planning your Support Trust.

1. *Initial phase.* Your family members initially will be hit by the shock of your death. They will go through feelings of disbelief that you are gone. They likely will be confused and disoriented. They will have a profound sense of loss and sadness and also will become acutely aware of their own mortality. This can be the beginning of a spiritual crisis for all or some of your family members. They possibly will start to channel their pain into anger, which is natural, but this also can lead to bitterness. The emotional, physical, and even spiritual exhaustion of handling the details surrounding your death will be immense.

2. *Bereavement phase.* The grief will intensify as your family realizes the full impact of your death. Usually the funeral service is held less than a week after someone dies. The survivors cannot come to terms with the reality of a death in a week. It will not be felt fully until well after the funeral. Weeks and months later, when everyone else has gone on with *their* lives, your family members likely will reach the pinnacle of their grief. They may feel depression, guilt, fear, resentment, regret, anger, bitterness, and loneliness and will still have a profound sense of sadness and loss. In this phase, the potential remains for your survivors to experience a crisis of faith.

3. *Ongoing phase.* Your family members will begin to reconstruct their lives. Although you will continue to live in their hearts, they finally will begin the process of living without you and going on with their new lives. The journey to reach this phase is difficult, and your family members may never fully recover from certain as-

pects of the aftermath of your loss.

> "Grieving is not a short-term process; it's not even a long-term process; it's a lifelong process."
>
> — Ashley Davis Prend[7]

Familiarity with these phases of grief, as well as with the individual needs of each person in your family, will enable you to develop a Support Trust that will be instrumental in your family's healing process. The circumstances of each person's death are highly unique, and the ways in which each survivor deals with grief are equally unique. Some reach the final phase of grieving within a couple of years. Others take much longer.

EVALUATING YOUR FAMILY

As you develop your Support Trust, you must be courteous and sensitive to your family's needs. There is no place for self-centeredness. Ask your family members how a Support Trust would have real value to them if something were to happen to you. Think about your family as individuals — how each would be uniquely affected by your death.

Spiritual Trusts are not about ego. They are about helping. The three key words are sensitivity, sensitivity, and sensitivity! For the most part, you will create your messages from a rational perspective. Your family members, however, may receive your rational messages at a time when they are still experiencing severe emotional grief, especially if your messages are delivered in the initial and bereavement phases. Timing is important so you don't risk sending your loved ones into deeper grief.

> Spiritual Trusts are not about ego. They are about helping. The three key words are:
> sensitivity, sensitivity, and sensitivity!

SPIRITUAL SUPPORT METHODS

Based largely on the three general phases of grief and bereavement, the Support Trust explained here will follow the stages of initial support, bereavement support, and ongoing support.

Initial Support

Support in this first phase is intended primarily to help your family members through the immediate shock of your death and dealing with the reality of your passing. During this phase you will have the chance to tell them again that you love them, and you will be able to say goodbye. You can inform them of the Spiritual Trusts you have created and arrangements you have made and set the tone for your funeral service. The Prayer Trust you have established (See Chapter 3) will be set in motion, and the spiritual foundations for coping with your death can be laid.

You can provide various kinds of support in the initial support phase. Because of the shock your family members will undergo soon after your death, you should make your support available to them only when they are ready to receive it. You should not force any component of a Spiritual Trust on grieving family members. Rather, you should let them know what is available and allow them to receive the information when they are ready. The types of support you can offer are addressed below.

> You should make your support available to them only when they are ready to receive it.

Goodbye Messages

Whether your death comes from a life-threatening illness or from an unforeseen event such as a car wreck or heart attack, a goodbye message gives you an opportunity to talk to your family at this crucial time — a time when your family would give anything just to hear your voice again. This message gives you the opportunity to tell family members that you love them and that you will be with them always, and to say goodbye for now, until you are able to see them again in heaven. A goodbye message can be in the form of a letter or an audio recording, but the most powerful format is video.

Steven, John's best friend, is the executor of John's Spiritual Trust. After Susan called to tell him the news, Steven and his wife went directly to be with Susan and the kids. Later that night, Steven went to a certain place in his home and took out a portable safe. He opened it with his key and pulled out more than a dozen large manila envelopes and numerous small boxes. He held the top envelope in his hands as he read John's handwriting: "Okay, Steve, here we go!"

The following day, Steven went to Susan's home to begin fulfilling the obligations he had promised John he would carry out. The atmosphere of grief and disbelief was so thick you could cut it with a chain saw. Flowers were arriving, and the phone was ringing perpetually as the word of John's death spread.

Steven took Susan aside in private and told her that John had prepared a video message to her. He asked her (as John had instructed him) if she would like to watch it now or if she would rather wait a while. Susan knew about his Spiritual Trust, and through the fog of her grief, Susan began to remember what John had told her. As these memories returned, the look in Susan's eyes left Steven no doubts that she not only wanted to see the videotape but that she wanted to see it right *now*. Steven, his wife, and Susan went into the study to watch John's video privately. This is an excerpt of what John said:

Hi, honey. I'm so terribly sorry that you have to watch this. I know that my death is going to hit you and the kids hard. If I were in your shoes right now and I had just lost you, I'd be devastated. As strange as it may sound, I'm thankful that it was me who went first. I have such confidence in you and know that you and the kids will make me proud. But right now I know it's tough. I know you're in shock and you're so sad. But please, Susan, don't be bitter. Don't let the trust in God that we have lived our lives by falter because of my death.

You will have to depend on the Lord now more than ever, and it's my biggest hope that you will allow Jesus to comfort you and not turn Him away because you're mad at Him for allowing me to die. We've talked many times about how we never know when it's our time to go. Well, this was my time. It will be hard to see the purpose right now, and I suggest you don't even try.

Spiritual Trusts

We loved each other very deeply, so I know your grief will be deep, as mine would be if our situation were reversed. Oh, I love you so much. I'll be watching you and the kids as much as the Lord allows me.

I've left many messages for you, and the children to receive at different times. This way I can continue to be a part of your lives. Steve will give you a video for the kids to watch if you think it will help more than hurt. Please watch it in your own time, and use your judgment.

Steve is the executor of the Spiritual Trusts I've created for you and the kids. He will tell you what kinds of messages I have prepared. I also asked him to call David to inform him of my passing and to help facilitate getting you the life insurance check later this week. Don't worry about that at all. I've already taken care of it. When you're ready, I have a letter for you giving my input on where you should consider putting this money and on other financial matters.

Steve has agreed to handle the funeral details, and, as I'm sure you will recall, I've already arranged everything. I've prepared a eulogy to be played at my funeral service. Please watch it beforehand if you can, because even though it's very important to me to say some last words to my friends and other family, I don't want to make this any harder on you and the kids. I know it's sad for you, but I do want my service to be a celebration of my life and not a somber remembrance of my death. I had an awesome life, and I want that to be the focus of the service.

I'm sure that all that heaven holds for me won't keep me from missing all of you.

Although Susan's grief remained strong, she gained a great sense of comfort and support from John's message. It gave her an inner peace and the strength to carry on.

What would your home be like if you were to meet a fate similar to John's? Those who are left behind have to deal with a myriad of funeral arrangements at the same time they begin to realize they are never going to see or hear or touch you again. If you do not create messages for them, communication from you is over. Except for their memories of you, they fear that you will never be a part of their lives again.

A simple goodbye message can help your family through this stage. These messages also can help your friends and other loved ones you leave behind who will be mourning your loss.

Funeral or Memorial Messages

Death is merely the opening of the door to eternal life, for to be absent from the body is to be with the Lord (*2 Corinthians* 5:8). Death is defeated, and we will go to be with our heavenly father in an awesome spiritual realm. A believer's funeral should be a celebration. It seldom is, however, because friends and family are so distraught at the reality of the death, especially if the death was unexpected. Through your Support Trust, you can help make your funeral a blessing for your family and those who will be attending the funeral or memorial service.

Eulogy

The word "eulogy" comes from the Greek word *eulegein*, which means "to speak well of." The most common use of this word is to speak well of, or praise, a person who has died.

One of the most meaningful parts of a funeral is the eulogy, in which a loved one or a minister tells a little about the one who has passed away. Most eulogies are hastily prepared. If a minister delivers the eulogy, it may sound like a standard form with the name changed and a few personal stories added. Why not prepare your eulogy, to be delivered by — you! Creating your own eulogy message can turn your funeral into one of the most memorable events that those attending your funeral will ever experience. It's not nearly as difficult as you may think and, with the right mindset, the process can be rewarding.

The most basic eulogy is a written message. A person of your choosing can read to those attending the service the letter you wrote before your death. Your message will have more impact if it is relatively brief — in general, not longer than 10 minutes. A powerful eulogy can be less than a page long. You also may request that a copy of your letter be given to those in attendance. This way, all of the attendees will have a meaningful remembrance of you — your last words — to take home and read whenever they want.

Or you could record your eulogy on a voice recorder. (See Chapter 8 for details about voice recordings.) Your voice will have much more impact than someone else reading your words. You could have the text of your message transcribed and made available to the attendees, or you could give them the voice recording on cassette or CD.

Alternatively, you could make a video of yourself talking to your funeral audience. (See Chapter 8 for details about video recordings.) This can be the most powerful format because people you love and who love you will get to both hear and see you. They will be able to watch your body language and facial expressions. Like audible eulogies, you can have a copy of your video transcribed and given to attendees or have VHS copies available for those who want one. Most funeral homes have a television or viewing screen that can be used. If not, your executor or a family member can arrange to have one brought in.

Have you ever thought about what your funeral might be like? Who will be there? What they will be saying? Imagine the minister standing before your family, friends, and associates. He talks about you and says that you have a message for everyone in attendance today. A screen then is lowered into view. The lights are dimmed. Then you appear on the screen smiling. The audience is silent, watching and listening to a message from a very special person in their lives whom they never will see on earth again. I assure you that you will have everyone's undivided attention.

You thank them for coming to pay their respects. After your short introduction — and perhaps taking the time to show your appreciation and love for certain people — you might say something like what John said. We'll pick up close to the beginning of John's eulogy video message:

You may have heard that I have died. I assure you that I am more alive at this moment than I ever have been. I want this to be a celebration of my life and not a somber remembrance of my death. I'm in a better place. Believe me, earth doesn't compare to heaven! I'm in paradise with my Lord Jesus, who lived in my heart when I was on earth, and now I will live in his home for eternity. This is a celebration. Please rejoice with me. I appreciate that I'm missed, and I wish I could have had more time with all of you. But death is an obvious part of life, and all us will go to meet our Maker — probably when we least expect it.

If you can see the body in that casket over there, I want you to know that I'm not there. That body was just a vessel that held my spirit while I was on the earth. Can't you tell that there is a soul just by knowing me and then looking at that body? I have a spiritual form now. It is up to you to determine where your soul will go when you die. Never have I been as grateful as I am at this very moment that I decided that my soul belongs to Jesus.

I once read that we think that we are living in the land of the living on our way to the land of the dying, when we actually are living in the land of the dying on our way to the land of the living.[8] *Everyone in this room will end up at your very own funeral sooner or later. It is my deep and sincere wish that Jesus will own your soul before you have that appointment. Yes, my human body has perished. But my spirit has just begun an eternal journey of inexpressible wonders. If Jesus is not the Lord of your life, I pray that you will make Him so. All you have to do is open the door to your heart and He will enter. You'll never be sorry you did — I promise you.*

Please pray for and look out for my family, I love them so. Please keep them in your hearts and prayers, not just right now, but in the future as well. God bless you all.

The screen fades to black. Imagine the faces and reactions of those who were watching John's video message. Most likely they had never before experienced a funeral like this. Imagine the reactions of *your* family and friends if you were to leave them a message like this!

This is just one example of a eulogy. To the people who attend your funeral, your eulogy can be the most powerful witness they have ever experienced. You have a captive audience that is collectively wondering about its own mortality. Your eulogy will stick in their minds and pierce their hearts. Many will vividly remember this moment for the rest of their lives. Some may renew their faith. Some may decide to go to church the next Sunday for the first time in years. Some may ask Jesus Christ into their heart right then and there. Many will be moved by your words and will honor your request to pray for your family. Your children might have their boldness for Christ strengthened by observing your boldness for Christ. You can seize this moment and make it count for all eternity.

To the people attending your funeral, your eulogy can be the most powerful witness they have ever experienced.

Here are some things to think about in creating your own eulogy message:

- Will your funeral have a spiritual theme?
- How do you want to be remembered?
- What are the most important things you want to share with those at your funeral?
- Do you want to mention certain people?
- Do you have a specific verse by which you have tried to live your life?
- What scriptures do you want to quote?
- Will copies of your eulogy be made available?

Byeulogy

In a eulogy, the living speak well of, or praise, the dead. In a byeulogy, a person who has died speaks well of, or praises, the living. You won't find this word in the dictionary, but we're working on it! In your byeulogy, you can send messages to be delivered at the time of your death, or shortly thereafter, to your loved ones. Your messages can express love, appreciation, respect, and similar sentiments. You might thank people for something they did for you, tell them how much their friendship meant to you, point out their special qualities, tell them you love them, tell them why you cared so much about them, tell them how their life contributed to yours, and tell them what you learned from them.

You can send byeulogy messages to special people you know will be at your funeral: brothers and sisters, moms and dads, mentors and friends. This is an excerpt of such a message that John created for his brother, Dustin. John's executor, Steven, discretely gave John's brother this letter in a sealed envelope:

My dearest brother,

I'm taking this opportunity to tell you how much I love you and how much I've valued our friendship throughout life. Perhaps no one knows me in the way you do, and as I'm writing this letter, I'm smiling as the memories of our youth flood my mind. Even though you're my baby brother, I've always looked up to you in many ways (including literally — ha!). Your character and convictions have given me strength more times than you know.

I learned a lot from you, and I hope you've learned half as much from me. Remember when we were at the lake? You were — what — 14 or 15 at the time? You had skied a couple of times and got back in the boat. We were going to be leaving soon, and I was trying to get you to go back out one more time. You said no, that you were tired. I persisted. You again told me no, that you just didn't want to do this at all.

So I started dancing around the boat singing some stupid song about how much of a sissy you were. Dad cracked up and joined in. You finally relented and said fine, that you would go one more time. You were mad as you put your life jacket back on, and we couldn't get you to even crack a smile as you got back into the water while we were cheering for you like you were a war hero or something.

You got up on the water just fine and did great for about 10 seconds. Then you crashed. Your ski hit your forehead right between your eyes and gashed it wide open, leaving a permanent scar. I think you had 12 stitches. I bet that in this one day I taught you not to go against your instincts, not to succumb to peer pressure, and not to care if others make fun of you. Now that I think of it, maybe I taught you more than you taught me!

I have such good memories of our childhood and our friendship that I just wanted to tell you so and let you know one more time how much I love you. Look out for Susan and the kids, will you, bro? I'm sending you a video message as your Christmas present this year. That way, you'll be the only one on your block to get a video from someone living in heaven.

I had a good life, Dustin. You know better than anyone — I lived it to the fullest. Tell my kids some funny stories, and try to keep everyone encouraged today. I'll tell Gramps "hi" from you.

I'll talk to you this Christmas.

Love always,
John

Byeulogy messages can be in letter, audio, or video format. They also can take the form of short, one-paragraph notes. One such note I found humorous was a two-word message that John wrote to his boss, part of a private joke the two of them had going: "*I quit!*"

Most of John's byeulogy messages were delivered to those who were the most important to him directly at their homes. He also arranged for seven byeulogy message letters and notes to be discretely passed out at his funeral service.

I recently received the benefits of a heartfelt byeulogy in my own family. My uncle Bob was diagnosed with cancer. Shortly after learning this, I was in his state on a previously scheduled trip to visit my grandparents and videotape their stories of the last half-century. I met with Bob, set up my camcorder and recorded his byeulogies and other thoughts for his children, parents, and siblings. He didn't get too wordy, just told it like it was. The video conveyed how much each member of his family meant to him and how much he loved them. This is meaningful in life, but hearing these words from someone who has passed away is even more powerful.

Bob didn't want any of the family to know what he had recorded until the tape was shown after he had passed away. After the funeral the family went to one home, where the family gathered in the living room to watch the video message from Bob. It was moving, and I'll never forget the faces of my family members as they watched Bob talk about and to them. My family appreciated Bob's thoughtfulness in taking the time to do this. Each person was given a copy of Bob's byeulogy and messages to take home and view whenever they wanted to see and hear Bob again.

In as little time as a few hours, you can prepare a funeral message like the ones mentioned here. Your recipients will treasure your messages for the rest of their lives.

Video Montage

A video montage is a short (perhaps 3 to 10 minutes) "movie" of your life. In a way, it's a short multimedia presentation about the life you lived or a particular aspect of your life. It focuses on the themes you want to emphasize. You select pictures and even short video clips from your life and have them edited into the video. Background music and voiceovers can be easily inserted. This montage of your life can be played in the funeral home foyer or can be part of the funeral service.

If you prepare your own eulogy, it could play as a prelude to your eulogy. You can prepare a video montage with any of the following themes: chronological events of your life, family and friends, your faith, or special moments. Or you could combine these themes into one production. Most video studios will prepare these productions, or you can visit our website for more information and resources at www.spiritualtrusts.com/videomontage.

Messages Defending Your Death

Nothing brings faith in God to the surface more quickly than the death of a loved one. Your death likely will cause a religious crisis of faith for at least one member of your family. As a result of your death, members of your family will be susceptible to anger toward God, and Satan uses these opportunities to exploit doubts about God.

Your death is likely to cause a religious crisis of faith for at least one member of your family.

Your children are particularly susceptible because they usually have little experience with death and dying and the accompanying feelings. They may question God's motives and intentions. They may wonder about God's purpose in allowing, or even causing, your death. If God is good, all-powerful, and full of love for us, why didn't He prevent this? It's hard for adults to understand and can be even more difficult for young children.

Although children are the most at risk, even adults with a strong faith can undergo a crisis of faith. The author C.S. Lewis fell into a state of despair that hurled him into a crisis of faith when he lost his wife. If you read his book, *A Grief Observed,* you will see how a devout man of God, who has blessed so many others by his books, was not immune from experiencing a crisis of his faith and severe spiritual pain. If it can happen to C.S. Lewis, it certainly could happen to your spouse, your children, or your parents.

Think about the members of your immediate family. Take a long, hard look at their spiritual maturity, personality, and life experiences. Might one or more of them turn away from God if you were to die in a tragic, unexpected way, or were struck with a disease and suffered through a prolonged dying experience? If so, you should support their faith in specific and targeted ways.

Given that one or more members of your family could suffer a crisis of faith upon your death, it is crucial to support their faith through a personalized message at the time of your death. One of the most effective ways to support your family spiritually in the event of your death is to *defend your death*. Although this process of struggling with spirituality and questioning God is natural, you don't want any of your family members to *wallow* in spiritual doubts, anger, or bitterness.

> "Some will tell you not to struggle, not to question. Yet it is in the struggle that we are strengthened. We use emotional and intellectual 'muscles' that may have never been in service before."
> — Sue Holtkamp, Ph.D.[9]

By defending your death, you can help get your family members through their struggles and on the road to healing grace. You can help stop them from going down the road to resentment and bitterness.

Although John had some concern about a crisis of faith for Susan, he was concerned mainly for his children and what their views of God would be if something were to happen to him. John's concerns were especially acute for his two sons because of John's unique perspective of their personality and spiritual maturity. This is the letter John wrote to his family defending his death against a crisis of faith:

Susan, Lauren, RJ & Tyler,

My dear family,

I've left you many messages covering various topics, and these will be delivered to you at specific times in each one of your lives. But this is perhaps the most important message of all. If you do not accept this message in your heart, you probably will not accept any of my messages and my messages will not have the impact or usefulness I intended and hoped for when I created them. If you are to embrace the truth of any message I have created for you, I pray that it is this one.

The message is simple: Please do not be bitter about my death, and don't blame God. Don't let bitterness poison your life. As you have heard me say before, death is a fact of life. Death is what makes life so precious. There's no way of getting out of it. God is not responsible for my death. If you want to be angry at the circumstances of my death — whatever they were — fine, but don't *be angry with God!*

Nothing would make me sadder or disappoint me more than to think that everything I stood for in life was unraveled in my death by bitterness, resentment, and doubt. Just because I died doesn't mean that God doesn't love you or me anymore. The whole reason Jesus came to earth and died on the cross was so that when I would die, I would be able to spend eternity with Him.

Please don't let my death shake your foundation of faith. I want your faith to get stronger, not weaker, after I die. Our family is no more immune to death than any other family. I'm not saying to you, "Don't grieve." To the contrary, I would be disappointed if you did not mourn my death. What I am saying is that God is grieving with you because He knows you're hurting. It is not His fault that I died. It is His desire, however, to help you through this difficult time. He is the great comforter. His love is so unfailing. Allow God to use the grieving process to bring healing to your heart.

If I had only one wish about my death that could come true, it would be that in dealing with my death, each of you would grow stronger in your faith and develop a deeper relationship with Jesus Christ.

All of you will die someday, too. Remember that Jesus died for us so that when we die, we can be with Him. We will all be together again someday. Make me proud of you up here, will you? I want to be able to go over to a group of angels and point down to you and say, "Now there goes a person of God!"

Love always,
Dad

Your death likely will send your family on a spiritual journey. You would do well to provide a road map and spiritual rations to nourish them on the way. The goal is for them to attain a stronger faith and dependence on Jesus as a result of their loss of you. You can help make that happen with appropriate messages delivered after your death.

> Your death likely will send your family on a spiritual journey. You would do well to provide a road map and spiritual rations to nourish them on the way.

Funeral or Memorial Arrangements

Most people don't get excited about preplanning their funeral, but it's not that bad — really. Although not as exciting as creating messages for those you love, making these arrangements beforehand will be of tremendous help to your family and will reduce their stress. This is a time when your family will be physically and emotionally exhausted from notifying people, taking phone calls, and dealing with all the attendant burdens. Making funeral arrangements in advance is a helpful way to support your family.

The thought of Susan having to go to the funeral home, select a casket, select a burial plot, arrange for the funeral service and burial, and then pay for it all made John cringe. So a couple of years ago he took a few hours out of his day to do this for her. As he went through each step at the funeral home, he found comfort, even gratitude, in knowing that Susan would not have to do this someday.

After John's death, Steven called the funeral home and had someone pull John's file. Then Steven and the funeral director finalized all the arrangements John had already planned. Susan didn't have to be concerned with any of the details of John's funeral service and burial.

Because the average person has to arrange, or help arrange, fewer than two funerals during his or her lifetime, people don't develop expertise in this area. Having your family members go through this learning process while they are grieving is so unnecessary. In one trip to the funeral home of your choice, you can make most of the decisions that will go a long way in easing the burdens on your family at the time of your death.

Support Trusts

Among the many decisions to be made are:

- Whether you want to be cremated
- Where your service will be held
- Details of the service itself (flowers, music, eulogy, etc.)
- Whether you want a large or small service
- Those you want to invite (old high school friends, people you used to work with or go to church with, mentors, etc.)
- Wording of your obituary
- Casket selection
- Pallbearers
- Cemetery or mausoleum where you will be buried
- Headstone selection and inscription
- How you will pay for everything

Regarding the last item — you can expect to spend five to seven thousand dollars for the average funeral service and casket these days. You can prepay or make payments over time. In some cases, you can make a down payment and have the balance paid by your life insurance proceeds.

Just reading the list of issues above can boggle the mind. Now imagine that you are suffering the most extreme emotional distress of your life and you have to make these decisions. That's why you should make these decisions now instead of having your family do this when you die.

In addition to the caring assistance rendered at a funeral home, you can use resources including our Support Trust Workbook; the books *Death Through the Eyes of a Funeral Director*, by William Ellenberg, and *Everyone Dies!*, by Ralph Hicks; as well as a multitude of Internet sites and other resources, to which you can find links at www.spiritualtrusts.com/funeralplanning.

When you make your arrangements, be flexible. Your family will need the ability to change things at your funeral. For example, a pallbearer you chose may not be available. In your Support Trust, acknowledge that some changes may have to be made, and give your family the freedom to make these changes without undergoing additional guilt or grief. Moreover, you should understand that your wishes might not be legally binding. Therefore, your family will be able to modify many of the arrangements you have made.

Your Obituary

You may or may not want to draft your own obituary. If you would rather not, you could ask someone else to prepare your obituary. To help out, select a black-and-white photo that you want to use, and list all the publications you want your obituary sent to. Your obituary will be a short (*very* short) summary of your life. Typical information in an obituary includes when you were born, major accomplishments, and who survived you. Most newspapers will not charge to publish your obituary if it fits within their maximum space allowed. If you or your family want a longer obituary, newspapers will generally charge extra.

Since this is your final, official statement to the world that you have "left the building," you may want to arrange for a more extraordinary farewell message. I have arranged for a rather lengthy obituary for myself. It briefly tells about my accomplishments and the family I left behind. Then I go into a message similar to the eulogy message John left in the previous example. At the end I even tell people, "In lieu of sending flowers, please get Jesus in your life, so when you're listed in these pages someday, you'll be in paradise!"

Legal and Financial Arrangement Support

When you pass away, your spouse and family will be left with the responsibility to resolve and reconcile your legal and financial matters. The support you provide *now* regarding these matters can relieve your spouse and family from substantial stress and effort. Your important financial and legal matters should be summarized in a simple list of accounts, directions, and contacts. This list should be kept in a safe place in your home, and the appropriate family members should know where it is. The same list should be given to your estate executor, your Spiritual Trust executor (if different), and your attorney, if you have one.

During this time of grief and mourning, your family shouldn't have to make an exhaustive search of your records to locate a document needed to resolve a pressing financial or legal issue.

You can help by addressing the basics well before you die. You should consult with your CPA (or accountant) and attorney specifically about these issues if you haven't done so. Ask for steps you can take to assist your family when you die. I am not just talking about having a will and insurance. I am talking about properly addressing all of your significant financial and legal matters with your family in a letter or other document that will alleviate their concerns about these matters upon your death.

Issues you should address, as appropriate, include:

- How your family will receive immediate financial support upon your death
- Major bills and how they are generally paid
- Location of and access to financial assets and other resources
- Recommendation for a financial planner
- Entitlements of which you are aware
- Life insurance policies, their amounts and agents
- Location of your will and other important papers

Designation of Personal Mementos and Heirlooms

I get into more detail about leaving a will in Chapter 5, Stewardship Trusts, but there are some important implications for this chapter. Unfortunately, numerous families have been hurt through squabbling and fighting over the deceased's personal mementos and other items. You can eliminate this possibility by designating now who will get these items that have sentimental value.

    Make a list of these items and their matching recipients, or attach notes to the items themselves when possible. This can be a difficult decision-making process, especially if several heirs may want the same things. Taking the time and effort to go through this process will help to unify the family during this most difficult time. You can make copies of photographs, documents, video and audio recordings, certificates, and the like. For these kinds of items, you could select a primary beneficiary and request that the copies be made and distributed to all who want them.

    For years, my grandmother has written on the back of framed photographs, artwork, and other items the names of those she wants to have that specific piece. She has four living children and dozens of grandchildren and great grandchildren, so, by having copies of special mementos and keepsakes, her descendants will be able to retain cherished memories of her.

Another way to address these issues is to make a video will. This is not a replacement for your written will. In fact, a video will in itself is not considered a valid will in most states. Rather, it is a way for you to explain decisions you have made in your estate distribution. For example, a videotaped will presents a marvelous opportunity for you to explain why you designated certain people to receive specific items in your estate. Even if you told them while you were living, this is your chance to tell them again. It also is a good time to explain that, regardless of the financial resources you were able to leave, the spiritual resources you built up over the course of your life and supplemented in your Spiritual Trusts are far more important. You should know that if a video will is inconsistent in any respect with a written and executed will, the latter generally prevails.

Bereavement Support

In the bereavement phase you can provide significant support to your family by sending FaithMessages and LifeMessages (which I will get into shortly) at certain benchmark events such as birthdays, holidays, and anniversaries, and by supporting them with resources on grief and bereavement.

Bereavement support is designed to assist your family through the protracted and often lonely bereavement phase. The support a family receives upon a member's death usually is front-loaded before, during, and immediately after the funeral. This initial support is vital during this critical time. The emotional and spiritual wounds, however, are far from being healed. Depending on the circumstances of your death, your family will continue to grieve intensely for months and longer after losing you.

During this phase of their bereavement, they will greatly benefit from your planned proactive support. Extended family and friends will not be there for your family daily or weekly as they were in the initial stage. Because they have gone on with their own lives, they might think it best for your family members to go on with their lives. People who never have lost a loved one might perceive grieving as a more rapid process from which your family will recover fairly quickly. They cannot comprehend the full scale of emotions and feelings that grief evokes and the time necessary to reconcile the grief.

> "When someone we love dies, we don't just say good-bye once. We say it over and over. And we don't just *say* good-bye, we *live* good-bye."
>
> — Carol Staudacher[10]

Your family will make the transition from *saying* goodbye to *living* goodbye. Although this still will be a difficult, painful process, you will be able to ease the pain by sending messages of support on important occasions, and by providing other resources to help your family cope.

Psychologists who specialize in grief and bereavement generally agree that the most intense portion of the grieving process lasts generally from one to three years. But we should hesitate to put any time limit on grieving. Each person handles grieving differently, and, depending on the circumstances, it could take more or less time. An old adage asserts that true healing cannot begin until the griever passes through each of the four seasons without his or her loved one.

Furthermore, each member of your family will have their own timetable. During this critical time of bereavement — especially the first six months or so after death — your family likely will be physically, emotionally, and spiritually drained. Chances are that your family will be the most spiritually vulnerable during this time.

> "Grief is an intensely personal thing, and different people handle it in different ways."
>
> — Zig Zigler[11]

In providing support to your family, you should plan ahead and not try to cut short the time needed to grieve. Grieving is important, and you could make matters worse by depriving your loved ones of this necessary emotional and spiritual process. The Bible verse quoted earlier comes to mind; to paraphrase it: There is a time to die, a time to break down, a time to weep, and a time to mourn (*Ecclesiastes* 3:1–4). This is your family members' time and season for such things. Once they weather this season, there will be a time to build up, a time to laugh, and a time to dance.

You can use this difficult and emotional time to help your family rebuild so each member will emerge with a faith that is stronger and more resolute. In providing this form of family support, your goals should be to help strengthen their faith and trust in Jesus Christ, and to promote their healing. If your family members suppress or ignore the grieving process, they may never realize the benefits that God can provide throughout. Instead, you can help them through the process.

God uses the grieving process as a healing process.

Your spouse in particular will experience acute grief. When you got married, you and your mate became one flesh. If you were to have an arm or a leg removed, how would that affect your life? How soon would you be over it? Would you ever be like you were before? Well, losing a person whose heart, spirit, dreams, and goals were an integral part of your life is much more difficult. Providing support to your spouse in the event of your death is one of the most precious acts of love and compassion you could ever do for him or her.

Your children, too, will experience intense grief even though they will go back to school and rejoin the activities that were part of their lives before your death. Because they are doing these normal things, they may appear outwardly to be normal. But they are not normal! It was explained to me this way:

> "Children grieve differently than adults. The adult process tends to involve a day-to-day grieving with day-to-day memories. Children have a tendency in their grief to deny the loss on a daily basis by becoming involved in school, friends, and activities and trying not to think about the grief. For children, grief is usually more pronounced during occasions and life transitions including holidays, birthdays, first dates, sporting events, personal awards and accomplishments, proms, graduations, marriage, and the birth of children. Leaving messages of support to be delivered at these benchmarks can be most helpful and meaningful to them."

— Steven Earll, MA, MS, LPC, LAC[12]

FaithMessages and LifeMessages

A FaithMessage is a means of supporting your family and loved ones through a message (written, audio, or video) that you have given to them, or arranged for future delivery of, at specific times, ages, and other benchmarks in their lives (discussed next). Although a FaithMessage can address a variety of issues, the underlying theme of a FaithMessage is — as the name implies — faith.

A LifeMessage, on the other hand, more broadly addresses aspects of your life you want to convey and the many "life" issues your family will face without you. A LifeMessage (written, audio, or video) also can be delivered at the time of your choosing, including long after your death. The message of a FaithMessage and a LifeMessage may overlap at times. The category isn't important; the content of the message is. The point is, these messages can be delivered on a variety of occasions, called benchmarks.

FaithMessages and LifeMessages can be used in any of the Spiritual Trusts, for many purposes. In the Support Trust the emphasis is on holding up your family after your death, which is the focus of this chapter. The Spiritual Trust System is flexible. You can decide the timing of your messages, based on their content or objective. You are the best judge of the support your family will need.

Benchmark Deliveries

Some of the most common benchmarks are the first month after death, 6 months after death, the 1-year anniversary of your death, your wedding anniversary, and certain holidays such as Christmas, birthdays, Mother's Day, and Father's Day. These days often bring to the forefront a desire to spend another moment with you, and they may be painful reminders that you never will be there to share these special days with your family again.

You, of course, are free to pick and choose from the benchmarks I cover in this section. You may not want to do all of them. In fact, some benchmarks depend on your personal family scenario and may be detrimental instead of instrumental in providing the right kinds of support. For instance, although your children and grandchildren will likely be happy to receive messages from you for decades, it may be inappropriate for you to arrange to keep sending messages to your spouse for decades if your spouse is likely to remarry within a few years or so after your death.

Personally, I have arranged messages to my wife for only 2 years after my death, because I expect that she will remarry and I don't want my messages to impede her healing or her relationship. In fact, the last message I have prepared for her encourages her to remarry in her own time. But this is not always the case. My wife's grandmother, Sue Ellen, would have loved to receive letters sent to her from her husband, Ernie, after his death, for the rest of her life. He died when she was 60, and she knew she would not remarry (not necessarily because of age, but by choice), and 20 years later she still talks of him often. Every time she speaks of him, you can see how much she still misses him.

If you are married, you and your spouse should discuss what benchmarks would be appropriate, especially after the first year. Factors to consider are age, how long you have been married, the likelihood of your spouse's remarrying, personalities, emotional makeup, and the like. Also, the recipient of your messages is under no obligation to accept or receive your messages. You will have to make your executor aware of this. If the recipient thinks your messages would do more harm than good, for whatever reason, they should not be delivered.

Although most of your messages will be just from you, I encourage couples to jointly create some of their messages to their children. Doing them together makes for a wonderful bonding experience.

Monthly Benchmarks

Monthly benchmarks don't have to be delivered every month. They can be set up for certain months such as the first month after death, the third, the sixth, and so on. Sending messages to your family at the one-month mark can be especially helpful because this is a significant short-term milestone. The reality of your death has started to sink in, and your family will be trying to get back into the swing of things. The shock of your death may have been replaced by deep sadness and emotional loneliness. The fullness of how deeply you are missed begins to emerge. This also can be a difficult benchmark for your family spiritually.

Many survivors feel regret, guilt, and pain about a specific thing they said or did when their loved one was alive. Dwelling on what could have been, or should have been, is a roadblock to healing.

"There are probably no survivors on this earth who do not experience regret, even pronounced emotional pain, about some specific thing they said or did when their loved one was alive."

— Carol Staudacher[13]

John knew that his wife likely would fall victim to this form of self-abuse and guilt. This is one paragraph from a LifeMessage John sent to Susan one month after his death:

Please understand and know that I don't care about anything negative you ever said to me, or anything you did or didn't do. Don't be upset if you didn't get the chance to say goodbye, or to tell me again that you loved me. Don't be concerned if something wasn't cleared up about an issue that I'm sure has little importance in the grand scheme of things. Honey, I know you love me, and I will always love you. Never let our love be tainted by a single issue that we didn't resolve, or that you wish we could have changed. We're not perfect, and not every aspect of our relationship was perfect. But it was perfect enough. I haven't the slightest regret about our life together except that I wish we could have enjoyed our relationship longer.

"After the death of a loved one, survivors often punish themselves with self-blame for not having been a perfect partner in the relationship that is now gone forever."

— Carol Staudacher[14]

As another example, here are a few excerpts from the message Susan prepared for John in case she met with death first. Susan created a five-page letter for John to receive at the benchmark of one week after the funeral instead of a series of messages to be delivered at various intervals. This also served as her goodbye message.

Honey, I love you so much. I know you miss me, and I know this is going to be a tough time for you. You will be concerned about the kids and certain aspects of running the household. Ask Kelsey for any immediate babysitting you need. She will be happy to help with this, and it will give you time to make longer-term arrangements. Tell Mary that I asked you to help you find the right long-term babysitter. I've mentioned it to her. Please let my mom help, John, at least in the short run. She would love to help. It will be good for the kids to have her there.

* * *

You will need to cut back on work. Fix up the desk like you've been wanting to do and work more from there when you can. The kids have to be your main priority now. You know that you will have to spend a lot of real quality time with them. You've got to see them through to graduation. They will need you there for them, and with my absence they will need you around more than when we shared this responsibility. I know you will continue to be a wonderful father.

* * *

Now to another topic that may be hard for you to read right now. Just tuck this away in your heart. John, I don't mind if you remarry some day. I want you to know that. I don't want you to feel guilty about that, because I do love you. You're going to need somebody, and I don't want you to feel like you can't remarry someday because of an unwarranted sense of guilt.

You need a wife. That's just the kind of person you are. I know that about you in life, and I give you my blessing to remarry after my death. Give it some time, John. For your sake and the kids' sake, don't rush it and make a mistake. My number-one request, however, is that she truly love our kids. And that she is the kind of person our kids will not only like but be very fond of, and even love. That would be my only request of you.

These kinds of messages do not have to be long. They can be letters, or they can be short notes. They can consist of a long or short audiotape or videotape. The important thing is that they provide support by offering encouragement and strength to the recipient.

In regard to this message that Susan left for John — you should give your spouse permission to remarry. Your spouse should feel secure in your support if he or she falls in love again. Giving this "permission" will head off unwarranted guilt by releasing your spouse from the thought that he or she would be betraying memories of you by remarrying. You also should leave a message to your children, letting them know that if their parent does remarry someday, you would support that decision and hope they will support it, too. If your feel other family members might have a difficult time in accepting the idea of remarriage, you should consider sending them a messsage as well.

First Wedding Anniversary After Your Death

The first wedding anniversary after a spouse's death is particularly painful. For Susan, this was no exception.

Susan slept in. She just couldn't seem to get out of bed. As she lay there, she went through anniversary memories in her mind. She knew this was going to be another long day. Later that afternoon, while the kids were at school, she was sitting on her couch flipping through the pages of a worn scrapbook. She alternated between smiling and crying as she came across the various pictures of her and John. Sometimes, she cried and laughed at the same time.

She came to one page and stopped. It was the picture she was looking for — of her and John on their first wedding anniversary. John is holding Susan in his arms as if he was carrying her somewhere. They both were smiling from ear to ear. She remembered how happy that day was. She was holding a bouquet of yellow flowers. She looked at the opposite page of the scrapbook to see those very same flowers, dried and preserved, protected behind the plastic sleeve. She thought how special it was for John to have given her those yellow roses, her favorite, and how he had presented her with a bouquet of yellow roses on every anniversary day since then.

The doorbell rang. Deep in thought, Susan was startled. When she opened the door, she saw a deliveryman standing on her front porch with a bouquet of yellow roses and a letter. After thanking him, she went inside with the flowers and sat down on the couch. She smelled the flowers, set them on the table next to her, then opened the letter.

As she read the letter from John, her eyes teared. She picked up the scrapbook and embraced it tightly to her chest. She looked up and whispered, "Thank you, honey. I needed that."

You can't guarantee that every message will have this kind of timing. Even though you can't plan it exactly, you can pray that God will bless your messages of support and, through your Trust executor, will arrange the details.

First Anniversary of Your Death

"Confronting the first anniversary of the death day is also a major psychological challenge."
— Ashley Davis Prend[15]

The first anniversary of your death is a significant and difficult benchmark. One year represents a psychological milestone in the grieving process. John's family received messages from John a year after the date of his death. In one excerpt, he wrote to Susan:

I'll be waiting for you, but I expect you to begin a new life when you're ready. You will have to. Tuck me away in your heart, but begin to live again. Rejoin the world and get back into life. Continue with the obligations I know you have, and don't feel guilty. Have fun! You and I will always have our memories, and nobody can ever take them away. But awaiting you are new memories, new experiences, and new challenges.

Birthdays

Birthday cards, letters, and even sentimental gifts can have special meaning to your recipient on his or her first birthday after your passing. You can arrange to have a letter sent along with flowers, or tickets to a show, a play, or a sporting event. All can be easily arranged by your Trust executor per your instructions. Chapter 4 goes into specifics about four unique kinds of birthday messages.

Holidays

Holidays are likely to be difficult for your family without you. The holiday could be Mother's Day or Father's Day. It might be Thanksgiving. It could be a holiday such as Memorial Day weekend, if your family traditionally spent that holiday together in a special way. Look at all of the key holidays and determine which ones will be the most difficult for your family. Then prepare a message of support for each member of your family or for the family as a whole, tailored to the holiday and the memories they will have of you at that time.

The First Christmas Afterward

For most families, the first Christmas after your death will be the hardest holiday time. Susan had dreaded this day for a couple of months. The traditions the family had established for the last 18 years just didn't have the same meaning or significance anymore.

The entire extended family was at her house this Christmas Eve, as had been the case for the last 10 years. Everyone was in the traditional semicircle in the living room, next to the Christmas tree, opening presents. The atmosphere was fairly jovial on the surface, but underneath it all, everyone was missing John. He was the life of holiday events, always joking and laughing, and everyone relied on him to set the tone of the event. John also was especially good at picking just the right Christmas presents for family members. He had an eye for the unique and unusual, and the gift you got from John was going to be your favorite, or certainly the most interesting.

After those who had gathered by the tree had opened their presents and were talking about their upcoming plans for the holidays, the doorbell rang. Susan wondered who would be at the door on Christmas Eve and thought it must be a neighbor. Her dad answered the door, and she could hear him greeting the visitor. It was Steven.

Her heart leaped. She told herself to contain her excitement, but she just knew Steven was delivering a message from John. Steven greeted everyone with a hardy, "Merry Christmas!" Susan couldn't take her eyes off of the nicely wrapped box with the big, red, velvet bow tucked under Steven's arm. Lauren ran to the tree and pulled out the Christmas present for Steven. He gave her a hug.

Lauren asked, "Is that for us?"

Steven looked at Susan and said, "It's for all of you, but your mom is the one who is supposed to open it."

Knowing that her hunch was correct, Susan said, "It's from John, isn't it?"

Steven nodded yes, and a hush descended in the room as some stared at the present and some at Susan. Suddenly Lauren, RJ, and Tyler began jumping up and down as if this were the only present anyone had ever given them. "Mom! It's from Dad! It's from Dad!"

Susan untied the bow and gently, almost reverently, laid it next to her. Lauren, RJ, and Tyler anxiously stood in front of her. She pulled out another, smaller wrapped box and said, "This one is for RJ," then another for Lauren and another for Tyler. The children sat down at Susan's feet, ripping the wrapping paper off their presents as fast as they could. Susan pulled out envelopes and started calling out the names of those whose names were written on them.

She pulled out a small present with her name written on it and said she would open it later, to the dismay of the curious family. Then she pulled out a VHS tape with a label saying, "Merry Christmas to all of my family — play now." She motioned to her sister sitting next to her and announced to everyone, "It seems that John has a Christmas message for all of us." Susan's sister turned on the television and put in the tape. While everyone was watching John's video message, Susan kept thinking, "John, you still never cease to amaze me."

How do you think John's family members will rate this Christmas gift? Probably at the top of their list. But every family is different. A Christmas message might *not* be the best kind of message for *your* family members — or it may be the ideal kind of message. You certainly do not want to ruin their Christmas. You want to bless it. As with other kinds of support, you should evaluate your family as a whole and individually, looking at their personalities, characteristics, and spiritual maturity, before determining the kinds of support messages you create.

Direct and Indirect Support

You can provide support in two basic ways during this time: direct and indirect. With direct support, you send your messages directly to your family, even though the messages will be delivered by your Spiritual Trust executor or other trusted messenger. With indirect support you send messages *to others*, such as your executor, friends, minister, or other family members, requesting *them* to provide your family support. In the first case, your family receives support from you; in the second case, your family receives support from someone else. Both types of support can be helpful to your family.

Direct Support Messages

When you send messages of direct support to you family, consider inserting at appropriate places in those messages some of the following points.[16] They will have extra meaning coming from you.

- Do cry. Crying is a natural response to pain.
- Do talk about your feelings, needs, and memories, good and bad.
- Do accept help.
- Do seek counseling on grief and bereavement from a qualified counselor.
- Do ask all of the questions that are in your head.
- Do get plenty of rest.
- Do question.
- Do be patient.
- Do forgive yourself.
- Do trust yourself.
- Do keep following your dreams.
- Do tell others what you need.
- Do tell others when they have helped.
- Do take care of yourself.
- Do consider mutual help/support groups.
- Do mourn. Mourning is like healing a serious and deep wound — The more healthy support a wound receives, the better is the quality of the healing in the end.
- Do record your thoughts and feelings in a journal.
- Do avoid making major decisions immediately following your loss.
- Do find someone who has been through the experience.
- Do reach out to others.
- Do take a trip you always have wanted to take.
- Do spend time reading the Bible.
- Do read the Psalms.
- Do ask the children about their grief on a regular basis. They may try to hide their grief to protect you.
- Do let the children see you grieve. It gives them permission to grieve.
- Don't invent guilt for something you did or didn't do.
- Don't feel guilty if you are having a good time.
- Don't worry about tomorrow.
- Don't try to hide the pain of your grief.
- Don't accept advice without questioning.
- Don't give away your rights.
- Don't go against your natural inclinations.
- Don't make decisions in haste.
- Don't ever give up.

Spiritual Trusts

Indirect Support Messages

> "Most people will accommodate whatever needs the griever has if they know that is what the griever wants."
> — Andrea Gambill[17]

Those you will ask to provide indirect support to your family members could use some suggestions as well. In your messages to them, feel free to make suggestions about how they can best support your family throughout the bereavement period. Some of the following tips may seem obvious, but I suggest you insert them appropriately in your messages.[18]

- Do be patient. Real support is not a quick fix.
- Do listen. Bereaved people benefit from telling their story again and again.
- Do be available.
- Do be sensitive.
- Do share a special memory about me, either in person or on a sympathy card.
- Do volunteer to drive them to the gravesite; some people don't want to go alone.
- Do offer to help with the thank-you notes.
- Do drop off food that just has to be reheated. When you make a meal, fix a plate for them and drop it by.
- Do ask about specific ways in which you can help.
- Do offer to take the kids to an afternoon movie or other fun event.
- Do invite them over for dinner on a specific night.
- Please DO say:
  - I'm sorry.
  - I really care about you.
  - What can I do that would be helpful for you right now?
  - What helps?
  - I'm praying for you
- Do make contact. Go for the visit. Make the phone call. Send the card or note.
- Do encourage them to eat.

- Do remember that you don't have to be perfect in your attempts to comfort those suffering from a loss. You don't need the ideal words. All that is really needed is compassion, open arms, and prayers for healing.
- Don't give too much advice on how *you* think they should grieve.
- Don't make judgments.
- Don't stay away.
- Don't worry about saying the wrong thing, but listen and be sensitive.
- Please *don't* say:
  - It was God's will.
  - God needed another angel in his garden.
  - Your loss is heaven's gain.
  - Your situation reminds me of my situation…
  - You need to forget about the past.
  - You need to go on with your life.
  - Don't cry, don't be sad, and don't be afraid.
  - I know just how you feel.
  - Time will heal.
- Don't just say, "Call me if you need anything." Drop by to see how they are really doing, and observe what they might need. If you can't visit, make a point to call them once a week or every other week for at least three months.

"Yet what people going through sorrow need most is consolation, not explanation. A warm hug and a few minutes of patient listening mend more hearts than the most learned theological lecture."
— Harold S. Kushner[19]

Supporting Your Children

Your children must not be forgotten, as they, too, will experience enormous grief. Although they may resume their normal schedule (school, sports, activities, and so on), they are *not* normal. Adults may have sympathetic adult friends to help them through their grief. Children may or may not have adult friends to help them, and the child's younger friends usually don't have the knowledge and experience to help their peers through something as difficult as the loss of a parent.

Take a friend of mine, Skip. He was 14 years old when his father died. The two had a wonderful and close relationship. Skip's dad was his baseball and football coach. They fished together, played together, and loved each other very much. Skip's dad, unfortunately, had a family history of heart disease, and his own heart attack came hours after he had coached Skip in a football game.

Skip saw his dad in the hospital, and he seemed to be in fair condition. As usual, his dad made some jokes. Back in 1964, people were placed in oxygen tents that covered their entire head and upper body. Skip's dad joked that if he were to break wind (not the term he used), he would gas himself.

Skip went home and prayed to God that his dad would be okay. A phone call at seven o'clock the next morning, however, conveyed the news that a blood clot had lodged in his dad's heart, and that he had died. Skip was crushed. His dad and best friend was dead, and God had let this happen.

Growing up, Skip had gone to church every Sunday and he sang in the choir, but nothing had prepared him for the tragedy of his dad's death. Shortly after the funeral, Skip concluded that if that's the way God is, Skip didn't want anything to do with Him. Skip continued to go to church because his mother made him go, but he had a deep resentment of God. That resentment lasted 20 years! Skip didn't go to church as an adult because he didn't have to go anymore, and really wanted no dealings with the God who had let his dad die so unfairly.

When Skip was 34 years old, a friend who happened to be a Christian invited Skip to go to a retreat, and he went because single women would be there. At this retreat, Skip again felt the love of God and asked Him back into his heart.

Although Skip now knows he will be with his dad again in heaven, not all stories have this happy ending. Children who turn off to God because of the death of a loved one can be deceived by Satan forever. Perhaps a message addressing this issue from his father could have prevented Skip from turning off to God for more than 20 years.

Besides the many examples I have given thus far on supporting your children, Chapter 4, Legacy Trusts, includes many examples of how to provide spiritual support to your children at various ages and stages of their life. Messages to your children may be especially difficult for you to prepare, particularly if they are young. Their importance to your children during bereavement, however, cannot be overestimated. Satan will attempt to sow fear, anger, bitterness, confusion, and doubt in the hearts and minds of your children. You can help to stave off these attempts through messages of faith and encouragement to your children.

Your adult children could use supporting messages from you as well. Erin Kramp makes an excellent point in her book *Living With The End In Mind* when she says, "As for adult children, never underestimate the "child" in all of us. None of us, no matter the age, is prepared for the death of a loving parent."[20]

Ongoing Support

The ongoing support phase is dedicated to providing your family and others with spiritual and emotional support for many years to come. This can be done through FaithMessages and LifeMessages (introduced in the previous discussion), sent at certain benchmarks in your recipients' lives, as well as through your Prayer Trust and Legacy Trust components. In this phase you lovingly remain a part of the lives of your family members while allowing and encouraging them to move forward with their lives.

John had learned a lot from his life and wanted to pass on this wisdom to his kids. In case he was not able to finish the task during his life, he made sure he would be able to do so afterward through ongoing support messages. John didn't let his death stop him from providing spiritual and emotional support, and others can follow his example.

Your Messages

Sending messages into the future lives of your children or grandchildren is a meaningful way to provide ongoing support and also is a way to deeply imprint your legacy onto their hearts. This is why many examples of these kinds of messages are included in Chapter 4, Legacy Trusts. Besides the many benchmarks I've mentioned in this chapter and in the upcoming chapters, you can focus your messages on more general issues such as answering the questions your children or grandchildren will have as they grow older. From an ongoing support perspective, this falls under the purview of LifeMessages or FaithMessages.

When you create these messages, avoid setting specific expectations or lofty goals for them. You do not want to convey wishes that they may not be able to live up to. You have to be careful in setting goals for them that may not be the direction in life they want to take. I'm not talking about setting general objectives, such as that they will be a person of character, or a person of faith. I'm talking about setting specific goals for marriage, college, a certain occupation — that sort of thing. Of course, you can create messages to be delivered if these things become a reality, but you should not to try to parent from the grave and continue to guide them throughout their life. A wide variety of circumstances could occur that make your specific goals or expectations impossible to achieve in their life. Furthermore, they will have to make decisions that will be best for them during their life — and those decisions will not always match the choices you conveyed to them sometime in the past.

Living parents and grandparents can change their hopes and wishes for their loved ones as life unfolds, but when messages are created and then delivered long after death, these messages cannot be changed. Therefore, you should word your messages carefully so as not to cause a sense of guilt or failure if they don't live up to the wishes you had for them when you were alive. Your approach should be one of sharing with them instead of telling them what to do.

Memories of You

> "Memories are of tremendous importance to all survivors. They keep us going, give us strength, and can be passed on to others who cared about our loved one."
> — Carol Staudacher[21]

A lady I know told me that when her husband died, she searched her entire home looking for something from him to her. She was hoping to find a note or a letter maybe tucked away in a book or a drawer but found nothing. She said she would have cherished anything like that and was depressed that she wouldn't have a tangible memory to cherish.

It doesn't take a lot of time or even effort to spend an afternoon or evening and write a few letters to your loved ones. If you have children or grandchildren especially, you should take the time and make the effort to prepare messages to them. The birth of a child or grandchild, also provides a wonderful opportunity to prepare messages to the child to be delivered well into the future. It only takes a few hours to prepare handwritten letters to a new child or grandchild to be delivered at key benchmarks such as when he or she turns 12, 16, 21, or gets married. David Dennis, the Assistant Executive Director of the Devereux Foundation, Florida, articulated to me the difference such letters can make to the children or grandchildren left behind:

> "When I was almost four I remember being called into the living room of our little home, where I crawled up on the couch, with my sister, and we were told our Daddy was gone. I never got to know him. I never will. As a Licensed Professional Counselor, Licensed Marriage Therapist and a person who has worked professionally with children and families for over 20 years, I know all the right "treatment modalities" for grieving, but nothing will stop the simple, painful truth that I just wish I could have known my Dad, or know more about him, *from him*. Even one letter from him would have made a tremendous difference in my life. The pain of that deficit will never be healed, or it's space filled. Nor will my life be made better, or my children's lives, because I learned things from my Dad."[22]

Don't underestimate the difference one letter, or an audio or video recording from you can make to your child or grandchild if something were to happen to you. If you are able to deliver these Trust components yourself when the time for delivery arrives, that's great and you can explain why you prepared it. If you are no longer around to deliver them yourself, your messages will be treasured by your recipients. They *will* make a difference!

The memories your family members have of you will be extremely important to them for the rest of their lives. After you pass away, one of the first things your family is likely to do is to gather all of the physical manifestations of these memories — photos, audiotapes, videos, letters, and so on. These items serve as a memory bank of *you*, tangibly speaking. Your family will treasure them.

You can supplement that memory bank with deposits of tremendous value. Those deposits are the components of the Legacy Trust discussed in Chapter 4. If you leave your family with your LifeStory, your loved ones will be comforted by the knowledge that memories of you are preserved for themselves and for future generations. This is an excellent example of how the parts of the Spiritual Trust System work together. Your Legacy Trust is perhaps the best way to provide ongoing support to your family.

When it comes to preserving a memory bank, consider these three issues:

1. Fading memories
2. The wrong memories
3. No more memories

Fading Memories

"C.S. Lewis and I share, too, the fear of the loss of memory."

— Madeleine L'Engle[23]

Survivors typically fear that the details of memories of their lost loved one will fade. They might not be able to remember exactly the sound of your laughter, or the precise look on your face when you were happy. To prevent memory decay, memories must be reinforced by repetition. When people die, they no longer are there in person to reinforce the memories. After time, the "outer edges" of our memories begin to wear down.

To prevent memory decay, memories must be reinforced by repetition.

This in no way implies that our loved ones will forget us after we die. But memories do fade. What can you do about it?

First, make sure you have a lot of pictures and videos showing you and your family laughing and having fun together. As you live your life, keep in mind the value of these pictures and video memories for your family later.

- Be sure you get close-up shots of you with each member of your family.

- Take advantage of the times you are being videotaped at a family event or just playing with the kids or grandkids. Look into the camera and say something meaningful. Don't rehearse it or script every detail. Just talk. Be natural. Be real.

- Tell the family member shooting the "action" that you love him or her. These kinds of verbal expressions of love fit into the context of any family video.

- Create a written, audio, or video memories message in which you simply chat about the fond memories you have. Include family memories and memories of individual family members.

- Make a video montage (discussed earlier in the chapter) on you and your spouse, and on you and each child. There are plenty of occasions to do this: anniversaries, graduations, weddings, and so on. Build a strong memory bank of family memories through your pictures and video.

John prepared a video that was nearly 2 hours long. He did this in three different settings, then segmented the 2-hour video footage into eight chapters and put them on a DVD. This way, his family can scroll through the chapters like a DVD movie. They can find the topic they want to watch and hit "play." They will see John talking about his family memories. Putting your video onto DVDs is simple, and the cost is modest. See www.spiritualtrusts.com/digitaltransfers.

You can talk about all kinds of memories. Here are a few topics to get your mind accelerating:

Family:

- Reunions

- Family trips and vacations

- Birthdays

- Holidays

- Family meal conversations

- Events, neighborhoods, and homes

- Churches attended

Spiritual Trusts

Spouse:

- The first time you met
- When you knew you had fallen in love
- When you first realized your spouse was the one you wanted to marry
- Favorite things to do
- Dreams achieved
- Obstacles overcome
- Jobs and careers

Children:

- The life you had before they were born
- Their birth
- The first times they talked, walked, rode a bike, told you they loved you
- Sports and other interests
- Friends and dating
- School — milestones, accomplishments, teachable moments, graduation
- Funniest memories, proudest moments, and so on

Creating meaningful memories with your loved ones can be a cherished byproduct of living your life while following the Spiritual Trust System. If you create a Legacy Trust, you will be assured that your family will not forget the details of their memories of you.

Wrong Memories

Your death — the most recent memory of you — likely will be in the forefront of your family members' minds for a long time. These loved ones can easily fall into the trap of concentrating almost entirely on the painful memories of the circumstances of your death instead of remembering your life as a whole.

Memories of your death are not the memories you want your family members to re-live. If they are haunted by the image of a loved one in a hospital bed hooked up to machines and a dozen tubes, for instance, they will be consumed with emotionally painful memories. Your ongoing support messages can help them concentrate on memories of the wholeness of your life and help to sweep away those negative memories. This will aid them in their healing process.

Here is an excerpt of a message John sent to his family members after his death to try to keep them focused on what he wanted them to remember:

I'm not sure exactly how I left this earth except that I know it wasn't planned. If it was expected, I would have changed this message accordingly. I hope you don't concentrate on the memories of my death too much. No matter how I died, how it happened, or why it happened, no matter if I suffered a lot or none at all, I want you to know this. The very moment, yes that very second that my spirit left my body, I went to be with our Lord, Jesus Christ (2 Corinthians 5:8).

I promise you that on my way to be with Jesus, I wasn't thinking about any of the circumstances of my death. I didn't have any physical pain or memories of pain at that time. Please take comfort in this. You will do my life a great injustice if you dwell only on my death instead of embracing the memories of my life.

I hope you will concentrate on the essence of who I was and how I lived, not on how I died. Wrestle with these memories, but allow God to take away the power of these memories and heal them. Remember how much I loved you, all of the things we did together, all of the laughs we had. I had a wonderful life because of all of you. I crossed the bridge to heaven, where the joys and wondrous things I am experiencing are so glorious that I couldn't describe them on paper if I wanted to.

Spiritual Trusts

When you think of me, think about the life I had and the life I'm now living. Don't concentrate on the bridge in-between.

You can help your family overcome the wrong memories by reinforcing the right memories. Once again, your Legacy Trust components are a fine way to do this.

No More New Memories

Equally as disturbing as the fear that their memories of you will fade is the somber feeling that family members will not be able to create *new* memories *with* you. Even though you can't change this reality, you can do the next best thing: Create new memories for them. Through your messages to them during the ongoing support phase, you can share stories that they haven't heard before.

In one of his ongoing support messages to Susan, John relived his memory of the day he asked Susan to marry him. In the message, he related feelings he had that day, which he had never told her before.

Susan, I never told you this, but the most nervous day of my life was the day I asked you to marry me. I was so nervous, in fact, that I didn't eat one thing that day. I must have rubbed my sweaty hands on my pants a hundred times. After I did ask you to marry me, that night when I dropped you off at your home, I got into my car as the happiest man in the entire world. I felt like climbing a mountain or something because so much adrenaline was racing through me.

But before I got out of your neighborhood, tears were streaming down my face. I was suddenly overwhelmed with the reality that you would be my wife and I would be your husband. I was so thankful to God for giving you to me. The euphoria, excitement, and deep sense of responsibility made me cry (in a good way!). I kind of embarrassed myself, but I knew it validated how much I loved you and how happy I was that I would be spending the rest of my life with you.

New insight into old memories is the next best thing to new memories. When you are developing this kind of memory bank, you're not just sharing old memories; you're telling the people you love how those memories made you feel and how they changed your life. This memory sharing can give your family a feeling of *discovering* you, as opposed to losing you.

> New insight into old memories is the next best thing to new memories.

Mentors and Advisors

An excellent form of ongoing support is to arrange for your children to have mentors. Steven Earll, whom I have quoted in this chapter, lost his wife, Rachel, to breast cancer. Focus on the Family featured Steven and their story on a video entitled *Physician Assisted Suicide, Not Worth Living*. Before Rachel died, she arranged for two women in her church to be mentors to her two daughters. She selected women who loved her children, and her children knew and were comfortable with. She chose each mentor to fit each child's personality. These mentors have played an important role in the lives of Steven and Rachel's daughters, and the girls continue to have a special relationship with them to this day.

If you do not feel comfortable with establishing mentors, you can suggest people that your children might want to talk to or seek advice from on a host of different issues. For instance, you might suggest a person to consult with when they need adult input in addition to the other parent. If you are a woman with a daughter, you might suggest a certain woman to talk to about "women's issues" that may be difficult to discuss with her father. This in no way is meant to circumvent the authority of the surviving parent. It is meant to supplement your children's support.

You also might consider recommending people for your spouse to talk to about certain issues —financial, parenting, school, or other issues. Think about the areas in which your spouse might need some assistance and the best person to seek out for help for each of these issues.

DOUBLE TROUBLE

This chapter is based on the premise that *you* will be the first to go and that your spouse will remain behind. That's not always the case. Your spouse may predecease you, or you both might die at the same time in an accident. As terrible as these thoughts are, you should contemplate this potential scenario, discuss it with your spouse, and prepare at least the following:

1. Messages to the person or couple who will serve as guardian to any children.
2. Some joint messages to each child, of the types outlined here.
3. Some joint messages to friends and family with requests and instructions to be followed in the case of a tragedy that takes both of your lives.

Most of the messages and other support you prepare individually will serve their purpose even if you and your spouse die together. This rare but real potential emphasizes the need for both the husband and wife to develop Spiritual Trusts to cover all eventualities.

If you are a single parent, you have many other concerns if the other parent would not be able to care for the children for any reason. For example, if the other parent is unfit or has passed away already, child custody arrangements should be made in advance. These issues are not within the scope of this book but should be carefully evaluated. The book *Living With The End In Mind* by Erin and Douglas Kramp (with Emily McKhann) is a good book to read about selecting caregivers for you, young children in this scenario.

RESOURCES FOR YOUR FAMILY

In developing a Support Trust, you should consider having at least one book on bereavement and grief ready for your family in advance. This book could be included in your Trust, or you could have your executor purchase a specific book or books you have preselected. Another option is to send a message to your minister with a request to provide your family with a book that is spiritually sound and rooted in Biblical principles.

Many good resources are available on the topics of grief and bereavement. Of all of the books I have read, several definitely will be in the hands of my family when I go to be with our Lord. Three of my favorites are Zig Zigler's *Confessions of a Grieving Christian*, Gerald Sittser's *A Grace Disguised*, and Carol Staudacher's *A Time to Grieve*. In my opinion, these are "must reads" for any family dealing with the death of a loved one.

Three good sources to locate publications on grief and bereavement are:

- Centering Corporation (www.centering.org or call 402-553-1200 to request their catalog of grief resources).
- Good Grief Resources (www.goodgriefresources.com or 719-277-0093).
- *Bereavement Magazine* (www.bereavementmag.com; 888-60-4HOPE). In addition to being an excellent source for books, this spiritual magazine (and website) is packed with helpful resources, tips, stories, and other valuable information. I have arranged for my family to receive a subscription for the first year after my passing.

If you leave books for your family, consider writing a short note inside the cover explaining what about the book appealed to you and why you believe it will be of help. A list of suggested books is given in the Recommended Resources, below.

IN SUMMARY

Leaving a Support Trust to your family members can be an enormous benefit to them regardless of the circumstances surrounding your death. It will help them in each phase of grieving as only you can do. The three phases of support — initial, bereavement, and ongoing — are as overlapping as the three phases of grief. Suggestions given for the bereavement support phase might be equally good for you to use during the ongoing support phase. There are no rigid guidelines. What may comfort one family may be painful for another, and the support you provide for your family may be quite different from mine. Creating a Spiritual Trust is a highly individualized process.

Throughout the grieving process, the timing of support is important. Gradually, your family members will work through their grief and embark on a new life of their own while retaining memories of you and the support you provided through your Support Trust.

In all cases, the important thing is to frame support messages in ways that promote healing and provide support, not ways that could impair the progress your family has made and set them back in their grieving process. Through careful thought and prayer, you can make arrangements that are sensitive to the needs of those you leave behind and will positively influence their emotional and spiritual realities.

The best kind of support you can provide your family members is the grounding you give them *during* your life, not after. Discussing death and eternal life with your family members appropriately will help you formulate your Support Trust and get your family accustomed to communicating about an issue that impacts everyone. This is all apart of living with eternity in mind!

Recommended Resources

Becton, Randy. *Everyday Comfort*. Baker Book House, 1993.
Dobson, James. *When God Doesn't Make Sense*. Wheaton, IL: Tyndale House, 2001.
Felton, Deirdre, *The Compassion and Bereavement Tape Series* (available through Bereavement Publishing, Colorado Springs, CO: www.bereavementmag.com
Gambill, Andrea. "Do and Don't Suggestions for the Bereaved and Their Caregivers" [booklet]. Colorado Springs, CO: Bereavement Publishing, 1993.
Heatherly-Landorf, Joyce, *Mourning Song*. Salado, TX: Balcony Publishing, 1994.
Hicks, Ralph. *Everyone Dies*. Tuscon, AZ 1-888-556-1350.
Holtkamp, Sue. "Bereavement and Spirituality" [booklet]. Colorado Springs, CO: Bereavement Publishing, 1995.
Kushner, Harold S. *When Bad Things Happen to Good People*. New York: Avon Books, 1989.
Lewis, C.S. *A Grief Observed*. New York: HarperCollins, 1996.
Manning, Doug, *Thoughts for the Grieving Christian*. Oklahoma City, OK: InSight Books, 2001.
Mitsch, Raymond, and Lynn Brookside. *The Grieving Process*. Vinebooks, 1993.
Prend, Ashley Davis. *Transcending Loss — Understanding the Life long Impact of Grief and How To Make It Meaningful*. New York: Berkly Books, 1997.
Schweibert, Pat. *Tear Soup*. Portland, OR: Grief Watch, 1999.
Sims, Darcie. *If I Could Just See Hope*. Louisville, KY: Big A and Company, 1993.

Staudacher, Carol. *A Time to Grieve*. New York: HarperCollins, 1994.

Sittser, Gerald. *A Grace Disguised*. Zondervan Publishing House, 1998.

The Journey Through Grief. Fort Collins, CO: Companion Press, 1997.

Wolfelt, Alan. *Healing the Bereaved Child*. Fort Collins, CO: Companion Press, 1996.

Zigler, Zig. *Confessions of a Grieving Christian*. Nashville, TN: Thomas Nelson Publishers, 1999.

2002 Bereavement Resources and Gifts of Hope and Healing. Colorado Springs, CO: Bereavement Publishing.

Websites

www.bereavementmag.com or 1-888-604-HOPE
www.centering.org 402-553-1200
www.goodgriefresources.com or 719-277-0093
www.compassionconnection.org

Additional resources appear on our website at www.spiritualtrusts.com/supporttrusts

Some scriptures you may consider using in your Support Trusts:

Matthew 11: 28-30
Come to Me, all who are weary and heavy-laden, and I will give you rest. Take My yoke upon you and learn from Me, for I am gentle and humble in heart, and you will find rest for your souls. For My yoke is easy and My burden is light.

John 14: 1-3
Do not let your heart be troubled; believe in God, believe also in Me. In My Father's house are many dwelling places; if it were not so, I would have told you; for I go to prepare a place for you. If I go and prepare a place for you, I will come again and receive you to Myself, that where I am, there you may be also.

John 14: 19
After a little while the world will no longer see Me, but you will see Me; because I live, you will live also.

Spiritual Trusts

John 14: 27
Peace I leave with you; My peace I give to you; not as the world gives do I give to you. Do not let your heart be troubled, nor let it be fearful.

1 Peter 5: 7
Casting all your anxiety on Him, because He cares for you.

Psalm 55: 22
Cast your burden upon the Lord and He will sustain you; He will never allow the righteous to be shaken.

Isaiah 57: 1
The righteous man perishes, and no man takes it to heart; And devout men are taken away, while no one understands. For the righteous man is taken away from evil.

Romans 8: 28
And we know that God causes all things to work together for good to those who love God, to those who are called according to His purpose.

2 Corinthians 5: 8
We are of good courage, I say, and prefer rather to be absent from the body and to be at home with the Lord.

Psalm 147: 3
He heals the brokenhearted and binds up their wounds.

Matthew 5: 4
Blessed are those who mourn, for they shall be comforted.

John 11: 35
Jesus wept.

Philippians 4: 13
I can do all things through Him who strengthens me.

Romans 8: 18
For I consider that the sufferings of this present time are not worthy to be compared with the glory that is to be revealed to us.

Psalm 46: 1
God is our refuge and strength, A very present help in trouble.

Jeremiah 31: 13
Then the virgin will rejoice in the dance, and the young men and the old, together, for I will turn their mourning into joy and will comfort them and give them joy for their sorrow.

2 Corinthians 1: 3-4
Blessed be the God and Father of our Lord Jesus Christ, the Father of mercies and God of all comfort, who comforts us in all our affliction so that we will be able to comfort those who are in any affliction with the comfort with which we ourselves are comforted by God.

Psalm 23: 4
Even though I walk through the valley of the shadow of death, I fear no evil, for You are with me; Your rod and Your staff, they comfort me.

Nahum 1:7
The Lord is good, a stronghold in the day of trouble, and He knows those who take refuge in Him.

Romans 8: 38-39
For I am convinced that neither death, nor life, nor angels, nor principalities, nor things present, nor things to come, nor powers, nor height, nor depth, nor any other created thing, will be able to separate us from the love of God, which is in Christ Jesus our Lord.

Psalm 34: 17
The righteous cry, and the LORD hears and delivers them out of all their troubles.

ENDNOTES

1. Randy Alcorn, In *Money, Possessions and Eternity*, (Wheaton, IL: Tyndale House, 1989), p. 137.
2. Randy Alcorn, In *Money, Possessions and Eternity*, (Wheaton, IL: Tyndale House, 1989), p. 138.
3. Interview with Steven Earll, September 2002.

4. Alan Wolfelt, *The Journey Through Grief* (Fort Collins, CO: Center for Loss & Life Transition, 1997), P.94.
5. Carol Staudacher, *A Time to Grieve* (New York: HarperCollins, 1992), p. 37.
6. Carol Staudacher, *A Time to Grieve* (New York: HarperCollins, 1992), p. 185.
7. Ashley Prend, *Transcending Loss* (New York: Berkley Books, 1997), p. xv.
8. Zig Zigler, *Confessions of a Grieving Christian* (Nashville, TN: Thomas Nelson, 1999), p. 101.
9. Sue Holtkamp, *Bereavement and Spirituality* [booklet] (Colorado Springs, CO: Bereavement Pub, 1995).
10. Carol Staudacher, *A Time to Grieve* (New York: HarperCollins, 1992), p. 155.
11. Zig Zigler, *Confessions of a Grieving Christian* (Nashville, TN: Thomas Nelson, 1999), p. 135.
12. Interview with Steven Earll, September 2002.
13. Carol Staudacher, *A Time to Grieve* (New York: HarperCollins, 1992), p. 43.
14. Carol Staudacher, *A Time to Grieve* (New York: HarperCollins, 1992), p. 139.
15. Ashley Prend, *Transcending Loss* (New York: Berkley Books, 1997), p. 5.
16. In part from: Andrea Gambill, *Do and Don't Suggestions for the Bereaved and Their Caregivers*, [booklet] (Colorado Springs, CO: Bereavement Pub, 1997).
17. Andrea Gambill, *Do and Don't Suggestions for the Bereaved and Their Caregivers*, [booklet] (Colorado Springs, CO: Bereavement Pub, 1997).
18. In part from: Andrea Gambill, *Do and Don't Suggestions for the Bereaved and Their Caregivers*, [booklet] (Colorado Springs, CO: Bereavement Pub, 1997).
19. Harold Kushner, *When Bad Things Happen to Good People* (New York: Avon Books 1989), p. viii.
20. Kramp and Kramp, *Living with the End in Mind* (New York: Three Rivers Press, 1998), p.60.
21. Carol Staudacher, *A Time to Grieve* (New York: HarperCollins, 1992), p. 72.
22. Interview with David Dennis, September 2002.
23. C.S. Lewis, Foreword in *A Grief Observed*, (New York: HarperCollins, 1996), p. xiii.

THREE

Prayer Trusts

"God will do nothing on earth except in answer to believing prayer."

— John Wesley

What is the single most important thing we can do on earth to prompt God's hand, protection, and provision? Most of us probably would say "prayer." Yet this most effective thing is possibly what we do the least in our spiritual lives.

Christians have the privilege and duty to pray, during our lifetime, for God's intercession on behalf of our families. A Prayer Trust enables us to continue to do so long after we have passed away. Prayer Trusts are inextricably related to Support Trusts, and both should be planned and executed together.

WHAT IS A PRAYER TRUST?

A Prayer Trust is a "prayer coverage policy" for loved ones. It is a unique way by which you can unleash and harness the power of prayer for your loved ones not just in the present but in the future as well. As a powerful weapon in your spiritual arsenal, prayer can continue to wage war on evil long after you have passed away.

> A Prayer Trust is a "prayer coverage policy" for loved ones.

In your Prayer Trust, you ask others to pray, after you pass away, in accordance with your specific requests. Most of these prayers will reinforce the prayers you made during your life. When the time for the requested prayers arrives, your Prayer Trust will be implemented by the prayer partners you selected when you created your Prayer Trust.

This chapter covers who and what you can pray for through your Prayer Trust, how to line up prayer partners to pray for your family in the future, and when to initiate prayers through your Prayer Trust.

> "The law of prayer is the highest law of the universe — it can overcome the other laws by sanctioning God's intervention."
>
> — B.J. Wilhite[1]

DIVINE AUTHORITY TO CREATE A PRAYER TRUST

God is ready to answer your prayers today, tomorrow and a hundred years from now. Perhaps this is because God is omnipotent and omnipresent. He exists yesterday, today, and tomorrow. You will not confuse God by asking Him to answer prayers in the future lives of your children, grandchildren, and great-grandchildren. He knows what is going to happen and when it will happen, and He wants to answer your prayers.

God has the power to answer your prayers (*Genesis* 25:21; *2 Samuel* 21:14; *I Chronicles* 5:20; *Ezra* 8:23), whether they are for the present or the future. He is able to provide for our needs beyond *all* that we ask or think (*Ephesians* 3:20).

God is ready to answer your prayers today, tomorrow and a hundred years from now.

Faith is a requirement for answered prayer in life, and it is no different for a Prayer Trust designed to activate interceding prayer after life. God takes pleasure in answering prayers from a faithful heart (*Luke* 18:8; *Matthew* 7:7,17:20, 21:22; *James* 1:5, 4:2, 5:15; *Romans* 12:12).

MEET MARY

Mary is a loving and nourishing mother and grandmother. She has two daughters (and sons-in-law) and four grandchildren. Mary's mother passed away from breast cancer, and 3 years ago Mary discovered that she, too, had "the cancer." Her attitude toward life didn't drastically change upon her diagnoses. For more than 30 years now, Mary has made it a point to live each day as if it were her last — a lesson we could all learn.

She has believed in the power of prayer for as long as she can remember. She has seen its power demonstrated again and again. She has witnessed answers to prayer in her life and in the lives of others so frequently that if you ask her, she can relate for hours incidents in which God has blessed and touched lives through answered prayer (trust me, I was there). Throughout her life, praying has brought her serenity like nothing else.

Mary is at peace about where she will be going when she passes away, but she has carried the responsibility of praying for her family and others for many years. It is her ministry in a way, and she spends time each day in fervent prayer, interceding for her family and others whom the Holy Spirit lays upon her heart. Her Prayer Trust gives Mary comfort in knowing that she has arranged for people of faith to continue praying for her family after she passes away.

Everyone's situation is different, but Mary believes that without her Prayer Trust, continuing prayer support for her grandchildren will be minimal to nonexistent when she dies. Her Prayer Trust helps Mary continue to stand in the gap for her grandchildren after she is no longer here. Although I believe Mary will be able to pray for her grandchildren from heaven, there is good reason to arrange prayer support for them with those who remain on earth. If they are praying for Mary's grandchildren, they also are more likely to take an active role in her grandchildren's lives. You will learn more about Mary's Prayer Trust in this chapter.

THE "WHO" OF PRAYER TRUSTS

Who will be the beneficiaries of your Prayer Trust? I will answer that question with a question. Who do you currently pray for consistently? Your answer probably will encompass your spouse, children, and grandchildren — but you don't have to stop there. Prayer Trust beneficiaries could include other family members, friends, church members, spiritual leaders, ministries, neighbors, the unsaved, and co-workers. The Prayer Trust you create can address all of these beneficiaries either separately or in combination.

> "First of all, then, I urge that entreaties and prayers, petitions and thanksgivings, be made on behalf of all men."
> (*I Timothy* 2:1)

THE "WHAT" OF PRAYER TRUSTS

To cover all of the things for which you can pray and for which you can arrange prayer for your Prayer Trust beneficiaries would take a book instead of a chapter. Here I will touch on some key subjects that should help you determine what to ask your Prayer Trust prayer partners to pray for. In addition, I encourage you to read some of the many excellent books on prayer listed at the end of this chapter.

Spiritual and Emotional Comfort and Strength

After you pass away, the first kind of support you can provide your Prayer Trust beneficiaries is for their spiritual and emotional comfort. They will be greatly affected, perhaps devastated, by your death. You can arrange needed prayer for them during their grief and bereavement — prayers that petition God to comfort them and to make them spiritually stronger instead of weaker. You can ask your prayer partners to pray that your family and other Prayer Trust beneficiaries will know in their hearts that you are alive and with God and that they will see you again in heaven.

Protection

If you are an Amy Grant fan like me, you may recall her hit song, "Angels Watching Over Me," in which she refers to "near misses all around me, accidents unknown." Through your prayers, you can call upon God and His angels to protect your family from a host of maladies. In all likelihood, you do this while you are alive. Through your Prayer Trust, you can arrange for prayer partners to watch over your family and to carry on for you after you are gone.

Prayers of protection are like preventive maintenance on a car. Surely you maintain your car — buy new tires when the tread wears thin, change the oil regularly, get tune-ups — all to keep the car running properly. Likewise, you shouldn't wait for a breakdown or crisis to start praying.

All believers need protection against attacks from our enemy. In *1 Peter* 5:8 Satan is depicted as roaming about as a lion, seeking those he can destroy. A real lion seeks out the weakest in a family first.

I sometimes think of my own family as my "herd" that I'm trying to steer from one realm (earth) to another (heaven). Throughout the journey a lion is trying to pick off me and my family. I've viewed too many nature shows on television to think that the lion and its pack will suddenly do a turnabout and begin to feel sorry for my family when I perish. I believe in Satan's total lack of mercy. Pray now and keep praying for the protection of your family.

Salvation

When I was growing up, my parents would have taken everything they had and joyfully traded it for my salvation. I proved to be quite the spiritual challenge. I know they prayed long and hard — and they were rewarded in God's time. There is no greater prize in the whole world than to know that the ones you deeply love also have Jesus living in their hearts and are destined for eternal bliss rather than eternal torment.

There is no greater affliction for believers than to know that someone they deeply love would be eternally separated from a loving God if they were to die today. If you have such a person in your life, his or her salvation should be the focus of many a prayer during your life. So why not utilize a Prayer Trust to keep the salvation of this loved one at the forefront of your prayer partners' prayers after you are gone? A Prayer Trust simply arranges for others to pick up the torch and carry it for this person's salvation. This is particularly important if you are the only person praying for another's salvation.

This example is Mary's request for salvation for her grandson. It is the basic prayer she offers up for him during her life, and it is the same one she will be asking others to continue praying after she has passed on:

Lord, I continue to pray for the salvation for my grandson, Chris. Though he shows a hard heart toward you, I know that within him there is a soft place. I pray that your Holy Spirit will call him, that He will convict him. May he know that without you there is no hope, no future. I ask that you place others in his life to grow the witness of the spirit within him.

May he be crossing paths with other believers who will love him and help him to see Jesus for who He really is. I pray that Chris will grow weary and tired of the world. May he be like the prodigal son and come back to your open and forgiving arms.

In Jesus name, Amen.

Blessings

Praying for God to pour blessings on your children is a superb way to utilize a Prayer Trust. Some of the blessings you might consider arranging for your loved ones are to bless their marriage, children, and work, and generally to anoint them with favor from God and men.

> "Blessed be the God and Father of our Lord Jesus Christ, who has blessed us with every spiritual blessing in the heavenly places in Christ."
> (*Ephesians* 1:3)

He has granted to you His precious and magnificent promises (*2 Peter* 1:3, 4). He blesses you with heavenly blessings (*Genesis* 49:25). His blessings will come upon you (*Deuteronomy* 28:2). Blessings are on the head of the righteous (*Proverbs* 10:6). The faithful man will be abound with blessings (*Proverbs* 28:20).

Here's a blessing that Mary has prayed for her granddaughter since the day she was born:

Oh Lord, please bless my Kaitlyn with every spiritual blessing. Cover her with your protection. Grant her favor all the days of her life. Open the doors of opportunity to grow in you, and give opportunities to be used of you. Show her your mercy, kindness, and provision. May you guard her heart; may she stay tender to your ways. May there always be the angels of heaven by her side, to keep her, protect her, and provide for her. I pray that she would escape the corruption of the world and recognize that you have blessed her with all that she needs.

My precious Jesus, I thank you for this wonderful girl, and pray that you would walk with her all the days of her life. Amen

All Good Things

We can sum up much of the above supplications in a simple prayer explained in Bruce Wilkinson's wonderful little book, *The Prayer of Jabez*: "Now Jabez called upon the God of Israel, saying, Oh that you would bless me indeed and enlarge my border (territory), and that Your hand might be with me, and that You would keep me from harm that it may not pain me! And God granted him what he requested"(*I Chronicles* 4:10).

This prayer sums up the above by praying that God will:

1. Bless them indeed (blessings).
2. Enlarge their territory (prosperity).
3. Place the hand of the Lord on them (salvation).
4. Keep them from harm (protection).

I love this simple, yet effective, summary of what we can pray for and have others pray for in our stead.

You cannot possibly foresee *everything* your Prayer Trust beneficiaries might need prayer for, and you should not attempt to do so. Instead, ask your prayer partners to seek the guidance of the Holy Spirit about how they should intercede for your family and other Prayer Trust beneficiaries through the various phases of their lives. In *John 14:26* Jesus calls the Holy Spirit our Helper. Ask your prayer partners to pray for each other and to pray specifically that they will be open to the Spirit's prompting.

"In the same way, the Spirit helps us in our weakness; for we do not know how to pray as we should, but the Spirit himself intercedes for us with groanings too deep for words; and He who searches the hearts knows what the mind of the Spirit is, because He intercedes for the saints according to the will of God. And we know that God causes all things to work together for good to those who love God, to those who are called according to his purpose."
(*Romans* 8:26–28)

PRAYER PARTNERS

"For the eyes of the Lord are toward the righteous, and His ears attend to their prayer . . ."
(*I Peter* 3:12)

Close friends cannot be expected to become prayer partners after you're gone without your prompting and encouraging. You need to line up your prayer partners now. Although friends and family likely are the first choices to come to mind, I strongly recommend that you seek those who are solid in their faith. Some believers may have a deeper understanding of your Prayer Trust goals and objectives, as well as an appreciation of the power that prayer provides through your Prayer Trust. They also are more likely to honor their prayer commitments.

There is no age or other specific requirement. The Holy Spirit can bless a person with spiritual maturity as He wills. Peter Wagner says, "Certain Christians, it seems to me, have a special ability to pray for extended periods of time on a regular basis and see frequent and specific answers to their prayers, to a degree much greater than that which is expected of the average Christian."[2]

The best way to line up prayer partners for the future is to join with them as a prayer partner now. Those you pray with today are well suited to carry out your prayer requests in the future since they will know you and most of the people for whom you want them to pray. I can't stress enough the benefits of having people in your life who are praying and interceding on your behalf *now*. The best way to have this now is to pray for *them* and communicate with them regarding existing prayer requests and future prayer requests.

The best way to line up prayer partners for the future is to join with them as a prayer partner now.

Keeping the above in mind, let's take a look at how to arrange for prayer partners to pray in the future for your Prayer Trust beneficiaries. I offer you two methods that should be used in conjunction with each other: the micro method and the macro method.

The Micro Method

In the micro method, you start with your own inner circle and work outward. The most obvious potential prayer partners are family members and close friends. You also should consider people you know from your Sunday school class and church, your minister and church staff, teachers, members of any prayer group or similar small groups to which you belong, and those on any prayer chains of which you are a member. Think of the many people in all walks of life whom you know and who know you.

People who know you reasonably well are probably familiar with your Prayer Trust beneficiaries. Many people feel an innate loyalty to honor a prayer request from a brother or sister in Christ whom they know personally. Make a list of the people you think might pray for your Prayer Trust beneficiaries regularly if you were to pass away.

You should approach your potential prayer partners before you establish your Prayer Trust. Tell them about the spiritual concerns you have for your loved ones now and in the future. Talk to them about the Spiritual Trust System, and explain the vision of your Prayer Trust. Let them know you are creating a Prayer Trust and are looking for prayer partners now who will implement it later. Ask them if they would consider praying for certain needs and in general for your family after you pass on.

Making a commitment to be a prayer partner for a Prayer Trust is a serious responsibility that should not be taken lightly. After you first bring it up to them, you should meet again to determine their interest and commitment, and to pray together for your Prayer Trust and its beneficiaries.

The Macro Method

Many who don't personally know you or your Prayer Trust beneficiaries may still welcome the opportunity to pray passionately for your beneficiaries after your death. Thus, after you have considered the micro method, you may move out from your inner circle into the national and even international flock of believers. Although these people won't know you personally, the sheer number of potential prayer partners is enormous.

You can arrange for hundreds, even thousands, of praying people to bring your loved ones up to the Lord. Among the many avenues are ministries, prayer chains, other churches, and the Internet.

Ministries

Ministries are an excellent resource for seasoned prayer partners. Most ministries attribute their success to prayer. But how do you get a ministry to pray for your loved ones *in the future*? One way is to have the executor of your Prayer Trust contact ministries upon your death. Ministries you supported during your life, or ministries to which you have left a bequest, are a great place to start.

List these ministries for your executor. Upon your death, your executor will contact the ministries and inform the proper person of your prayer requests. Because many ministries are not set up to track long-term prayer requests, this may work best in supporting your family with prayer during the initial phase of their grief and bereavement. In addition, you may ask your executor to contact the ministries you identify periodically after your death to renew prayer requests for specific things or events.

Some ministries, particularly smaller ones, might be willing to commit to being prayer partners for your Prayer Trust in the future. Ask the ministries you support if they would be willing to help you implement your Prayer Trust. Also, you might want to evaluate some prayer ministries. Some ministries either are prayer ministries or offer to pray for the needs of others. One such example is Marilyn Hickey's ministry. You can find more information at www.mhmin.org or call 877-661-1249. Another example is Intercessors International found at www.intercessorsinternational.org In any case, ministries are an important resource to evaluate.

Prayer Chains

As part of your Prayer Trust, you could ask those in your circle of friends and family on your prayer chains to pass along your prayer requests to other prayer chains to which they belong. Additionally, if you search the Internet by using "prayer chains" as your search words you will find dozens of prayer chains that you can contact or have your executor or prayer partners contact.

Other Churches

You might go a step further and ask friends and family members to take your prayer requests to their churches. They could ask that your requests be mentioned in their Sunday school classes and church services or posted in the church bulletin. You basically are getting your circle of prayer partners to reach out to their circles of prayer partners. We trust in the Holy Spirit for prompting, but we can do a little nudging.

The Internet

Dozens of sites on the Internet allow people to post prayer requests. Although somewhat impersonal, this method can reach dedicated prayer partners who are looking specifically for someone for whom they can pray. They may be chomping at the bit, eager to intercede. You can request that your executor post your prayer requests on specific prayer sites visited by people all around the world.

On our website we list ministries, churches, other websites, and even individuals who have expressed a willingness to pray for the behalf of others. You can find this page at www.spiritualtrusts.com/prayertrust. If you are interested in becoming a prayer partner, you can contact the same address.

Your Prayer Partners: Quality and Quantity

Prayer changes things! As you have just read, you can arrange for prayer partners of quality and quantity that can make a real difference in the future for your Prayer Trust beneficiaries. Numbers do make a difference.

Spiritual Trusts

> "Again I say to you, that if two of you agree on earth about anything that they may ask, it will be done for them by my Father who is in heaven. For where two or three have gathered together in My name, I am there in their midst."
> (Matthew 18:19–20)

And Scripture tells us that one puts a thousand to flight, but two — ten thousand (*Deuteronomy* 32:30). Even one man or woman of God can make a significant spiritual difference for your Prayer Trust beneficiaries. God's ears are attentive to the righteous man's prayers (*I Peter* 3:12) and a righteous man's prayers are effective and can accomplish much (*James* 5:16).

Prayer changes things!

Having those who were close to you sincerely praying for your beneficiaries also makes a difference. Therefore, as you establish your Prayer Trust, you should pray about both the quality and quantity of your prayer partners.

Supporting Your Prayer Partners

If you expect others to pray for your family in the future, you should provide prayer support for them in the *present*. Consider how you can support the prayer partners you have selected and who have agreed to participate in your Prayer Trust. Ask how you can pray for them. When they see a commitment of prayer from you, they will be even more likely to follow through with the prayer requests you send them in the future. This action operates on the "you will reap what you sow" principle — a principle that is as certain as the law of gravity.

Take a moment and make it a point to pray for the living members of the family of a deceased person you knew. Start sowing now.

WHEN TO INITIATE PRAYERS
THROUGH YOUR PRAYER TRUST

In reading Chapter 2, you became familiar with the three phases of grief and bereavement and the corresponding phases of a Support Trust: initial support, bereavement support, and ongoing support. Your Spiritual Trust executor should also be familiar with this information so he or she can formulate prayer requests accordingly.

Initial Prayer Support

> "Thinking back upon it now, I realize how much the prayers of the rest of my family and my Christian brothers, sisters, and friends all over the world have meant to us through this grieving period."
> — Zig Zigler[3]

Through your Prayer Trust, you can encourage members of your church and others to harness the power of prayer to spiritually support your family. You can arrange for dozens, hundreds, or even more to pray for your family during this particularly painful initial phase.

When your church is notified of your death, some prayer support will go up for your family by the sheer nature of a caring church. Many churches will provide meals and housekeeping assistance in addition to prayer. Usually an announcement is made in church about the passing of one of its members. Some members of your church and its leadership likely will attend your funeral and go to be with your family at your home afterward. You can encourage this care and prayer for your family through your Prayer Trust.

One way is to write a letter to each person in the leadership of your church and have your executor deliver your letters shortly after your death. These letters ask each to sincerely and deeply pray for your family during the immediate shock and grief following your death.

Let's pretend that John and Bill (from the example in Chapter 2) went to *your* church. You may not have been really close to either of them, but you knew each other on a first-name basis. At church, you heard the announcement that John and Bill had passed away. You solemnly joined the congregation in praying for the families left behind. You made a mental note to find out when and where the funerals will be, and you plan to attend.

The next day you receive a letter at your home from John. When you see his name on the envelope, you are surprised and quickly open it. You read:

Dear [your name],

I hope this letter finds you well, and I pray that your family is healthy and blessed. I'm sure you are surprised to be receiving this letter from me. I wrote it some time ago in case I went to be with the Lord. I'm sure you've heard by now that I've done this very thing.

You and I weren't best friends, but I enjoyed knowing you over the years. I considered you a mature Christian and respected your beliefs, character, and convictions.

Now I want to ask a favor of you: Would you please lift up Susan and the kids in prayer for me? I'm not talking about casual prayer either. I beg you to get on your knees and deeply pray for my family right now. I know they're suffering, and that thought nearly breaks my heart.

I have sent this request to you because I hope you will help me provide spiritual support to my family during this most difficult time. I hope you will pray for my family and ask others to pray for them as well.

There is power in prayer, and I'm asking you to release that power by having you and your family pray for my family. Please pray that the Lord will cover them with His grace and love right now. Pray for spiritual protection for my family. Pray for protection against the evil one sowing thoughts of doubt and bitterness into their hearts.

Please don't let my family down. They need YOUR prayers. I'm counting on you.

My appreciation is boundless. I will thank you personally when I see you up here someday.

God bless you,

John

If you were to receive a letter like this, would the intensity of your prayers for John's family increase? I suspect it would! This kind of letter personalizes the death and the grieving family, creating much more of an obligation and a conviction to pray repeatedly for your family.

You might have this sort of letter sent to people in leadership at your church such as your minister, elders, deacons, music leader, youth minister, associate minister, small group members, and so on. The same type of letters could go to people you know who belong to other churches: family, friends, co-workers, neighbors, and so forth. You would request them to ask their church, Sunday school class, prayer meeting, small group, and others to pray fervently for your family. And you could ask them to place your family on any prayer chain they belong to.

Bereavement Prayer Support

Many believers like to think that other believers will automatically provide prayer support for their families if something happens to them. Although this often is true in the initial phase, most people live hectic lives, and as time passes, they are likely to pray for your family less and less often. Their grieving process will be *substantially* shorter than what your family is going through.

As part of your Prayer Trust, you can send messages to your friends, church fellowship, and others, reminding them that your family still needs their prayers and specifically indicating what you would like them to pray about. This will ensure that your family and other Prayer Trust beneficiaries will have prayer coverage to help insulate them from attacks during the bereavement phase.

John sent the following letter to his minister as part of his Prayer Trust. He sent a similar letter to seven different people. John's executor, Steven, mailed these letters to John's selected recipients 30 days after the funeral.

Jack (John's minister) came home from working all day putting out fires at his church. He walked into his kitchen and laid his car keys on the counter. On top of the stack of the day's mail his wife, Sylvia, had laid out for him was a hand-addressed envelope, and she was anxiously waiting for him to read it. He picked up the envelope, and said, "This is from John. How is this possible?"

"I don't know. Open it up and see what he has to say," his wife replied.

Jack pulled out a chair and sat down at the kitchen table. He began reading aloud:

Dear Jack,

I wanted to write you personally and thank you for being there for Susan and the kids during the time after my death and at my funeral service. Knowing that you have been praying for them means so much to me, and I'm grateful for your concern and help.

It now has been a month since I went into the direct presence of our Lord. Time goes by rather fast up here, but I know this last month has seemed like an eternity to Susan, Lauren, RJ, and Tyler.

I'm writing to ask you to renew your prayers for each of them, individually and as a family. Please don't let down your spiritual support for them now that some time has passed. The reality of my death is really sinking in now, and the deeper stages of grief are starting to take hold. They need your prayers now more than ever.

Please help me by praying for their healing, emotional comfort, and spiritual protection from the evil one. Although it is healthy for them to complete the grieving process in their own time, I don't want my death to launch even one of them into a spiritual crisis.

Please pass the word for others to pray for them as well. I ask you to commit to getting seven other people to pray for my family at this time. Please commit to this; I'm counting on you, Jack.

I would be most grateful if you would give Susan a call, or swing by just to visit and check in on them. Please let them know that you're still praying for them. Heaven truly is more glorious than you can imagine. I thank you for your continued prayers and support.

God bless you and Sylvia!

Until we meet again,

John

    Jack and Sylvia held hands right then and there and prayed passionately for John's family. Afterward, Sylvia picked up the phone and said to Jack, "I'm putting Susan and the kids back on the prayer chain right now."

    Jack responded, "When you're done, let's give Susan a call."

    She nodded in agreement.

    John asked for prayer, and he also asked for a commitment to get others to pray for his family. Steven will be sending similar letters to the same seven people every 6 months for the first 2 years after John's death. That is a total of four letters to each person. Each letter requests the recipient to provide prayer support for his family and to get others to do so as well.

    You can send letters similar to this one and do even more. Sometimes your friends will be wary of intruding on your family and not call or visit as they did before your death. Extending them an invitation and encouraging them to keep your family in their prayers will help ease the awkwardness that some people feel in dealing with a family that has suffered a profound loss.

    Let's look at the quantity of prayer support John arranged. John sent letters requesting prayer to:

Jack
Deborah
Jeff
Bandi   = seven people and their families praying
Rick
Carla
Todd

If each person honors John's request and gets seven other people to pray for his family, that is 49 praying people *and* their families. With those people also taking John's request to prayer chains, churches, prayer meetings, Sunday school classes, and other small groups, this could mean hundreds of people praying for the spiritual support and protection of John's family.

You don't have to stop at seven people like John did. I personally have written 20 letters of this kind, and there is no maximum. But you don't have to write as many either. Even two people committed to getting two others who will get two others (and so on) praying for your loved ones can generate a multitude of prayers. There are no negative consequences, only positive results from the prayer support you build for the members of your family.

> **There are no negative consequences, only positive results from the prayer support you build for the members of your family.**

Ongoing Prayer Support

As your spouse and family come to grips with your death and move forward with their lives, they still need and benefit from continuing prayer support. Through your Prayer Trust, you can arrange numerous prayers for your family and other beneficiaries at various intervals and benchmarks in their lives. Essentially, what you are doing is ensuring prayer coverage for your family members for specific things and at specific times, even though you are not there personally to pray for them. Once they reach these milestones, or benchmarks, your Spiritual Trust executor will see that the prayer requests go out.

As discussed in Chapter 2, family members reach specific benchmarks or milestones during their lives. These include birthdays, teen events, school honors, activities, and graduations, the first day of college, marriage, career, becoming a parent, and so on. For any such benchmark or milestone, you can arrange, in your Prayer Trust, for prayer for their spiritual and emotional strength, protection, blessings, and so on. When they become teenagers, you can ask for prayer for their morality and purity, or that God will take an active role in their selection of a mate.

On an 18th birthday, you could have prayer for perseverance, development of their faith, and spiritual maturity. One example of ongoing prayer support is the prayer Mary wrote for her granddaughter's benchmark of turning 16:

Oh my gracious and merciful Lord Jesus Christ, I humbly but boldly come to you in prayer, asking that your promises will be fulfilled through these requests I bring before you. Lord Jesus, I ask you to pour out the Holy Spirit upon Kaitlyn, covering her with your Spirit, and washing her with your loving grace. I ask you specifically Lord to give your angels charge over Kaitlyn's life and guard, protect, and defend her from evil in all of its forms.

May she increase in faith, wisdom, and purity of heart. Lord, I pray that she will embrace morality and flee from the youthful lusts that will tempt her. May she seek you in all her ways and embrace your Word and embed it into her heart.

I bind Satan in the name that is above all others, in your name, Lord Jesus Christ. I have total faith in you Jesus, and absolute faith that you hear my prayer and will answer this prayer in Kaitlyn's life. I gratefully thank you and praise you for who you are, and for turning back the enemy in Kaitlyn's life.

In the name of Jesus Christ, Amen.

When you arrange these kinds of benchmark prayers, you also may have your executor send a copy of the specific prayer (if you have scripted one) to the prayer beneficiary, letting this loved one know that committed believers are offering a specific prayer. By doing so, you will alert beneficiaries to the spiritual side of the benchmark they have reached and help them to develop or maintain the right spiritual mindset. This also will help to instill a strong sense of the value of prayer in your beneficiaries and may encourage them to seek a stronger prayer life as well.

IN SUMMARY

We need faith now for what God will do tomorrow. God is omnipotent. He is not going to get confused about what you are asking of him. God is familiar with the concept of paving the way by preparing and implementing a spiritual plan. He should be. He is the master planner. Knowing this, you can lay a foundation of prayer during your life that will carry on long after your death. Another way of living with eternity in mind. Now is a good time to go to God in prayer, seeking guidance and direction for whom and how your Prayer Trust should be implemented.

Recommended Resources

Alves, Elizabeth. *Becoming a Prayer Warrior*. Ventura, CA: Renew Books, 1998.
Eastman, Dick. *Dick Eastman on Prayer*. Global Christian Pub, 2000.
Hayford, Jack. *Prayer Is Invading the Impossible*. Plainfield, NJ: Logos International, 1977.
Jacobs, Cindy. *Possessing the Gates of the Enemy*. Grand Rapids, MI: Chosen Books, 1991.
Omartian, Stormie. *The Power of a Praying Parent*. Eugene, OR: Harvest House Publishers, 1995.
Sheets, Dutch. *Intecessory Prayer*. Ventura, CA: Regal Books, 1996.
Sherrer, Quin, and Ruthanne Garlock. *How to Pray for Your Family and Friends*. Ann Arbor, MI: Servant Publications, 1990.
Wagner, C. Peter. *Prayer Shield*. Ventura, CA: Regal Books, 1997
Wilkinson, Bruce. *The Prayer of Jabez*. Sisters, OR: Multnomah, 2000.
Willhite, B.J. *Why Pray?* Lake Mary, FL: Creation House, 1988.

ENDNOTES:

1. B.J. Willhite, *Why Pray?* (Lake Mary, FL: Creation House, 1988), p. 91.
2. C. Peter Wagner. *Your Spiritual Gifts Can Help Your Church Grow* (Ventura, CA: Regal Books, 1979) p.74.
3. Zig Zigler. *Confessions of a Grieving Christian* (Nashville, TN: Thomas Nelson, 1999) p. 31.

FOUR

Legacy Trusts

"We now have technologies and methodologies that allow us to capture the past, preserve the present, and send them to the future in unprecedented ways. In your Legacy Trust you have the option of using these technologies, through the methodology of the Spiritual Trust System, to ensure that your family history, heritage and essence is preserved and richly conveyed for present and future generations."

— Dr. Milton Smith[1]

Many people believe that legacies are the province of the rich, famous, and powerful. They see libraries, schools, and other institutions bearing the names of these people. They see monuments erected in nearly every city and town paying tribute to such people. Symbols like these, however, cannot approach the power and influence *your* legacy will have on *your* family and descendants. The Legacy Trust is an effective instrument to help your children, grandchildren, and descendents discover who they are within the rich tapestry of their family history and heritage.

If you want to leave a godly Legacy Trust, you will need to *live* the legacy that you want to leave. A Legacy Trust is to be a manifestation of the legacy you live. Creating a Legacy Trust can result in spiritual enlightenment through the self-revelation that comes from creating it. You will find that by starting the process of creating a Legacy Trust, you will derive the motivation and encouragement that will help you live the type of legacy you want to leave.

WHAT IS A LEGACY TRUST?

Oral family history has always been an important part of our culture. You might have only a few worn pictures of your great-great-grandparents, but you probably have heard stories of how they migrated here, planted crops, fought in one of the wars, and so on. Unfortunately, our children are hearing fewer and fewer stories that make the faded pictures come to life.

A Legacy Trust enables you to leave, through a message or series of messages, a godly inheritance by capturing the essence of who you are, what is important to you, and what you want to tell your family and descendants about your life and faith.

Legacy Trusts encompass your family history, heritage, faith, stories, beliefs, advice, creeds, insight, and messages. A Legacy Trust can help establish and reinforce a strong sense of identity for your living family and those yet to be born. A Legacy Trust can create a family culture, define family spiritual values, and reinforce family traditions that will thrive for generations. In a world filled with chaos and confusion, it is a blessed gift to pass on a legacy that affirms worth, establishes identity, communicates Christian values and principles, and imbues the recipients with a sense of their spiritual heritage.

Legacy Trusts can be sufficiently flexible to accomplish a number of your spiritual objectives for your family.

Your Legacy Trust can be delivered to your family whenever you choose. It can be made available to your family now, in whole or in part, or portions of it can be given to your loved ones at specific times and benchmarks in their lives. Legacy Trusts can be sufficiently flexible to accomplish a number of your spiritual objectives for your family.

In our culture, people typically leave their descendants property and wealth, but our history, philosophy, faith, morals, traditions, and wisdom gleaned from a lifetime of experiences are often forgotten over time. Aren't these intangible aspects of our character and essence more important to leave to our descendants than material possessions? And if they are important to leave to your family, aren't they just as important to preserve for your descendants?

THE MORAL NEED FOR YOUR LEGACY TRUST

American society has changed so much over the last 50 years that children seldom grow up around their grandparents and great-grandparents these days. Moreover, as a result of the high divorce rate in our society, including the Christian community, children often don't grow up with *both* parents anymore. This state of affairs takes a substantial toll on our ability to keep our family history alive.

The need for Legacy Trusts is pressing and surely will intensify. The spiritual and moral decline in our society is increasing at an alarming rate. Look how much things have changed! What our society shunned decades ago it embraces today. Our families are bombarded daily with immorality and decadence. Movies, magazines, television, radio, video games, and the Internet have a pervasive impact.

Recently, my family went shopping in our local shopping mall. After leaving the food court, we were walking through the center of the mall. As we passed the Victoria's Secret store, my boy was subjected to life-size posters of nearly nude women looking at him with sexually alluring facial expressions and poses. Or were they looking at me? You get my point. At a different level of the mall, my daughter asked me why a store was saying such bad things about God. Glancing in the direction she was looking, I saw satanic propaganda and foul obscenities about our Lord printed on the merchandise that was displayed in the window. For our families and children to be subjected to these assaults on their godliness by just walking in an advertised "family mall" is appalling.

Given the nature of our society and the direction it is going, strong links to the past are becoming more and more important. The authors of *Family Traditions* state that, "When we become aware that our behavior and values have an impact on generations that follow, we begin to sense a responsibility to pass on a strong heritage."[2] Although we all should pray for a revival in our great country, the direction in which we are heading is not promising.

> Given the nature of our society and the direction it is going, strong links to the past are becoming more and more important.

HOW WILL YOU BE REMEMBERED?

In addition to the spiritual insight and family history that Legacy Trusts pass along, they serve as a fond remembrance of those who created them. Psychologists specializing in grief and bereavement report that a common fear of survivors is that their memories of a loved one who has passed away will fade. What can you remember about a parent or grandparent who passed away more than 10 or 20 years ago?

Although you probably still have some vivid memories, many details fade like old pictures. Very young children who lose a parent or grandparent will have lost, by adulthood, many, even all, of the memories of those close family members. If a loved one passed away when you were young, as one of mine did, you have experienced this yourself.

Moreover, even though you relate your memories of a lost loved one to your children, after your death they probably will not be able to recall much of what you shared with them. They likely will not be able to effectively pass on to *their* children many of the memories you shared with them. This is a tragic loss of family history and family heritage.

Your legacy is a priceless gift to your family. For the sons and daughters who shared your life, your Legacy Trust will be one of their most cherished possessions. It will reinforce their memories of you and help them pass along those memories to their children and grandchildren.

> Your legacy is a priceless gift to your family.

Those in your family who are young or not yet born at the time of your passing will not be able to connect with your essence as a person and as a believer simply by looking at some old photographs or hearing some stories. Take yourself as an example.

Do you have insight into the real essence of a parent, grandparent or a great-grandparent who died before you got the chance to know that person yourself? Not likely. But you could have gained a lot from that person through a Legacy Trust.

How you are remembered and the intensity of those memories can have a powerful influence on the lives of your descendants. Tangible memories of you don't have to be relegated to just a picture on a wall or in an old scrapbook. I have used my Legacy Trust as a tool to be a part of my children's lives, after I am gone, in an active way. Whenever they want, my children will be able to hear me talking and see me visiting with them. By creating a Legacy Trust, you can positively influence your family's lives for generations after your death.

How you are remembered and the intensity of those memories can have a powerful influence on the lives of your descendants.

Some of your relatives might remember that you were a believer or a "man or woman of God" whether you do or don't create a Legacy Trust. They might hear stories from other family members or friends who knew you. But through a Legacy Trust you can determine your own spiritual legacy. You can tell them not just that you believed in God, but *why*.

In *your* words, you can witness to your children, grandchildren, and others. You can tell them why you hold the convictions you do, recite the scriptures that mean so much to you, pass along tangible messages and stories of your life to encourage them, and let them know your essence as a person so they might have the opportunity to know you better and more intensely carry you in their hearts and minds. Family photographs are great — but they are much more meaningful if supported by a Legacy Trust.

TYPES OF LEGACY TRUSTS

This chapter presents a variety of options to consider as components of your Legacy Trust. Some of these may appeal to you more than others. Some are more complex than others. Your personal desires, available time, resources, and health issues all will help you determine the elements to include in *your* Legacy Trust, and in what order you will create them.

The two general categories of a Legacy Trust concern your heritage and your messages.

1. ***Your heritage.*** This focuses on capturing the past, preserving the present, and sending them to the future. This includes your life history, stories, beliefs, creeds, traditions and insights. Your heritage can be thought of as a broad tapestry of your life.

2. ***Your messages.*** This includes sending messages about your life and life issues in general. I call these kinds of messages "LifeMessages." In addition, there are those messages about your faith and faith issues, which I call "FaithMessages." Both types of messages can be delivered during your lifetime or after you have passed away.

YOUR HERITAGE

Your heritage can be thought of as a broad tapestry of your life.

If you've ever watched the History Channel or the A&E Network, you've probably seen one or more of the biographical productions of famous people that these networks do so well. Now imagine watching one of these channels from your living room couch and hearing Roger Mudd say, "Stay tuned for the biography of Isham Manis and the interesting tales and insights into this man's life." Your first reaction would be puzzlement, as I'm sure you don't know who Isham Manis is, but *my* reaction would be one of shock and excitement. He's my grandfather, who passed away when I was a young man. Now, instead of Isham Manis, insert a name of one of *your* relatives in this hypothetical scenario.

The background music starts and the standard introductory shots flash on screen as the music builds. Then Roger Mudd, sitting behind his desk, says, "You're going to be treated to a biography about [your relative's name], a person of humble beginnings who made their mark pursuing the American dream." Would you be changing channels at this point? Would you be getting up to go see what's in the fridge? Or would you be glued to the television set wondering what this segment was going to reveal about your parent or grandparent?

This hypothetical example is intended to get you thinking about the Legacy Trust you can create for your family. Who cares if it won't be aired on A&E or the History Channel. What does it matter if it's not filmed and produced by the top professionals in the business.

If you record *your* autobiography for your children and the generations that follow, it will mean more to them than all of the famous biographies ever produced. Your forbears lacked the technology to create a video life story for you, but *you* have more than enough resources to create one for your family and descendants.

> "A good man leaves an inheritance for his children's children."
>
> (*Proverbs* 13:22)

Right now, think about a loved one you have lost. What do you remember most? How vivid are your memories? Imagine that this loved one had the technology and foresight to record a video talking to you. What would you want to hear about?

Most of us have not received messages from our parents, grandparents, or others who have passed away. Moreover, most of our parents and grandparents who are alive have not created legacy messages. Most people do not inherit a tangible legacy. In determining the kind of legacy you will want to create for your family, a good starting place is to think about the kinds of messages you would like to receive or would have wanted to receive yourself.

To provide a valuable inheritance, you don't have to leave money or possessions. You can leave a spiritual legacy with spiritual nuggets of wisdom and truth that far surpass the physical worth and value of material wealth and possessions. Your Legacy Trust will have an impact on future generations of your family. How much of an impact, in part, is up to you.

If you have gained life-changing wisdom, it's a valuable asset to leave in your legacy. A wealthy spiritual legacy is fostered by the previous generation's passing on its wisdom and spiritual wealth to the next generation, not by each new generation starting from scratch. Succeeding generations, in turn, will add to the Legacy Trust, and the next generation will receive an even more blessed spiritual inheritance.

You can draw upon hundreds of topics to create a spiritual inheritance. You may wish to share your insights about Jesus, the Bible, the Holy Spirit, Satan, prayer, spiritual maturity, faith, grace, morality, and love. Anything that will spiritually help your loved ones constitutes a thoughtful inheritance. We can pass along *why* we believe what we believe. A side benefit is verifying your own convictions and understanding of who you are spiritually.

> "I will open my mouth in a parable; I will utter dark sayings of old, which we have heard and known, and our fathers have told us. We will not conceal them from their children, but tell to the generation to come the praises of the Lord, and His strength and His wondrous works that He has done. For He established a testimony in Jacob and appointed a law in Israel, Which He commanded our fathers that they should teach them to their children, that the generation to come might know, even the children yet to be born, That they may arise and tell them to their children. That they should put their confidence in God and not forget the works of God, but keep His commandments."
> (*Psalms* 78:2-7)

LifeStories

A LifeStory is a powerful and innovative means of preserving your special voice and personal history. The story of your life will be a priceless legacy to your family and descendants. Although this section of the book talks about a LifeStory about *you*, the discussion here is equally applicable to a LifeStory about an individual or about a husband and wife. Actually, a couple with a long history would be most effective in creating a joint LifeStory. Such couples typically start with individual chapters covering their lives before they met, and their individual family histories. Then they proceed to the story of their life together and focus on their immediate family.

Doug Weiss, who is a popular author and marriage counselor conveyed to me the benefits of a couple creating their Life Story together in this way,

"In my practice, I find that communication between husbands and wives is a key to good relationships. Consequently, I am always looking for ways to help couples improve their communication. The process of creating a Life Story provides tremendous opportunities for meaningful communication about topics that are central to happy and fulfilling relationships. In looking back over their lives, couples can relive their good times and the difficult times through which they have persevered together. This provides an opportunity for reflection and appreciation. By focusing on these qualities, they are motivated and encouraged to live their legacy *today*."

-Douglas Weiss[3]

A LifeStory is a powerful and innovative means of preserving your special voice and personal history.

In its simplest format, a LifeStory is a compilation of stories and facts about the events of one's life in a way that reveals the essence of that life. This can be in the form of a stroll down memory lane, or highlights from any "chapter" in your life, such as early childhood, school years, military career, college days, romance and relationships, parenting, or grand parenting. Or it might be a summary of your life experiences organized into broad themes such as spiritual journeys, personal callings, lessons learned, traditions cherished, or experiences worth sharing.

Through the introspective process of preparing your LifeStory, you might discover a purpose you never realized, or an awareness of the fullness of your life. This process is for the giver and receiver alike, honoring lives, stories, and families.

Passing on your LifeStory will have an impact on each generation of your family. It will help your children and their children understand and connect with your essence as a person. It will soften the grief of those remaining at the time of your death. It will give future generations a documented heritage and establish a record of family history that they will want to supplement and continue to pass down.

Everyone has a story! Your descendants will look at your LifeStory, smile at the stories you tell about yourself and those who surrounded you, and tenderly recall the person who cared enough to record the stories.

You are in a unique position to pass along your LifeStory. You know your story better than anyone. You know what is important to you and about you. Creating your LifeStory can be fun. It certainly will be a lasting and memorable gift for your family, friends, and descendants to treasure for generations to come.

A LifeStory, like all other components of the Spiritual Trust System, can be created by using written words, video recordings, or audible recordings, or by using a multimedia combination of all of these forms.

> **You are in a unique position to pass along your LifeStory. You know your story better than anyone.**

The three basic types of LifeStories are:

1. Chronological
2. Essence
3. Spiritual

These LifeStories can be done as individual segments or can be woven together into a broader autobiography containing aspects of all three. I address each type separately to more clearly explain the purposes and benefits of each. As with any component of the Spiritual Trust System, you can combine these and use them in any way that makes sense and fits your style and preferences.

Chronological LifeStory

Your chronological LifeStory relates the major events of your life from birth to the present. It is your LifeStory in its broadest context. It is a historical account. By reviewing and telling your own personal history, you likely will understand it better yourself! Nevertheless, I don't recommend that you attempt to record every little detail and experience of your life in a drawn-out tale. This is not just a collection of facts. Your family will want to know what you were feeling and thinking as you experienced the *major* events of your life.

Your chronological LifeStory relates the major events of your life from birth to the present.

To start, you will find it helpful to divide your LifeStory into chapters. Consider the following. Not all will apply, and you might want to add others.

Childhood
Elementary school years
Teenage years
High school days
College
Military service
Career
Courtship and marriage
Family
Retirement

After you select your life chapters you want to address, start with just a few stories for each chapter. Ask yourself whether each story satisfies one of these criteria:

1. Does it teach a valuable lesson?
2. Does it reveal why you are a certain way today?
3. Did it change your outlook on life?
4. Does it reveal some aspect of your essence?
5. Does it provide insight into a certain period of your life?
6. Does it evoke strong feelings or emotions in you even today?
7. Are you compelled to make sure it is never forgotten?
8. Is it interesting?
9. Do you have pictures, video, or other items that you can include with the story?

Appendix C contains questions and ideas that you might consider for your LifeStory.

Essence LifeStory

Whereas a Chronological LifeStory presents the stories and events of your life, an Essence LifeStory brings life to ... well ... your life. In an Essence LifeStory, you explain what kind of a person you are emotionally, spiritually, intellectually, and socially, and why you are that way. This allows the beneficiaries of your LifeStory to connect with your essence. The LifeStory focuses on the person behind the chronological events and experiences of your life. Often, important events of your life are linked to your essence, so you may address these together. Don't feel compelled to separate them just because I treat them separately for purposes of the discussion here.

> **In an Essence LifeStory, you explain what kind of a person you are emotionally, spiritually, intellectually, and socially, and why you are that way.**

An Essence LifeStory enables you to explore many topics that will be of great interest to your family and descendants. You can review lessons you learned from major experiences of your life and explain the importance to you, for example, of creating an atmosphere of security and love at home. You can discuss your views on certain emotional issues and highlight the skills you believe are necessary for cultivating healthy, stable relationships and interacting with others.

In this LifeStory you will have to think on a deeper level, through an intellectual and emotional process of self-exploration. You must reflect on who you are deep inside, and what made you that way. This can be difficult. In consulting with people, I have developed a list of open-ended statements. By going through each statement (the order is not important) and completing the statement from your personal perspective, you will be able to articulate and convey the essence of "you" to the future. Examples of these statements are included in Appendix C.

If you are like many people I have consulted with, you likely will have your eyes opened to aspects of your essence of which even you were unaware. The only rule is that you must be honest with yourself in finishing these statements. Honesty can be difficult because we all have faults and failures that we would rather ignore or that we would like to shield from our loved ones. Issues such as these, however, often are ones that, when communicated honestly, disclose our humanity. When they are related to our spirituality, these topics can be revealing and offer a compelling witness.

For a real eye-opener, get your spouse, parent, child, and close friend to propose key words or phrases that they think reveal your essence. Many times, the way others see us is quite different from how we see ourselves. This can reveal aspects of you of which you might not have been aware and give you the opportunity to self-reflect on how your views of yourself match the views that others have of you.

> **Many times, the way others see us is quite different from how we see ourselves.**

Spiritual LifeStory

Spiritual LifeStories center on your spiritual beliefs, ideologies, convictions, practices, and, most important, your witness. A Spiritual LifeStory reinforces values, creates a sense of family heritage, and strengthens emotional and spiritual bonds. By creating a Spiritual LifeStory, you can rest assured that your religious values, beliefs and traditions will be conveyed into the future.

Richard Peace has written a couple of excellent books about spiritual autobiographies and spiritual journaling. He describes a spiritual autobiography (Spiritual LifeStory) in this way: "What distinguishes a spiritual autobiography from an ordinary autobiography is the lens through which we look at our lives. In this case, we view our lives through the lens of the spiritual by searching for God's footprints. We focus on aspects that reveal the activity of God."[4]

A Spiritual LifeStory can address topics from your spiritual perspective and plant deep and sturdy roots from which your family can grow and develop spiritually. In this LifeStory, you can discuss your spiritual perspective of Jesus Christ, the Bible, the Holy Spirit, and so on. You might explain what being a believer has meant in your life and what you have learned through your life experiences. Through this vehicle, you can share God's timeless truths, and your personal experiences with those truths, as a powerful witness to your family of God's abiding love, mercy, and grace.

The importance of passing down a family history that establishes a godly heritage must not be overlooked. If you didn't inherit a spiritual legacy, you can start that tradition with your family. As Richard Peace says, "Writing a spiritual autobiography usually brings great insight. We notice patterns in our lives that we have never seen before. We understand better who we are and where God is leading us. We are clearer about our purpose on this planet."[5]

Take Patricia, mother of seven children (no, that's not a typo) and grandmother to eighteen grandchildren (and still counting). During the latter half of her life, she began exploring and researching her family genealogy. She told me that she has spent hundreds of hours investigating her roots and collecting every bit of information about her ancestors that she can.

Patricia has a long and well-documented family tree, going back more than 300 years, with hundreds of past relatives. As Patricia put it, "Of all the information I collected personally and all the information given to me by other relatives who have researched the genealogy of the Christman clan, not even *one* message tells the next generation about the details of the faith that was widespread throughout the history of my family. *My* contribution to my family will be the birth of a tradition of leaving a spiritual heritage, rich in content, to all current and future generations of the Christman family."

In your own Spiritual LifeStory, you, too, can be a strong witness to generations of your family, impacting the future spiritual realities of many lives. Scripture tells us that "he who is wise wins souls" (*Proverbs* 11:30). The greatest benefit of your Legacy Trust will not be that your personal legacy will be remembered in a meaningful way for generations. The greatest benefit is the power of the Holy Spirit to utilize your Legacy Trust to move the hearts of your children, grandchildren, and descendants to perhaps save their souls through your words and actions.

What better inheritance can you give your children and future descendants than the message of eternal life? The most powerful witness is a person's own story. In your LifeStory you tell your story from the spiritual perspective. What are the tales of your spiritual journey, and how do they relate to your witness? Again, from Richard Peace: "By reviewing our past, we also begin to recognize the footprints of God in our life. They weren't always clear at the time, but in retrospect we can see patterns. We come to understand how God was at work, shaping us in unique ways".[6]

To help you evaluate your spiritual life for a spiritual LifeStory, I have created another list of open-ended questions that will give you a glimpse into your spiritual essence. You can find examples in Appendix C. Chapter 8 also gives specifics of how to create your LifeStory.

A LifeStory of Your Living Parents and Grandparents

If you are going to create your own LifeStory, you probably recognize the value of having a LifeStory from your parents and grandparents. If they are alive, and are able to do a LifeStory themselves, you can find a way to help them do it. You can give them this book and tell them why you hope a LifeStory will be a part of the inheritance they leave you and your children. You can tell them that when they die, you want to inherit their LifeStory so you can pass it on to your children and grandchildren.

Some seniors appreciate the value of doing their LifeStory but lack the energy or other resources to complete the project. If they feel uncomfortable being in a video LifeStory, the next best thing would be to get audio recordings of them. One method I have helped people use many times is to have the person look at photographs and use a voice recorder to capture their memories of the photograph, and what their life was like at that time. You would then have the photographs scanned and put on a video and use their voice as the narrator. This makes a great mini-documentary that can be copied and given to all family members. For many, this is an easier way to talk about their life — by simply giving the background and details of photographs from their lives. It often spurs on other topics they are reminded of and want to discuss. You might consider helping them with their LifeStory or getting your siblings together to help. It can be a wonderful family project.

For those of you who are close to your parents (or grandparents), this is an excellent way to spend time with them and further strengthen your relationship. If your relationship with any of these family members is strained, you might find a healing benefit in doing this project. You might gain a perspective or understanding that eluded you before. Although attempting a LifeStory in situations like this can be difficult, I have seen it lead to the road to reconciliation. Many people who have undertaken it have told me that they wish they had done it sooner!

Spiritual Trusts

If you or your siblings cannot help your parents or grandparents do their LifeStory, another alternative, especially if your parents or grandparents do not live near you, is to hire someone to work with them to prepare their LifeStory. In that case, siblings often share the cost and make the LifeStory a gift for an anniversary, birthday, or other occasion. Your parents and grandparents will be honored that you love and appreciate them enough to be willing to arrange to have their story, their essence, recorded and preserved so future generations will know them in a special and personal way.

If for some reason your parents (or grandparents) cannot do *their* LifeStory, the next best thing is to get them involved in *your* LifeStory. Go to them with your "work in progress" and spend time with them to capture their legacy and all the family history they can remember. Devote a separate chapter in your LifeStory to each parent, grandparent, or other family member on whom you have sufficient information. Combining your parents', grandparents', and ancestors' legacy with your legacy will give your descendants that much more of a rich family heritage.

For ancestors who already have passed away, include what you know about their lives in your LifeStory. This could be a family tree of sorts with facts such as names, dates and places of birth, where they lived, occupations, and the like. You should try to capture as much of that history as possible and preserve it for the future. In doing this, you should contact uncles and aunts, friends who are still alive, and other family members who knew them. Almost every family has a "family historian" of some sort. You likely will find that they will be more than willing to share with you facts and stories about past members of your family. They just might have a priceless story they would be happy to relate to you.

The farther back the family tree you go, the harder it is to obtain information. The important thing is to include what you reasonably can learn. All these facts will be of interest to your children and grandchildren when they are grown. Anything you can reveal about your ancestors' essence and spirituality will be doubly appreciated.

LifeTributes

A LifeTribute is another special component of a Legacy Trust. It is essentially a LifeStory created by you *about* a person who has already passed away, as a tribute to a parent, grandparent, sibling, or

Legacy Trusts

other loved one. Although that person may not have prepared a LifeStory during his or her lifetime, the memory of the loved one can be preserved for future generations through a LifeTribute. A LifeTribute can encompass the lives of a couple as well as an individual.

Preparing a LifeTribute involves most of the concepts covered with respect to a LifeStory. A LifeTribute also should encompass a combination of the chronological, essence, and spiritual aspects of his or her life. You can write about the person and use video and audio clips and interviews, or use all in combination. In a LifeTribute the use of pictures and other visual aids is particularly important because the person whose life is being captured in the LifeTribute will not be present to talk about the stories.

A LifeTribute is an excellent way to preserve prized stories and memories about a lost loved one for generations. Although you may do much of the organization of a LifeTribute, others can add to the final product. For example, a LifeTribute on your mother might have sections in which family members appear on video and talk about their fondest memories of your mother. They can capture the type of person she was by telling stories that illustrate her character, faith, and other important qualities.

One benefit of creating a LifeTribute is consolidation. Many times when a person has passed away, family members and friends have different tangible memories and personal stories of that person. For instance, one person might have video of the person joking around at a family reunion. Another may have some rare photographs or film of the family member taken during early adulthood. Yet another may have letters or documents about him or her. Instead of each family member's having fragmented tangible memories of the person, the family members can combine all of their memories into one LifeTribute — contributing a copy of what they have toward a consolidated memory on one format.

You also can use LifeTributes, or excerpts from Life- Tributes, as part of the family history chapter of your LifeStory. You can combine segments of LifeStories and LifeTributes in many ways. For example, one client asked his uncle, who was the repository of family history, to participate in a LifeStory. The uncle proceeded to summarize over 100 years of family history in about an hour. That segment was used in the LifeTribute on the client's father and in the client's own LifeStory. All of these projects were formatted onto a DVD, with individual chapters identified on the Main Menu (these details are summarized in Part II, Chapter 9) and each family unit of the extended family received one.

YOUR MESSAGES

Your messages can be of two basic types:

1. *LifeMessages* — thoughts about your life and life issues in general.
2. *FaithMessages* — specific messages about your faith and faith related issues.

In Chapter 2, Spiritual Support Trusts, we discussed using LifeMessages and Faith Messages to provide your loved ones support during the bereavement and rebuilding phases of grieving. They can be used in Legacy Trusts as well.

LifeMessages and FaithMessages are typically shorter than LifeStories or LifeTributes, and more focused on one topic or issue. These messages can be delivered to your recipients during your lifetime, and they also can be delivered to your recipients at specific times in their lives long after your earthly life is over. I refer to these particular times or milestones as *benchmarks*. In addition, your messages can be in the form of Legacy Journals.

Benchmark Deliveries

You can create messages for delivery at benchmark events such as birthdays, graduations, weddings, the births of children, holidays, and others. Sending your messages at these specific times affords opportunities for you to be involved with your family during significant events in their lives irrespective of whether you are there in person. You may not want to create every option presented here. Your personal situation, family members, time availability, and other circumstances — all are determining factors as to the benchmarks for which you may want to create messages.

One couple, Rick and Deborah, have jointly created four videos for four different benchmarks for their only son, Cale, now 8 years old. Cale will receive the first message on his 21st birthday, the second when he gets engaged, the third when he is married, and the fourth when he has his first child. Cale will get these messages regardless of whether Rick or Deborah have passed away. They want to record these benchmark messages when they are still relatively young. Cale probably will be close to the same age as his parents are now by the time he watches the fourth video.

Rick told me that he found a great deal of satisfaction in knowing that if one or both of them die before Cale reaches these benchmarks, Cale still will receive the advice and guidance they want to provide at these important events in Cale's life. If both Rick and Deborah are still living, it also will be meaningful to watch them together as a family during the benchmark times.

> "These words, which I am commanding you today, shall be on your heart. You shall teach them diligently to your sons and shall talk of them when you sit in your house and when you walk by the way and when you lie down and when you rise up."
> (*Deuteronomy* 6:6-7)

Birthday Messages

Perhaps because birthdays are such natural milestones, they are popular selections for the delivery of messages. Here are some innovative ideas that put a unique twist on birthday benchmarks. They are categorized into four types:

1. Milestone birthday messages
2. Time-warping birthday messages
3. Generational birthday messages
4. Sequential birthday messages.

Milestone Birthday Messages

Milestone birthday messages are to be delivered on key birthdays such as the 16th, 18th, and 21st. The advent of ages 30, 40, and 50 are other possible designations, as these ages, too, are considered benchmarks.

This is an excerpt from the video message Cale will receive on his 21st birthday. Rick, wearing a blue sweater and khaki pants, is sitting in a brown leather recliner chair next to his wife Deborah, clad in navy blue pants and a red blouse. A lit fireplace is to the right of them. Here are two excerpts from this message, Rick is speaking.

Hi, Cale. We're excited to be talking to you. It's a chilly January evening, and we recorded this video because we want to share with you some important things. We hope this video will bring a smile to your face. It is our deepest wish that both of us will be sitting next to you watching this video with you when the time comes. If something has happened to end my life on earth, I'm doubly grateful that I have created this message to you. First — Happy Birthday, son! Twenty-one. Wow. I have spent many hours thinking about what kind of man would be watching this video...

* * *

If I could choose only three things for you to remember about ME, it would be that I love Jesus, I love your mom, and I love you.

Rick and Deborah's video is nearly two hours long, filmed with breaks. Sometimes they would speak individually about certain subjects and sometimes they jointly shared with Cale. Rick reflected about being a man and shifted his narrative occasionally to the topic of women — what to look for in a wife plus a couple of fun stories about when he was dating Cale's mom. Deborah discussed the qualities she sees in Cale, how important it is to treat others with respect and dignity, and character traits she prays he will grow up to have. Individually and jointly, they discussed many other issues with Cale, including responsibilities, goals, and spiritual realities. Rick and Deborah were able to talk to Cale about subjects that would not have been prudent to discuss until Cale became an adult.

Throughout the message, they connect with their son and impart wisdom, but they always come back to Jesus as the top priority in life. They reiterate how everything else in Cale's life will fall into place as long as the most important thing, Cale's salvation and walk with God, comes first.

Legacy Trusts

Time-Warping Messages for Parallel Birthdays

In a time-warping message, you record a message on your birthday to be delivered on your child's birthday when he or she reaches the same age — their parallel birthday! For example, let's say you are going to be 40 years old on your next birthday. On your birthday, or thereabouts, you prepare a birthday message to your son or daughter — to be delivered when he or she turns 40. This means that you will be 40 years old talking to your son or daughter when he or she is 40 years old.

The earlier you start doing this, the more you and your children will benefit from it. If you are no longer alive on their parallel birthday, your birthday message will be a cherished and priceless gift. If you are still alive, you will deliver the messages anyway so your children will be able to see, read, or hear you talking to them when you were the same age. Either way, this is a superb opportunity for your children to appreciate the essence of who you *are*, or *were*.

Time-warping presents a superb opportunity for your children to appreciate the essence of who you are, or were.

Time-warping communication will strengthen bonds between you and your children and give them the unique opportunity to learn of your insights at the same stage of life. It will be refreshing for them to see you talking to them at a parallel age instead of always thinking of you as a person a couple-or-so decades their senior. Of course, this can be done in the same way with grandparents to their grandchildren.

In preparing your time-warping messages, use your imagination. Think about what you would tell your son or daughter if he or she were sitting next to you right now and were *your* age. What do you discuss with other adults your age? How to be a good parent or grandparent? Funny stories about your children and the things they did and said? Social, political, and spiritual issues? What would you like to talk to your parents about if they could become the same age you are *right now*? There. You already have a good starting place to begin time-warping.

Generational Birthday Messages

In a generational birthday message, you interview your children or grandchildren on their birthday each year and deliver the interview to *their* children when they reach that same age. On video, or through audio recordings, you can capture your children or grandchildren talking about their world, including friends, activities, and the other things kids talk about at that age. Ask them what they want to be when they grow up (you likely will end up with a different answer every year). Ask your very young children to explain who Jesus is, for example. Ask them for their opinions on all sorts of things (this is really fun with young children). Capture their essence at the various ages.

Then take each interview, preserve it, and give it as a birthday gift to their children when they become the same age as their parent (your child) was when the birthday interview was conducted. This is similar to time-warping, but you're helping your children get started on it for the next generation at a much younger age than you did.

When your children are old enough, you can get them more involved in communicating to their future children. Let's say you have a daughter or granddaughter who will be 16 years old tomorrow. Have her record a message to her future son or daughter when the future child will become 16. This will be one of the more interesting traditions you can establish for your kids. Ask them if they think it would be "cool" to receive a video message from you when you were a "hip" 16-year-old. They'll get the picture.

Recording and storing these messages for your children until they are old enough to store the messages themselves is a precious gift of foresight. Your children *and* grandchildren will come to cherish these generational birthday messages far more than any toy or sweater.

Sequential Birthday Messages

Sequential birthday messages are to be sent to your children or grandchildren on successive birthdays, but you prepare them well in advance. This way, if something were to happen to you, they could still get a birthday card and short message from you for the next 10 or 20 years, or for however many years you have prepared.

One lady with whom I consulted, Evelyn, was going through a period in her life when she felt she needed to "get her house in order," as she put it. She was healthy (and still is) but wanted the peace of mind that comes from being prepared in case something would happen. She is a proud grandmother who sends all of her four grandchildren a birthday card without fail each year, with a handwritten letter folded and inserted inside.

This is something that Evelyn really looks forward to doing for her grandchildren. After hearing about my birthday precepts, she decided to put this one into action. She now has finished birthday cards and letters for each of her four grandchildren for the next 20 years! That means she selected 80 birthday cards (her local Hallmark store had to be excited about that!) and wrote 80 half to one-page letters. She wrote a couple of letters a day most days of the week, spending less than a hour each day, and the project took her a couple of months.

Evelyn will send the pre-readied birthday cards herself until she passes on. Then the cards will be given to her two daughters for them to deliver the appropriate card for the appropriate year to each of their children (Evelyn's grandchildren). If Evelyn passes away tomorrow, her grandchildren will receive this meaningful gift from her until they are likely to be parents themselves.

To do your own sequential birthday message cards, follow these easy steps:

1. Write your message on a card or insert a letter into the card.
2. Place card and letter into the envelope and write the name and birthday on the front. For example: "Elizabeth, for her 18th birthday."
3. Keep each recipient's cards separately in sequential order. For example, keep Elizabeth's cards from her 18th birthday to 30th birthday together in one bundle, Joshua's 15th birthday to 30th birthday in a separate bundle, and so on.

These messages do not have to be just birthday cards. They could be video messages or audiotaped messages. Cards are simply the easiest and least time-consuming method.

If you decide to prepare future birthday messages to be delivered beyond the first birthday after your death, you should take the time to create the messages for the longer term. After a few years, you will have instituted a real birthday tradition — along with the accompanying expectations. When you end your messages at some point, be sure to indicate in the final card that it will be the last.

When I was growing up, I eagerly awaited every birthday, and it seemed to take an excruciatingly long time to get to the next one. Time changes things. As I got older, I lost my enthusiasm for birthdays and wondered how they possibly could be flying by so fast. Few adults I know actually enjoy their birthdays like they used to. Most of us don't have meaningful birthday traditions to replace the party hats and noise-makers of childhood.

After personally utilizing these birthday message precepts, I've changed my attitude about birthdays. Creating the kinds of birthday messages described here can bring back an excitement that you might not have felt for many years. And it will have an impact on your children's and grandchildren's birthdays in the future in ways you've never imagined.

Graduations

Another opportunity to deliver meaningful messages comes with graduations. The following example was prepared by Sarah, who was diagnosed with cancer 5 years ago and recently passed on. She designated the message for delivery to her daughter, Hannah, on the day Hannah will graduate from high school. Because of Sarah's chemotherapy treatments, she had lost a lot of hair and weight and for that reason chose to record her messages on a voice recorder. She arranged to have the tapes transferred to a CD with her favorite picture of her and Hannah printed on the face of the CD.

In her message Sarah tells her daughter how proud she is of Hannah, relates some memories of her daughter growing up, and emphasizes her desire for Hannah to focus on good memories of her mother, not on the death. Here are some excerpts:

I've got to tell you, it's exciting for me to be talking to you right now. It will be nearly 10 years from now when you will be listening to this. It makes me happy to know that I have an opportunity to let you know my views on some serious life issues. I'll be watching as you listen to this. I hope you're smiling. I will be!

* * *

Hannah, if you're like me — and I know you are — you're going to go through an extensive search of who you are, why you're here on this earth, and what the grand scheme of things is. You no doubt will investigate God all by yourself, coming to that time in your life when you will determine for YOURSELF what your own beliefs are and not just accept what you have been told.

This inquiry has been a serious focus of mine ever since I was your age — and even more so lately, after I was diagnosed with cancer. I've recorded this message to you because I wanted MY shot at telling you the conclusions I've drawn from the knowledge I gained through sincere searches for truth and from my life experiences. This is important, Hannah. The conclusions you draw from your own personal search will have either eternal benefits or eternal consequences.

* * *

I've gone through a search for my soul, Hannah. You, too, I hope, have already done this. If not, you might find my words a little unsettling. I hope that if you have not discovered the true meaning of your soul and of your life, you will find this CD just what the doctor ordered for your spiritual health. I hope you grant me my wish and listen to my words with an open mind...

Throughout the CD, the tone in Sarah's voice reveals her unabashed faith and great concern for Hannah. Sarah knew this might be her best opportunity to personally influence Hannah's faith. It will not be her *only* opportunity, however, because Sarah recorded additional FaithMessages that will be delivered to Hannah at other benchmark events. All are part of Sarah's Legacy Trust.

<u>Weddings</u>

Weddings are such an important event in life that they are a natural time to share a message of hope and encouragement with a loved one who is embarking on this journey. Because this is such an emotional day, I suggest that you deliver these messages before the wedding day. The following is an excerpt from a letter Sarah (my above example) wrote for her daughter, Hannah. It is to be delivered by Sarah's Spiritual Trust executor one week before Hannah is married.

My precious Hannah, I know you're so excited about your wedding. I wish I could be there to help you with your dress and hair and hundreds of other things. I know you will be such a beautiful bride. I want you to know that, although I won't be with you physically, I will be there!

I'm certain your husband-to-be is a fine man. I wish I could have met him. Please give him a big hug specifically from me, and tell him that I love him and will be watching over both of you as you become one.

I recall the wonderful day I married your father as if it were yesterday. I can still see and smell the flowers. I remember the delight of walking down the aisle with your grandfather toward a new beginning in my life — a beginning filled with hopes and dreams. I hope your father is still alive and able to share this thrill with you. If he's not with you, he's with me and we both will be with you in spirit. We had a marvelous marriage, crowned by the joys of you and your brother.

Marriage is breathtaking in its joys and in its challenges. I've shared with you in past messages some of my views on this most important aspect of your life. And I have some future messages on this most important aspect of your life, too. I hope you will find some wisdom in my words of encouragement. But today I just want to tell you again how much I love you and how proud I am of you.

Other Benchmarks

Just as with the benchmarks discussed in the Chapter 2, Support Trusts, you can have your Legacy Trust messages delivered in any number of ways — holidays, anniversaries (not necessarily just wedding anniversaries), parenthood, achievement of goals you know specific members of your family will be trying to accomplish, and so on. Your legacy can be manifested in many forms of messages at a variety of times in the future lives of your family.

> **Your legacy can be manifested in many forms of messages at a variety of times in the future lives of your family.**

Legacy Journals

Legacy Journals are another highly effective conduit for leaving your messages to your children and descendants. They are created on a daily, weekly, or monthly basis, and they center more on topics upon which you want to communicate a specific message. A Legacy Journal is a message of love, and it requires you to make an ongoing, periodic time commitment toward your legacy.

A Legacy Journal is a message of love.

A Legacy Journal can be written into a journaling book or on notepads, typed into your computer, or audio or video-recorded. Each of these formats can help you create a priceless legacy component of your Legacy Trust.

Legacy Journals are not logs of appointments and events. Most of that information belongs in your daily planner. A Legacy Journal is the place where you record your thoughts, prayers, lessons learned, wisdom, feelings, fears, hopes, dreams, concerns, special moments, memories, and the like. In it, you record things your children or grandchildren say and do that you don't want to forget and that you want them to be able to read, hear, or see someday. You record the "firsts" of a variety of life events in your family as a whole and for individuals. In your Journal you reveal the situations in life that unveil the essence of you and each member of your family in the different times and stages of life.

This is not a typical journal that you might use solely for your own benefit. The entries in a Legacy Journal are always for the benefit of your family. These are messages to *them*. You are consciously recording each entry knowing that your children or grandchildren, and perhaps their children and so on, will read, view, or hear it someday. In doing this, you always have to keep this big picture in perspective. If you don't, you might include things that can be hurtful. Concentrating on the idea that your journal is for your family members will keep you focused on the proper priorities and objectives when you are recording your entries.

The entries in a Legacy Journal are always for the benefit of your family.
They are messages to them.

As with other Legacy Trust components, you should be yourself when you record your Legacy Journal. Because a Legacy Journal unfolds over a long time, reading it will give your children insights into your faith, spirituality, growth, and similar things that might not be as apparent in some of the other Legacy Trust options. For example, your children and descendants can see how your relationship with Christ matured over the years covered in your journal. They can see how you applied your belief and faith in a multitude of real-life experiences. They will be able to capture the innermost feelings you had through the learning process of being their parent.

The four main kinds of Legacy Journals are audio journals, written journals, computerized journals, and video journals. You can use them exclusively or, as with any element of your Legacy Trust, in some combination. I cover the details of using these different media tools in Part II of this book.

<u>Audio Journals</u>

Audio journals are my personal favorite because of their ease and convenience. An audio journal is just as it sounds (pun intended). You audibly record yourself talking into a voice recorder as your journal entry. Audio recordings tend to be more candid than written works because they are more spontaneous. Your audio journal can always be transcribed later.

The audio journal can be created in places where you cannot write, type, or video-record. You should consider your voice recorder the same as you do your wallet or purse — take it with you wherever you go. Voice recorders give you the freedom and convenience to record a message at almost any time and any place, including your commute to work and business trips.

This is an example of an audio journal entry created by David during his morning commute to work:

Ashley, last night you, your mom, and I were driving home from your kindergarten graduation. Out of nowhere, you asked us if we wanted to hear you recite Psalms 23. Your mom and I glanced at each other and smiled, and I said, "Sure, honey — let's hear it." I thought you were going to quote a verse from Psalms 23, but there you went, quoting the entire chapter! I couldn't believe it. I asked where you learned that, and you told me, "At school." We congratulated you, and you and mom chatted the rest of the way home. I was silent.

The rest of the way home, I was deep in thought. I felt guilty that you could have memorized this without my knowledge. I felt embarrassed that you knew such a sizeable portion of scripture that I didn't know word for word myself. I've got to spend more quality time with you! I want to be the spiritual leader in your life that I envision myself to be. I promise you I will. I have a feeling you're going to be keeping me on my toes as you grow older. I'm so proud of you, Ashley. I love you so much.

You also can use your voice recorder to capture priceless conversations with your children or grandchildren as journal entries. In this way you will retain the tone and pitch of their voices that soon will be lost forever as they grow and mature. You can record them singing songs, reciting scripture, or talking about what is important to them. Making them part of your audio journal will heighten *your* enjoyment as you create the journal — and *their* enjoyment years later when they hear themselves along with you on the tape.

Written Journals

Written journals, the most traditional form of Legacy Journals, have been used for years. Many people hold handwritten documents in high regard because they are done carefully and take time to create. Also, some people find that writing in a journal is more convenient than typing on a keyboard, and easier to read than looking at a computer screen. Furthermore, your children will be able to pick up your "book," get comfortable in their favorite chair, and read your thoughts or messages to them.

You could purchase a journal with blank pages for your entries or you could get a three-ring binder and insert your pages into it as you complete them. This gives you flexibility, as you can include pictures printed off your computer or copied onto paper, as well as other documents and keepsakes. Whatever format you use, it should be the one with which you are most comfortable.

Patricia, a healthy woman in her early 60s, wrote a FaithMessage in journal form for her family and descendants. Having studied the Bible for many years, she told me, "I want to make sure that the things I've learned about the Word and some of the insights the Holy Spirit has graciously given to me do not die with me. I want my children, and my grandchildren and great-grandchildren and so on, to appreciate the Bible as much as I do."

Here are a few excerpts:

The Bible is the most miraculous book ever written. It's the only book that can equally captivate both a child and a scholar. This book is from God himself, a part of God that tells and teaches us about Himself. This is His key that He has provided to show us the way to unlock the gates of heaven and a life manual that we might live by His will.

Your Bible is your spiritual food. Without it, your spirit will starve to death. As with physical food, to stay healthy, you should eat at least a couple of times each day. If you do this for the fleshly body whose purpose is to carry your spirit during your short time on earth and then return to the earth when you die, why not also feed your spirit so it will grow up big and strong? I would rather that any member of the Burns clan starve to death physically than to starve to death spiritually!

* * *

Don't discard the Old Testament just because we have the New Testament. Jesus himself often quoted from the Old Testament. In addition, the New Testament includes more than 600 Old Testament quotations and references linking both Testaments into a united whole...

* * *

Never just accept whatever you hear about the scriptures as true. I don't care if it's coming from your preacher or your father. God gave you the responsibility to test every doctrine and teaching against the word of God to see if it bears evidence of truth (Acts 17:11 & 1 Thesalonians 5:21).

Many books on journaling are available for you to consult for additional assistance. A few are listed at the end of this chapter. Journaling is a great habit to develop and can lead to years of thoughtful pleasure for you as you create your journals, and for your descendants as they enjoy them.

Computerized Journals

Computerized journals are the modern version of written journals. If you're one of the millions of people using a computer daily or weekly, you may prefer this format to a written journal. If you choose this kind of Legacy Journal, you can do much more than just type words. You can scan pictures, or any image, and insert them into your entries. You can insert audio files and video clips. As technology matures, you will be able to do more and more creative things with your computerized journal.

Although some people perceive a computerized journal as being less personal than a written one, I don't think the next generation will view a computerized journal as impersonal at all. In fact, it may be their most comfortable way of reading your journal. Moreover, they can print and reprint your various entries and annotate the pages. A word of caution: If this is the kind of journal you choose to do, *be sure to consistently SAVE and backup your Legacy Journal* entries.

Video Journals

The video journal is an extremely effective type of Legacy Journal because it bring into play more of your senses. Your children and descendants will be able to see you, hear you, and observe your nonverbal communication. This sensory combination can magnify the impact of your substantive message. Video journals, however, are generally the most complicated to prepare and require some different skills. Some people enthusiastically begin video journals only to have their journal entries decrease in frequency over time. Notwithstanding, because the video journal format can be so effective, I strongly encourage you to consider trying it.

First of all, you must find a convenient recording location where you can leave your tripod and camera between recording sessions. I usually store my video recorder on my tripod. When it is not being used for recording family memories, it is on the tripod waiting for me to record another video entry. This avoids my having to set up and take down the video equipment every time I want to record a journal entry.

If possible, then, leave your video recorder on its tripod at the proper height and distance from where you will sit. This way, whenever you want to record an entry, you'll just walk to your recording location, hit the power button, the record button, and start talking. Don't concern yourself with how you're dressed. Just make sure you are! If you make too many rules, you'll be recording less instead of more.

When it's convenient to record your entries in another location, seize the opportunity. That way, your video journal will be more interesting to watch. For example: Take your audience to work with you one day, showing where you work, who you work with, what you do — and thereby give a more vivid impression of what work is like for you.

As another suggestion, insert short video clips from a vacation, reunion, or just family memories into your video Legacy Journal. The more creative you are, the more interesting it will be for your children and descendants to watch.

If you ever start thinking that your video journals are getting to be too much work, go back and watch what you've recorded. Pretend that you are your child or grandchild watching it decades from now. This usually will give you ample motivation to continue. If you find that this kind of journal is not the best style for your personality and lifestyle, switch to a different format, but don't stop! Part II offers more tips on video recording.

The substance of your journal is far more important than the form. Whether you use professional-looking journals or less formal methods, it is what goes into the journal that will be treasured.

> **The substance of your journal is far more important than the form.**

Albums and Scrapbooks

Leaving photo albums and scrapbooks is a very common practice and such keepsakes will be cherished by your family and future generations. However, let me suggest a couple of ideas to increase the impact and sentimental value of your photo albums and scrapbooks. Consider taking a voice recorder and recording the date, background, and story behind each picture. This audible recording can then be placed with the album or scrapbook by attaching it to the inside cover of the album. I suggest you have your voice recordings transferred onto a CD. This will preserve such recordings for a much longer period, and fits better within an album. You can also take the photos and have them scanned onto a computer and then add the voice recordings as the audible narrative. Additionally your pictures and audio recordings may be captured into a video format. This is another way to utilize a video montage. Your albums and scrapbooks can then be watched as a movie, with zooming and transition options adding to the appeal of your photo memories.

Albums and scrapbooks can also be narrated and used in a digital LifeAlbum™, which is covered in Chapter 8.

Generational Witnessing

A final consideration for your Legacy messages might be called "generational witnessing." Again, Scripture tells us that "he who is wise wins souls " (*Proverbs* 11:30). There is no greater reward than helping to win souls in your own family by the direct or indirect result of the legacy you lived and the Legacy Trust you leave behind. The greatest benefit of a Legacy Trust is not that your personal legacy will be remembered in a meaningful way for generations — although that's reason enough to have one. The ultimate benefit is the power of the Holy Spirit to utilize your Legacy Trusts to move the hearts of your children, grandchildren, and those on down the line.

A good man leaves an inheritance to his children's children (*Proverbs* 13:22). What better inheritance can mothers, fathers and grandparents alike leave their children (and their children's children) than the message of eternal life?

> **Anything that will spiritually help your loved ones constitutes a thoughtful inheritance.**

Whether you believe your children will or will not be reared by other believers if something were to happen to you, you should share the salvation message of Jesus Christ with them and other family members. If you were to pass away tomorrow, your children likely will have grown up thus far in a home where faith in Jesus was emphasized and encouraged. Other members of your family and future descendants might not have that same advantage. As a result, their children (your grandchildren) could be reared quite differently. Generational witnessing helps to ensure that your descendants will receive a witness from within their family, regardless of intervening developments.

If the family members who receive your witness are saved, they will appreciate the foresight and love you had to share the good news of the Gospel with them. If they are not believers when they hear your witness, it is possible that they just might be moved to accept Christ as a result of your witness. Imagine how you would feel if you were to meet one of your descendants in heaven and learn that your witness, heard long after your death, was instrumental in their salvation.

Spiritual Trusts

This is an example of generational witnessing that Carl, a father and grandfather, has prepared for his family members, both present and those to come. It is a message of salvation, which, in his words, is the most valuable gift he could ever leave them. Carl told me that he has a heavy heart for his family, born and unborn, because some of his children have rejected Christ. He said he feels the burden to make sure his grandchildren and great-grandchildren will have the opportunity to hear the Gospel from a family member. The content of his message is directed to the unsaved. Here are just a few excerpts from his 12-page letter:

The evidence of God is all around you. You only need to open your eyes to see the overwhelming facts of His existence. Look at the stars and the vastness of space and the billions of galaxies it contains. Did this just come to be on its own? Look at the earth you live on. Did its creation, and the laws governing nature and the environment, accidentally materialize by itself?

Look at yourself, your body — your bone structure, your muscles and organs, your brain, your nervous system, your blood, and your protective skin that keeps it all together. Can you really believe that your body is a byproduct of some cesspool that somehow generated a fish that grew legs and became a reptile and then, eventually, somehow, became a human with a soul and the ability to reason?

Look at all of the species of life on earth — animal, insect, and plant life. This all happened by chance? Can you really convince yourself of such nonsense? Look at your fingerprints and miraculous individuality. No two people have ever been created exactly the same. Look at your intuition, personality, and ability to reason. How can you think that there is not a creator?

* * *

Life on earth is so very short. Life in eternity is, oh, so very long. I beg you not to live the few years you have on earth ignoring the zillion, billion, trillion centuries that you will live in eternity.

Other parts of Carl's FaithMessages address sin, hell, forgiveness, and other spiritual topics that Carl hopes will impact his future family members for Christ. These are just some of the topics you can address in your Legacy Trust messages.

LIVING YOUR LEGACY

To leave an accurate, truthful, spiritual legacy, you must *live* your legacy. In my opinion, one of the best resources for helping you do this is the Heritage Builders Association, a ministry of Focus on the Family. You can find its website at www.heritagebuilders.com.

I pray that by living your legacy, you will benefit from the self-awareness and enlightenment benefits that articulating and passing down your Legacy Trust provides. I know your recipients will.

IN SUMMARY

A Legacy Trust gives you the opportunity to pass on your rich legacy that your family and descendants can connect with, learn from, add to, and continue the chain through the generational branches of your family tree. Your future generations can challenge their future generations to keep the family legacy alive by contributing their own individual legacy and passing the torch to the next generation. You can make it easier for them by passing along the tools they will need, such as your copy of this book or other books and materials that you have used to develop your legacy. This is another way to live with eternity in mind.

Recommended Resources

Baldwin, Christina. *Life's Companion: Journal Writing as a Spiritual Quest*. New York: Bantam Books, 1990.

Daniel, Lois. *How to Write Your Own Life Story: The Classic Guide for the Nonprofessional Writer*. Chicago, IL: Chicago Review Press, 1997.

Klug, Ronald. *How To Keep a Spiritual Journal*. Minneapolis, MN: Augsburg, 1993.

Ledbetter, J. Otis, and Tim Smith. *Family Traditions*. Colorado Springs, CO: Heritage Builders, 1998.

Ledoux, Denis. *Turning Memories Into Memoirs: A Handbook for Writing Lifestories*. Lisbon Falls, ME: Soleil Press, 1993.

Meyer, Paul J. *Unlocking Your Legacy — 25 Keys for Success.* Chicago, IL: Moody Press, 2002.

Peace, Richard. *Spiritual Autobiography: Discovering and Sharing Your Spiritual Story.* Colorado Springs, CO: Navpress, 1998.

Peace, Richard. *Spiritual Journaling: Recording Your Journey Toward God.* Colorado Springs, CO: Navpress, 1998.

Polking, Kirk. *Writing Family Histories and Memoirs.* Cincinnati, OH: Betterway Books, 1995.

Trent, John. *Life Mapping.* Colorado Springs, CO: Focus on the Family Publishing, 1994.

Wakefield, Dan. *The Story of Your Life: Writing a Spiritual Autobiography.* Boston, MA: Beacon Press, 1990.

ENDNOTES:

1. Dr. Smith is President of LifeMessages® and contributing author to this book.
2. Otis Ledbetter and Tim Smith (Colorado Springs, CO: Cook Communications, 1998), p. 31.
3. Interview with Douglas Weiss, October 2002.
4. Richard Peace, *Spiritual Autobiography* (Colorado Springs, CO: NavPress, 1998), p. 59.
5. Richard Peace, *Spiritual Autobiography* (Colorado Springs, CO: NavPress, 1998), p. 49.
6. Richard Peace, *Spiritual Journaling* (Colorado Springs, CO: NavPress, 1998), p. 34.

FIVE

Stewardship Trusts

"God provides His children with material abundance not primarily to raise their standard of living, but to raise their standard of giving."
— Randy Alcorn[1]

A steward is someone entrusted with another's wealth or property and charged with the responsibility to use or manage it in the owner's best interest.[2] A Stewardship Trust is a dedicated approach to using or managing the wealth and possessions with which God has entrusted you for *His* glory, not yours. A Stewardship Trust is a spiritual application of financial planning and can become an important part of your legacy.

A Stewardship Trust is a spiritual application of your financial planning and can become an important part of your legacy.

Stewardship Trusts offer countless opportunities to make a difference in the lives of others during and after your life on earth. What can you do? You can help build churches and hospitals. You can pay for bicycles and homes for preachers in Third World countries. You can provide medicine, clothing, and food to the poor. You can fund scholarships for those in need. You can care for orphans, help widows, and feed starving children. You can provide for Bibles to be distributed in the United States, Africa, Mexico, or any country. You can be fiscally responsible for saving souls — hundreds, even thousands of them. A Stewardship Trust will help you do these and countless other good deeds during your life *and* after you have passed away.

A Stewardship Trust gives you the opportunity to systematically exercise your stewardship skills as you funnel the blessings God has given to you back into the work of the Lord. Your Stewardship Trust can be a central part of your life. The spiritual heritage you establish through your Stewardship Trust also can be a strong component of the Legacy Trust you live and leave.

Thus, being a good steward has both immediate and eternal benefits for you and your family. You gain satisfaction from being a steward, and your family benefits from your example. The good deeds you arrange through your Stewardship Trust can continue and proliferate after your death to the benefit of many people outside your family.

A Stewardship Trust enables you to make financial arrangements during life that reap spiritual dividends during and after your life. It encompasses your stewardship practices during your life and after-life directives through a variety of possibilities, customized to fit your situation and goals. A Stewardship Trust uses traditional financial planning tools, in whole or in part, to transform physical finances into spiritual wealth. A Stewardship Trust is a way to visualize, organize, and manage the stewardship of your finances.

Some of you may have a Stewardship Trust already; you just haven't formalized it. In this chapter I will show you how to memorialize your Stewardship Trust in a document that is part of your Spiritual Trust System. A basic format for this document is given in Appendix A. Although it is not a legal document in itself, much of the content of your Stewardship Trust consists of legal documents. A Stewardship Trust includes things such as financial trusts, a will, and life insurance. During your life you likely will be the executor of your own Stewardship Trust, and you will be able to modify your Stewardship Trust as you see fit. Once you pass away, an executor of your choice will make sure that your after-death stewardship directives are fulfilled.

This chapter introduces you to Stewardship Trusts and how to use them to convert your temporary earthly resources into eternal heavenly treasures. I explain the importance of Stewardship Trusts, establish the context of Stewardship Trusts, and describe how you create them. Many excellent books are available on the principles and details of stewardship that fall within the purview of a Stewardship Trust. The Recommended Resources at the end of the chapter includes some of my favorite books and other resources on stewardship and finances, covering topics such as setting financial goals, the danger of debt, typical financial mistakes, and tax and investment planning. Now, let's begin.

THE NEED FOR SPIRITUAL STEWARDSHIP

Jim Elliot, the famous missionary, once said: "He is no fool who gives what he cannot keep to gain what he cannot lose." I love this nugget of wisdom. It even feels good to say it aloud a few times. Go ahead and try it. Memorize this saying. It is fundamental truth. Moreover, it is spiritual motivation for you to create a Stewardship Trust.

Randy Alcorn has written several books on the topic of stewardship. He is frequently quoted, and if you read his books, you will see why. He explains:

> "Stewardship is not a subcategory of the Christian life. Stewardship is the Christian life. For what is stewardship but that God has entrusted to us life, time, talents, money, possessions, family, his grace, and even his Son? In each case he evaluates how we regard and what we do with that which he has entrusted to us."[3]

Although our pride may tell us that we are responsible for the financial blessings we have received, the Word of God tells us otherwise:

> "Otherwise you may say in your heart, 'My power and the strength of my hand made me this wealth.' But you shall remember the Lord your God, it is He who is giving you power to make wealth."
> *(Deuteronomy* 8:17, 18a)

Wealth comes from the Lord. It is the Lord's. We merely have temporary custody. Because God is responsible for the financial blessings we have received, we must use them wisely. Are you returning the blessings you have received? Or are you just a taker and not a giver? God gives to you because He wants you to give. He does not desire that you hoard the blessings He has provided.

> **Because God is responsible for the financial blessings we have received, we must use them wisely.**

WHAT DOES THE BIBLE SAY?

Many of us rationalize that scripture is not pertinent to our finances and investments, but that clearly is not the case. In fact, Jesus discusses issues of money and finances more than any other social topic — yes, more than *any* other topic. I don't think that was by accident. God has always considered financial issues as relevant to the way we lead our lives. He knows of the good that money can bring to our lives and the harm it can cause as well. A Stewardship Trust helps you use money and resources for spiritual good and provides a structure and system that can help you become the kind of steward Jesus wants you to be.

Much of what Jesus teaches on the subject of finances can be disturbing. Scripture does not tell us that possessions are sinful in themselves, but scripture is clear that financial blessings are not ours to keep. We hold these blessings in stewardship from God. Jesus put our finances in perspective when He asked, "For what will it profit a man if he gains the whole world in exchange for his soul? Or what will a man give in exchange for his soul?" (*Matthew* 16:26).

Richard Halverson gives this perspective,

> "Jesus Christ said more about money than about any other single thing because, when it comes to a man's real nature, money is of first importance. Money is an exact index to a man's true character. All through scripture, there is an intimate correlation between the development of a man's character and how he handles his money."[4]

Let me paraphrase just some of what the Bible says pertaining to stewardship, money, and resources:

- It is the Lord who teaches us how to profit. (*Isaiah* 48:17)

- It is the Lord who gives us the power to get wealth. (*Deuteronomy* 8:17,18)

- The Lord declares ownership of all money. (*Haggai* 2:8)

- Everything in the earth is the Lord's. (*Psalms* 24:1)

- Wealth comes from God. (*Psalms* 104:24)

- We are to give in proportion to what we have been given. (*Deuteronomy* 16:17)

- Give and it will be given unto you. (*Luke* 6:38)

- God loves a cheerful giver. (*2 Corinthians* 9: 7)

- How people use money reveals a lot about their character. (*Psalms* 37:21)

- We are to release all of our possessions to Him and His purposes. (*Matthew* 19:21)

- We are to store treasures in heaven instead of on earth. (*Matthew* 6:19–21)

- To whom much is given, much will be demanded. (*Luke* 12:48)

Scripture clearly teaches that financial blessings come from the Lord and we are merely stewards of those blessings on behalf of the Lord. Consider the following facts regarding the Bible:[5]

1. The Bible contains more than 2,000 scriptural references to wealth and property.

2. Jesus says more about money than about heaven and hell combined.

3. The Bible talks about stewardship, wealth, and property twice as much as about faith and prayer.

4. One in every 10 verses in the Gospels deals with some aspect of stewardship.

5. Sixteen of the 38 parables speak about the relationship of people and their stewardship.

6. Jesus spent 15 percent of his recorded words on the topic of money, resources, and stewardship.[6]

Given this clear message, if you have trusted God for your salvation and put your eternal life in his hands, why not trust God with "your" money?

Materialism and Consumption

The main reason we are reluctant to trust God with "our" money, I believe, is the attitude of materialism and the habit of consumption. Do you think the consumption mentality is of God? If God stresses the virtues of giving and repeatedly tells us to do so, would He favor America's obsession with consumption? No, that is not the plan for our lives that Jesus established. Jesus told us to give, not to consume. That's not always easy, though. It seems natural to gather all we can for our families and ourselves.

Many of us get defensive when the issue of spending, or even worse, giving, is raised. These are not comfortable topics for many, including myself. The spirit of materialism is so compelling and gratifying to our flesh that it blinds us to the spiritual perspectives and principles that Jesus expects us to see and also to implement.

Materialism is perhaps Satan's masterpiece in spiritually blinding believers from the reality of true spiritual stewardship. Its magnetism is so strong that it is hard to focus on the spiritual consequences of how we handle our resources. For much of my life I was not able to see clearly through the materialistic haze in which I was enveloped. I'm not alone.

Let's look at the facts. Many believers spend more on their hobbies than they spend on the work of the Lord. We justify our cars, trucks, SUVs, boats, club memberships, retirement plans, and financial security. We justify spending more on candy bars than on foreign mission work and even more on movies than on making Bibles available.

The evidence clearly reveals that professing believers, as a whole, pay lip service to God's direct instructions and then go on about their lives. We consume with an apparent indifference to the plight of the world. Are you ensnared in the materialism habit? To find the answer, go through your checkbook and financial statements and see in black and white what is really important to you, not just what you say is important.

Jesus understood this danger and that is why He talked about it extensively. The money or possessions themselves are not what is sinful. Our tendency to hoard God's blessings and turn those blessings into *our* treasures is what is sinful. It prevents full ownership of *our* hearts by Jesus. "For where your treasure is, there your heart will be also" (*Luke* 12: 34). A Stewardship Trust is an antidote to the spiritual poison of materialism.

> ## A Stewardship Trust is an antidote to the spiritual poison of materialism.

Are You Rich?

Jesus said that the rich are at a spiritual disadvantage (*Matthew* 19:23–24). Having a lot of money is so dangerous, in fact, that Jesus compared a rich man making it to heaven with a camel fitting through the eye of a needle (*Matthew* 19:24). That's not very encouraging, is it? God is not saying, however, that it is impossible for someone who is rich to make it to heaven. The Bible mentions many wealthy men and women, individuals of deep faith, who surely ended up in heaven.

The Bible also contains many verses about the Lord's desire to bless us. It is when we are richly blessed financially, however, that we seem to have the most difficulty drawing the correct line and striking the proper balance of stewardship and selfishness. And you don't have to be "rich" by our current standards to be confronted by these issues. Look at your financial net worth, then look at the financial resources Jesus used in His ministry. Do you think Jesus might consider you a "rich" person?

Just being born in the United States makes you one of the richest people in the world. In fact, it makes you one of the richest people *ever* to live on earth. Many of us focus on others who are "richer" than we are instead of looking at how rich each of us is in comparison to the rest of the world. To whom much is given, much will be required (*Luke* 12:48).

Taking the "camel through the eye of a needle" example, imagine that Jesus were to look through that eye of the needle into *your* life. What would He see? Would He say you are an example of how it can be done? Or does your life typify His example? You can be a vessel through which God can pour out his blessings, or a camel standing next to a needle, unable to enter. It's your choice. As Randy Alcorn says:

> "The problem, of course, is not that God doesn't love the rich. The problem is that the rich don't love God. They simply have too much else to love already."[7]

An Investment Tip for You from Jesus

You can use your Stewardship Trust to show where your love is directed. Jesus can help you do this. He counseled people who came seeking God to: "Sell your possessions, and give to charity; make yourself money belts that do not wear out, an unfailing treasure in heaven, where no thief comes near nor moth destroys" (*Luke* 12:33). From an investment perspective, does that sound like a good deal? To trade temporary earthly possessions for a permanent, unfailing heavenly treasure? Well, that's exactly what Jesus has promised. Jesus made this vow to you just as much as he did to the people to whom he was talking.

Too many people, however, in effect tell Jesus: "No thank you, Jesus. I'm short-sighted and would rather hold onto my wealth and worldly possessions for my earthly life. I don't want to trade my earthly treasure that will fail me for the heavenly treasure that won't fail me. Thanks anyway." I never said that aloud, but I've said it with my actions and, therefore, with my heart.

Ouch — That Hurts

This topic is uncomfortable for many. It was for me. I didn't want to hear about it or talk about it — sincerely anyway — because when I did, it shed light on an area of my heart that I was keeping from Jesus. I couldn't let Jesus into a place in my heart that revealed my materialism and greed, and replace it with the resources provided to me by God.

I'm not alone. We live in the wealthiest nation in the history of the world, a nation that has more potential to do spiritual good than any nation ever has. Yet we give only 2 to 3 percent of our incomes.

To justify my purchase of the golf clubs I gave to myself, I went out and bought a gift for my wife. And on the first Sunday after my family went to church in our new car, I gave a larger than normal offering. I had a habit of trying to justify my spending. It's not that I'm an extravagant person. It's not the amount of money that is the issue. It's how you view "your" money and act in stewardship of that money, whatever the amount. I justified spending "my" money on material possessions because, hey, I worked hard for it and my family deserves it. This is the very core of materialism.

Before I accepted Christ as my Savior, and even for some time thereafter, I analyzed the fundraising tactics of churches, ministries, and charities. Maybe it was because as a businessman, I was curious about the "business" aspects of religion. I heard preachers and evangelists on the radio asking for gifts and donations, sometimes selling a "gift" for a "donation" of $25. I never had a good feeling about all of this "spiritual marketing." In fact, shortly after I got saved, I inquired about whether there was some sort of "buyout plan" for tithing and gifting. I got a few raised eyebrows — but not the answer I was hoping for.

As I grew to see things from the spiritual perspective, I began to understand how much money really does matter — but for different reasons than I previously had thought. I used to look at money as a tool to measure success, prestige, security, and status. Now I see that God is using money to measure my character, my obedience, my stewardship, and my heart. Because where you spend your money determines where your heart is (*Matthew* 6:20–21). It's not the money that's the problem; it's what we do with "our" money that's important. In essence, God is saying, "Show me the money." The way we spend our money reflects our character, moral direction, and obedience to God. Establishing a Stewardship Trust can help us address these issues, focus on them, and ensure we are good stewards.

> The way we spend our money reflects our character, moral direction, and obedience to God.

Giving Patterns

Sadly, the spirit of materialism and the habit of consumption have dampened the motivation for far too many people to follow the Lord's instructions on what to do with what we have been given. An excellent study by John and Sylvia Ronsvalle[8] tracks Christian giving patterns. If church members were to tithe 10 percent of their income, they would give $131 billion more dollars each year than they presently give.

This study of 11 denominations also showed that giving, as a portion of income, was lower in 1998 than in 1921 or in 1933, during the depths of the Great Depression. In the 1990s, the average church member spent less than $20 a year on global outreach, including activities that provide temporal and spiritual aid to children dying around the globe. Yet, during this same year, Americans, including church members, spent an average of $164 on soft drinks, $657 on restaurant meals, and more than $1,000 on recreation activities per person.[9] Further, church-member giving is declining as a portion of income, and currently is around 2.5 percent.[10]

Is God Short on Cash?

Why is the state of giving so anemic? Where is the vision for the lost? Is it a lack of manpower? Hardly. There are more believers now than in any time in history. More than 152 million Americans were members of 176 Christian denominations in 2000.[11] There are more than 5 million Bible-believing congregations in the world today. Are available finances lacking? Certainly not. The accumulative wealth of all professing Christians is in the trillions.

The truth is that God already has provided the funding for His work and any other need. He has provided, and continues to provide, His flock with more than enough financial resources to fund every church, mission, charity, and ministry that exists today. It is not a matter of lacking financial resources. Sadly, it is a matter of properly reallocating through stewardship what has been provided to where it needs to go.

Before I got saved, I looked at tithing to a church, at best, as a way of paying the membership dues. At worst, I considered it spiritual extortion. After becoming a believer, I still looked at religious fundraising as intrusive and unwelcome. I rationalized that if God really wanted this to happen, He would find a way. Then I would get into my new vehicle, with my kids in their new Sunday clothes, and drive my family to a nice restaurant, where I would eat a steak and complain about my golf game. I would go on with my day without even considering that I could have, or even should have, helped with a specific need.

God isn't short on cash, I thought. It never crossed my mind that the reason I was blessed was so I could pass on those blessings. I was worried more about what the money God gave to me could buy me and my family or what kind of return I was getting on it. To be sure, God wasn't short on cash. I had His cash, and I was keeping it for myself.

A pastor once offered a good analogy in comparing you and your giving to a FedEx delivery. Let's say you send something by FedEx to someone who really needs what you're sending. But instead of delivering your package, the FedEx driver takes your package home with him and uses it himself with no guilt. You try sending the gift again, because the person for whom it was intended didn't receive it. Again the delivery person takes your gift home for his personal use instead of delivering it to the intended recipient. Would you keep using the same FedEx driver again and again, or would you eventually switch carriers out of frustration? Now imagine how God must feel while giving to us again and again and then watching us hoard the blessings instead of funneling a portion to His work as He has admonished.[12]

Imagine God looking at the needy and unsaved and then looking at the richly blessed Americans. Surely each of us will be held accountable for our stewardship of the blessings with which He has entrusted us. How will you respond when He asks you about your stewardship? Establishing a Stewardship Trust will help you address these issues, focus on them, and ensure you are a good steward.

Saving Versus Hoarding

> "Individuals who value a rainy day above the present agony of the world will get no blessing from God."
> — William MacDonald[13]

One of the pitfalls we often experience is to rationalize saving by equating it to being a good steward. To be sure, saving is a part of stewardship. But we sometimes claim we are trying to be good stewards of our resources when we really are being selfish and hoarding God's blessings. God rewards us for what we do for Him, not for what we do for ourselves. Although we should be a conduit for the Lord's blessings to be dispersed into the work of the Lord, many of us have chosen to be a bucket instead. Remember the parable of the rich fool.

> "Then he said, 'This is what I will do: I will tear down my barns and build larger ones, and there I will store all my grain and my goods.' And I will say to my soul, "Soul, you have many goods laid up for many years to come; take your ease, eat, drink and be merry."

> "But God said to him, 'You fool! This very night your soul is required of you; and now who will own what you have prepared?' "So is the man who lays up treasure for himself, and is not rich toward God." (*Luke* 12:18–21)

When we have good economic times, we justify hoarding our finances under the guise of saving for the future, saving for retirement, or saving for a rainy day. Of course, when the rainy day arrives during poor economic times, we can't give then either. Using this self-serving rationale, we cannot give in the good times or the bad times.

Some of you may be wondering if I'm against savings, retirement planning, and financially investing in your family's future. I am not, and I have made financial decisions of this nature for the benefit of my family. Scripture tells us that saving is a wise thing to do. "There is precious treasure and oil in the dwelling of the wise, but a foolish man swallows it up" (*Proverbs* 21:20). "Go to the ant, o sluggard. Observe her ways and be wise, Which, having no chief, officer or ruler, prepares her food in the summer and gathers her provision in the harvest" (*Proverbs* 6: 6–8). But, as we have discussed, Scripture also tells us about the consequences of hoarding His blessings.

Knowing where to draw the line between responsibly providing for your family's financial security and hoarding God's financial blessings can be difficult. Notwithstanding, it is an issue that each of us has to answer. To answer in the spiritually correct way, imagine that Jesus is your auditor. Are you excited to show Him your books, or do you want to avoid the audit? Believe me, He *is* your auditor. But, thankfully, He also wants to be your financial advisor.

> Money is not at the heart of the issue.
> Our heart is at the heart of the issue.

STEWARDSHIP AND YOUR FAMILY

A Stewardship Trust can have many benefits for your family. I highly recommend that you involve your family in creating your Stewardship Trust. It can serve as an important component of the spiritual heritage you live and leave. It is a heritage of *believing* that financial decisions are actually spiritual decisions and *acting* that way. The creation and implementation of your Stewardship Trust can instill character, strengthen convictions, reinforce responsibility, and set standards of spiritual maturity for you and your family. It will help your children learn how to preserve, utilize, and multiply the resources with which they have been provided, and to do so with a profound understanding of spiritual stewardship.

SPIRITUAL PHILANTHROPY

Philanthropy is voluntary action for the public good. Spiritual philanthropy involves voluntary actions for the spiritual good of others.

> Spiritual philanthropy involves voluntary actions for the spiritual good of others.

Look at the importance the Bible gives to the act of giving. "Since we have gifts that differ according to the grace given to us, each of us is to exercise them accordingly: if prophecy according to the proportion of his faith; if service, in his serving; or he who teaches, in his teaching; or he who exhorts, in his exhortation; he who gives, with liberality; he who leads, with diligence; he who shows mercy, with cheerfulness. (*Romans* 12: 6–8). From this, we learn that giving is a spiritual gift of the same stature as the gifts of mercy, prophecy, and ministry. That's pretty good company, and anyone can be a spiritual philanthropist.

Spiritual philanthropy doesn't require great wealth. Philanthropy is about attitude, not amount. Remember how Jesus praised the poor woman who gave two copper coins at the marketplace, saying her gift was more valuable than the "rich" people who actually gave more (*Mark* 12: 41–44). Her giving was sincere. It was heartfelt. She had the right attitude. The amount was inconsequential. This is a truly insightful view into the perspective of Jesus and how He views our giving. It's not about the dollar amount. It never has been. It's about our heart, and it always will be. "God loves a cheerful giver" (*2 Corinthians* 9:7).

> **Philanthropy is about attitude, not amount.**

With the Stewardship Trust mindset, you won't view your giving as a deduction from your earthly financial net worth. Instead, you will view it as a multiplier of your heavenly treasures. You will gain far more than you will give. You just have to be patient. Moreover, the Stewardship Trust mindset will help you be content with what you retain as you draw pleasure from what you give. If you are a spiritual philanthropist, your family will learn from you. Part of your spiritual heritage — an important part — will be your generosity with what God has given you.

Your Spiritual Portfolio

While your financial portfolio is measured in dollars, your spiritual portfolio is measured in heavenly rewards, crowns, treasures, promises, and blessings. Your financial portfolio can't go with you, while your spiritual portfolio keeps growing for eternity. A Stewardship Trust will help you transfer your temporary assets to a spiritual portfolio with long-term (eternal) holdings and a miraculous return rate.

Someone once defined "true wealth" as adding up all of the things that money cannot buy and death cannot take away. This kind of true wealth is what constitutes a spiritual portfolio.

The primary purpose of a Stewardship Trust is to help you substantially increase the size of your spiritual portfolio by filling it with "kingdom currency." Satan wants us to be preoccupied with our earthly portfolios. Perhaps it is time for you to decide which portfolio you want to be the focus of your investments. Paul tells us that "we must all appear before the judgment seat of Christ, so that each one may be recompensed for his deeds in the body, according to what he has done, whether good or bad" (2 *Corinthians* 5:10). You should spend as much time planning and evaluating your spiritual portfolio as you do your financial portfolio. It only makes spiritual sense.

You may have heard the saying "stepping over dollars to pick up nickels." That's exactly what we're doing when we pass up spiritual investments (dollars) because we're so determined to pick up as many possessions (nickels) as we can.

SPIRITUAL INVESTMENTS

Building your spiritual portfolio requires you to make deposits. The more deposits you make, the larger your portfolio will become. These deposits are the result of *true* giving. I consider true giving to be "spiritual investments" because when you give with the right motives, attitude, and sincerity of heart, you are funding your spiritual portfolio.

Funding your spiritual portfolio however, is not as simple as writing a check to your church, para-church, or other nonprofit organization. Spiritual investments do not have anything to do with the amount of financial funds given, or even the act of giving them.

To build your spiritual portfolio, your spiritual investing should:

- be joyfully given. (2 *Corinthians* 9:7)
- be given without self-interest or temporal benefit. (*Luke* 6:35)
- be given out of love. (1 *Corinthians* 13:3)
- not be given grudgingly. (2 *Corinthians* 9:7)
- not be given to receive praise from people. (*Matthew* 6:2)

If these giving criteria are violated, your financial gift may benefit others but you will have jeopardized any spiritual reward for yourself. Building your spiritual portfolio is about changing temporal wealth into spiritual wealth, but the action of doing so is not what makes the transaction successful. The attitude behind the action is what constitutes true spiritual investing into your spiritual portfolio. This is why the size of your financial portfolio has little to do with the growth potential of your spiritual portfolio. Rather, your motives, attitude, and sincerity of your heart is what builds wealthy spiritual portfolios.

Another aspect of investing in your spiritual portfolio is how good you are at being stewards of your wealth during your lifetime. Jesus asked, "If you have not been faithful in the use of unrighteous wealth, who will entrust the true riches to you" (*Luke* 16:11)? The "true riches" are the sum of our spiritual portfolios. If we have not been trustworthy in the sight of God with the financial portfolios He has provided to us while on earth, why would He entrust us with spiritual portfolios that are eternal? To invest in our spiritual portfolios, we must be good stewards of our finances *and* have the right motives, attitude, and sincerity of heart in reallocating His blessings back to others.

GIVING THROUGH SPIRITUAL INVESTMENTS

There are probably as many different perspectives on Biblical giving as there are churches, denominations, and theologians. Some believe that we should tithe 10 percent of our incomes. Some believe that we are not required to give 10 percent but should give as the Holy Spirit directs us through His grace.
Some believe in systematic, proportional giving. And there are other viewpoints as well, all quoting scriptures that can support their position.

Sadly, none of these beliefs seems to prompt action in accordance with that belief. Most who believe in tithing 10 percent do not do so. Most who believe in giving through grace fail to give in proportion to the grace that Jesus Christ has showed them. We simply aren't getting the job done. It's a sad scar on our faith that overall we give only about 2½ percent of our incomes. It tells the world that regardless of what we say, our actions are inconsistent with our beliefs.

Whatever its root cause, this giving shortfall has serious consequences to God's work on earth. The needs are many, and not enough money is being given to fulfill these needs. The financial needs of churches and missions would be amply met if we would be the kinds of stewards with "our" money that God wants us to be.

> It's a sad scar on our faith that overall we give only about 2½ percent of our incomes.

Spiritual investing is a way to use your money and other resources as deposits into your spiritual portfolio. You give out of love and obedience to a cause to which the Holy Spirit directs you. You invest your financial wealth back into the work of the Lord. The spiritual treasures, rewards, and other benefits this investment produces become the building blocks of your spiritual portfolio.

Every single one of us, no matter what our net worth, has the opportunity to invest in eternity through our stewardship. Some of us will use this opportunity to profit spiritually. Others will squander it and declare spiritual bankruptcy.

We are guaranteed to lose *everything* we spend our money on in this world for worldly purposes when we die. As we've been told, "You can't take it with you." Or, in the words of the Bible, "For we have brought nothing into the world, so we cannot take anything out of it either" (*1 Timothy* 6:7). Wouldn't it be better to invest in spiritual investments providing eternal rewards? Many investment options are available.

STEWARDSHIP TRUST INVESTMENT OPTIONS

You can build your spiritual portfolio in many ways during your life and after your death. Prayer will be required to determine which of the many worthy causes you should support. I'll offer some spiritual investment ideas for you to consider. You no doubt are aware of others as well. Although I include some resources by name, I'm not trying to endorse any specific organization or ministry. Many other choices and opportunities are available for nearly all of these investment options. In considering your Stewardship Trust options, you first should evaluate the needs you believe you are called to address through your spiritual investments. Then you can evaluate the various paths through which you can further those purposes.

The Needs

> "For we are His workmanship, created in Christ Jesus for good works, which God prepared beforehand so that we could walk in them."
> *(Ephesians 2:10)*

There are so many needs that you may have difficulty determining where you want to place your Stewardship Trust's spiritual investments. Here are some options for you to prayerfully consider.

<u>Your Church</u>

Churches play a vital role in the spiritual health of our country. Local churches nurture, train, teach, and support the believers in their local communities and prepare people for mission work abroad. Churches are the backbone of the spiritual support our society receives as a whole. Our churches must be strong because of the cascading spiritual ramifications that strong churches manifest in our communities. Churches don't just provide fish; they teach believers to be fishers of men. In doing so, they play a crucial role in other types of spiritual investments by supporting them directly and indirectly.

> ### Churches don't just provide fish; they teach believers to be fishers of men.

Without strong, indigenous churches, future generations may not have the spiritual opportunities we take for granted. The investment options suggested next are not meant to take away from spiritually investing in your church. They are meant to provide ideas from which you can chose *after* you have met your obligations to your church.

<u>Foreign Missions</u>

Even though our great country has many spiritual needs, you are likely to get more "return" from your dollar by investing outside of the country. The needs in other countries are so great, and the investments we make there are so small. Ninety percent of the world's Christian workers live in countries with 10 percent of the population. Their money tends to stay where they live (mainly our country). According to the American Association of Fundraising Counsel (AAFRC), international organizations, including relief agencies, exchange programs, research institutes, and others, received $2.71 billion in charitable support in 2000. Although this may sound like a lot of money, it is just a small fraction of total giving and even a smaller fraction of what is needed. International giving received only 1.3 percent of all giving in 2000.

Foreign missions is one of the least-funded areas of giving, yet it has one of the highest rates of return for your spiritual investment. Does this make sense? It wouldn't be prudent for a business to invest in a saturated market, especially if there were other markets where the initial investment was a fraction of the cost, the market was virtually untapped, and there was a great demand for the product. Yet we invest this way all the time, perhaps because foreign missions are just so, well, "foreign" to us.

Every believer has a duty to adhere to the Great Commission that Jesus Christ gave to us: "Go therefore and make disciples of all the nations, baptizing them in the name of the Father, and the Son, and the Holy Spirit" (*Matthew* 28:19). Not every one can go to other nations. Some are called by God to go, and some are called by God to send. If you are not personally spreading the Good News abroad, you should consider investing in those who do.

Some are called by God to go, and some are called by God to send.

Saving souls for Christ should be a motivation for developing your spiritual portfolio, and you can accomplish this by applying stewardship strategies to foreign missions. So how are we doing? Well, approximately 30 million un-reached souls are dying every year. There are 2.5 billion people who have not heard the Good News of the gospel. That's more than one-third of the world's population. If this concerns you, you should consider giving to your church's mission fund and to ministries and charities whose purpose is to win souls for Christ. Many fine ministries, large and small, are making an impact in world evangelism and mission work. One is The Christian and Missionary Alliance (www.cmalliance.org) another is Jimmy Hodges Ministries International (www.jhmi.ws).

I will use the example of Hunter to illustrate how you can invest in foreign missions and make a tremendous difference. He has made a certain ministry a partial beneficiary of his life insurance policy in the amount of $25,000. This amount will be given to this ministry for the purpose of winning of souls in Africa. This particular ministry[14] will use the $25,000 in an effort to bring approximately 10,000 Africans to Christ. How much time and money do you think Hunter would require personally to bring 10,000 people to Christ in Anywhere, USA? Supporting ministries that already are equipped to do this work is a wise use of resources and a shrewd act of stewardship. One such ministry could be your local church. In fact, your church's mission fund is a great place to start.

Providing the Word of God

Think how difficult it would be for you to grow in the Lord without a Bible, or one in your language. Without the Word of God it is far more difficult to know Him. We are lucky — 9 out of 10 adults in America own a Bible.[15] Most of those reading this book probably could find a half dozen Bibles in their home. The situation is far different in most other countries. Investing in ministries that provide Bibles to those who do not have one is a spiritual investment with huge returns.

Alternatively, or in conjunction, you could invest in ministries that translate Bibles into languages for which there is no Bible. Among the several excellent Bible distribution and translation ministries is Wycliffe (www.wycliffe.org). According to Wycliffe, more than 380 million people speak a language that has not been translated into a Bible. Other ministries you should look at are the American Bible Society (www.americanbible.org), the International Bible Society (www.ibs.org), and Bible Literature International (www.bli.org).

Church Planting and Building

America has many needs for church facilities — new buildings and expansions/renovations alike. If you know of a need and feel God leading you, find out what you can do to help through your spiritual investments.

Church building in Third World countries is also a great need. In some countries a rural church that will hold about 100 people can be built for about $500. This can be a wonderful way to maximize the benefits, dollar-for-dollar, of your spiritual investments.

Education

Many faith-based or religious schools, universities, and seminaries need funds. There probably is one near you. You might give to the general fund, building fund, or scholarship fund. If you talk to those in charge of fundraising, they will be pleased to explain their specific needs to you.

Youth

Investing in our youth is investing in the world's future. Among the many avenues are: youth programs at your church, youth camps, and mission trips. Some fine organizations you might look into are Young Life (www.younglife.org), Campus Crusade for Christ, (www.ccci.org), the Fellowship of Christian Athletes (www.fca.org), and Youth For Christ /USA (www.yfc.org).

Media

Has a certain radio or television ministry positively impacted your life? Through your financial contributions, you can help ensure that this show and others like it will continue. The Christian Broadcasting Network (www.cbn.org) and Trinity Broadcasting Network (www.tbn.org) are reaching tens of millions of people across the world with the Gospel.

Preachers and Evangelists

There is a tremendous need for training and support of preachers and evangelists at home and abroad. Scripture addresses the need to provide such support (see, for example, *Luke* 10:7; *Galatians* 6:6; *1 Corinthians* 9:3–14; *1 Timothy* 5:17–18). Many evangelists falter for lack of continuing support, and many others never start because they lack adequate financial support. Through your church or another ministry, you may be able to locate these preachers or evangelists. You will hear from them firsthand about their ministry and can support them in prayer as well as financially.

Humanitarian needs

Many ministries provide services to starving children, widows, orphans, and other people in need. We are called to do so (*1 Timothy* 5:3; *Proverbs* 28:27; *Luke* 14:14). Empty Tomb has reported that more than 35,000 children younger than five years old die *each day* from preventable poverty conditions. Many ministries seek to remedy these ongoing tragedies. Your spiritual investments can help.

Look at the work being done by Compassion International (www.compassion.com), World Vision (www.worldvision.org), Feed The Children (www.feedthechildren.org), Food For The Poor (www.foodforthepoor.org), Habitat For Humanity (www.habitat.org), Samaritans Purse (www.samaritanspurse.org) , Mercy Corps (www.mercycorps.org) and Christian Children's Fund (www.christianchildrensfund.org). These are just some of the many options to consider.

Other Worthy Causes

Other needs include family development, discipleship, and men's and women's ministries. A few of the ministries you might consider are Focus on the Family (www.family.org), The Navigators (www.navigators.org), Promise Keepers (www.pk.org), and Women of Faith (www.womenoffaith.org).

Paths by Which You Can Further the Lord's Work

You can take many paths to further the work of the Lord through your spiritual investments. As you evaluate your spiritual investment strategy, I believe you should begin with your church. So let's start our discussion with your church, then move to other options.

Church

The church you attend is the best place to start. The Bible encourages believers to consolidate their resources through their local church (*1 Corinthians* 16:2; *Acts* 4:34–35). Every church needs active givers, and few churches have enough of them.

Every church needs active givers, and few churches have enough of them.

Most churches will put your spiritual investment to good use in the Lord's work. Notwithstanding, I strongly suggest that you take an active interest in how your church uses your spiritual investments. Take a moment to evaluate your church's stewardship of the funds it receives. Most churches provide members a church budget. Take a look at how much money is spent on line items. Does your church have a missions fund? If so, what percentage of the church budget goes to missions? What are the church's most substantial expenditures?

Also evaluate how effectively your church handles the spiritual investments it receives. Is God actively moving in your church, making it an attractive spiritual investment?

Ministries

Ministries come in all shapes and sizes, both local and abroad. Some ministries have researched all of the ways possible for you to invest and share in their mission. An effective way to get more for your spiritual financial investment is to allocate your giving to ministries as matching funds. You give and encourage others to give by matching their contributions. This is an excellent way to motivate other givers, knowing that their gifts will be doubled. It affords you the opportunity to be a good steward while providing added incentive and encouragement for others to do so as well.

Ministries can be more difficult to evaluate than your church if you are not involved personally with a ministry. Unlike a church, you will not experience a ministry's fellowship or vision in person on a weekly basis, but some excellent tools are available to help you evaluate ministries. Any ministry you are considering should welcome your inquiry. Scripture supports this evaluation: "We want to avoid any criticism in the way we administer this liberal gift taking precaution so that no one will discredit us in our administration of this generous gift; for we have regard for what is honorable, not only in the sight of the Lord, but also in the sight of men" (2 Corinthians 8:20, 21). This was the practice of the Apostles, and it should be the practice of any ministry to which you give.

The Evangelical Council for Financial Accountability (ECFA) is well-respected and maintains stringent principles regarding the financial responsibility and accountability of its member ministries. ECFA member ministries have a commitment to evangelical Christianity, maintain high standards of financial integrity and ethics, offer full financial disclosure, have an independent board of directors, undergo annual audits, and follow strict fundraising guidelines. Billy Graham and Dr. James Dobson highly endorse the ECFA.

The ECFA has available an abundance of useful information about evaluating and investing in ministries, which can help you determine and validate your spiritual investment decisions. Through its website (www.ecfa.org) you can search its member list according to primary ministry objectives. There are 41 ministry categories from which to choose. You can even find a financial summary on each ECFA member. ECFA has a Donor's Bill of Rights and a list of questions you should ask a ministry before donating.

Another interesting website, jammed with information that is easy to find and easy to read, is www.ministrywatch.com. This independent source for ministry ratings rates more than 400 different ministries according to efficiency rating, overall rank, rank within sector, and transparency grade. It also provides information on the purpose of the ministry, comments by the analysts, ECFA affiliation, what supporters say, what critics say, and more about each ministry rated.

Religious Charities and Foundations

Many charities and foundations are doing wonderful works for the Lord. An excellent resource to locate a variety of charities is Christian Service Charities, whose mission is to provide donors (spiritual investors) with choices in religious charities. This organization works with charities in categories such as: children, disaster relief, hunger, health services, education and training, and international. You can visit the website at www.csoa.org. to peruse the lists of charities.

Other resources that list many charities, including "religious charities," are Share America at www.shareamerica.org and Charity Navigator at www.charitynavigator.org. For information on foundations, visit the Foundation Center (www.foundationcenter.org), the National Center for Family Philanthropy (www.ncfp.org), and the Council on Foundations (www.cof.org).

Separating ministries from charities and foundations can be difficult at times. In general, a ministry has a religious focus. A charity or foundation might have a religoius focus or might simply perform good deeds from a secular perspective. I suggest that you focus on the substance, not the form. Look at what the ministries or charities do, and how well they do it, then ask the Holy Spirit to guide you when you are considering an investment in a ministry, charity, or foundation.

Spiritual Mutual Funds

In developing a financial portfolio, every financial advisor will tell you to diversify — don't put all your eggs in one basket. This may be a prudent form of spiritually investing as well, depending on the value of your investments.

Ask Jesus to reveal to you if your spiritual portfolio should be diversified in spiritual investments. Depending on your financial condition, creating your own spiritual mutual fund may give your spiritual portfolio larger spiritual dividends over the long run than a portfolio with only one kind of spiritual investment. Alternatively, you may make more meaningful contributions if you invest in just a few or even one cause, particularly if you will be getting personally involved in a cause to which you contribute financially. The Holy Spirit may guide you in either direction. As in all your spiritual investments, being obedient to His guidance is the key.

FUNDING YOUR STEWARDSHIP TRUST

When you're making spiritual investment decisions that substantially affect your finances or your estate, your spouse should be involved so you agree about the financing and distribution of your Stewardship Trust. If warranted, you should seek the advice of a financial advisor, a CPA, or a lawyer who will understand your spiritual objectives and their legal implications (you can find such professionals on our website).

This chapter certainly is not intended to replace the counsel and advice of these professionals. The following discussion can get you thinking about options, but you should always follow up with the appropriate professional before you finalize your Stewardship Trust.

> "Without consultation, plans are frustrated, But with many counselors they succeed."
> *(Proverbs* 15:22)

Your Stewardship Trust can be funded while you are alive and at death. I will deal first with some options for giving during your life, and then go into how to "cash out" your financial portfolio and "roll it" into your spiritual portfolio at death.

Stewardship and Taxes

Good stewards care more about the reason they are giving and the spiritual benefits that will come from their stewardship than any tax benefits they receive. This is in harmony with the purity of motives necessary for true stewardship. Still, I believe that spiritually investing in a planned way to take advantage of available tax deductions is a legitimate part of being a good financial steward.

Therefore, I highlight certain tax benefits in the various ways to fund your spiritual investments. My purpose in doing this is *not* to offer you a temporal reward for giving. It is merely to show how planned stewardship can increase your giving by reducing requirements that otherwise would deplete the financial potential of your spiritual investments. These techniques allow you to give voluntarily to the church and nonprofits of your choice rather than to give involuntarily to the Internal Revenue Service.

If you give to nonprofits that the IRS recognizes, you may receive financial incentives such as a federal income-tax deduction for your charitable lifetime gift (you may need to itemize) and federal estate-tax deductions for charitable gifts made at your death.

The rules in this area are complex, and they change frequently. Therefore, I again recommend that you visit with a tax advisor who can help you maximize the tax deductions while accomplishing your stewardship goals. Your financial planner, church, or ministry also may have resources to guide you through the process. If you plan to make a major financial contribution, you should contact your church or nonprofit's director of major gifts or someone of an equivalent position and expertise. An excellent book to consult is *The Zondervan 2002 Church and Nonprofit Organization Tax and Financial Guide* by Dan Busby, CPA.

Funding Spiritual Investments During Your Life

During your life, the most common way to make spiritual investments is from your income or cash reserves. Most people do this directly from their checkbook. This is fine, although, as we saw in the beginning of this chapter, the giving patterns of most believers do not comport with applicable scriptural principles. As part of your Stewardship Trust, you should insure that your giving from your income and cash reserves is in line with the gifts you have received. There are also other ways to fund your Stewardship Trust. These other ways include family funds, appreciated securities, depreciated securities, stock options, real estate and other property, and charitable gift annuities.

Family Fund

You can establish a Family Fund in a savings or checking account called "The [your last name] Family Fund." You and other members of your family make contributions to this fund.

This is an opportunity to share with your family your stewardship and the joy of giving. A Family Fund can help pay for a friend's doctor bills, a short-term mission trip, a youth camp, Bibles, feeding the hungry, and on and on. It helps to develop a family heritage of giving back. You can finance your Family Fund through a percentage of income, bonuses, tax refunds, allowances, and the like.

Appreciated Securities

Giving appreciated securities can be a prudent form of stewardship. You might avoid paying capital gains tax on the appreciation and be able to deduct the full fair market value of the security at the time of the gift. For instance, Dustin bought a stock five years ago for $10,000. The stock did well and appreciated to $20,000. Dustin donated this stock to his favorite ministry as a part of building his spiritual portfolio. He took a $20,000 charitable-contribution deduction on his income tax (he itemizes). He also avoided paying the capital gains tax he would have incurred on the $10,000 appreciation had he sold the securities.

Depreciated Securities

If you are like me, you know all too well that not all stocks appreciate. I have some good news. You may be able to sell depreciated securities as part of your spiritual investment strategy and receive tax benefits. If you sell the depreciated security and give the cash proceeds to a qualified nonprofit organization or your church, you may be able to take a capital loss on your federal income taxes, as well as a charitable contribution deduction for the cash amount of the gift.

Stock Options

If you have stock options you may be able to exercise your stock options without any cash investment, and give the stock to your church or other nonprofit. You then may take a charitable contribution deduction for the fair market value of the stock.

Real Estate

Donating real estate could be a great way for some of you to fund your spiritual investments. If you donate real estate you have owned for more than one year, you may qualify for a charitable deduction equal to the fair market value of the property. You also will avoid the capital gains tax on the appreciated portion of the real estate that would have been required if you had sold it.

Property

In general, donations of property such as art, automobiles, and jewelry are treated similarly to donations of real estate. Like real estate, you may need a qualified appraisal to support the amount of your claimed deduction for property that has a value over $5,000.

Charitable Gift Annuity

A large variety of nonprofits offer many different and flexible annuity plans. Basically, with a gift annuity, you make a gift to the nonprofit and, in exchange, the nonprofit agrees to pay you a fixed payment each year for life. You may be able to take a charitable contribution deduction for the amount of the gift in the year you make the gift. You receive your payments in annual, semi-annual, or quarterly installments. Payout rates are calculated based on your age and life expectancy. Upon your death, any remaining balance goes to the charity.

You can set up as many annuity plans as you like throughout your lifetime. You can fund your annuity with cash, appreciated securities, or other property. The American Council on Gift Annuities (www.acga-web.org) gives standardized charitable gift annuity rates.

Funding Spiritual Investments at Death

If you are a good steward of the wealth and possessions with which God has entrusted you during your life, why stop there? With your Stewardship Trust, you can continue your stewardship after death and thereby continue to have a positive impact for God. You can use many of the options discussed in the prior section on Funding Spiritual Investments During Your Life to fund your spiritual investments at your death. These typically are part of bequests in a will. For example, you could bequeath property (such as cash, real estate, art) to a charitable organization of your choice (for example, your church, a ministry, other nonprofit).

Even though the church has many needs, most Christians don't think about their church as a beneficiary of their estate when they pass away. Nine in ten donors have not included a church as one of the recipients of a portion of their estate.[16]

Life Insurance

The primary purpose of life insurance is to provide financial security for your family in the event of your death. Life insurance also can be used as a powerful investment tool to fund your spiritual portfolio upon death.

Because life insurance is such an important way for most people to provide for the financial security of their families, I don't want to imply that you should neglect your family by dedicating all or part of your insurance proceeds to the Lord's work. But if you have an amount of insurance that is more than your family will need, or if you increase your insurance to provide for a charitable cause upon your death, life insurance can be an excellent method by which to fund a spiritual investment.

If you can't afford to make all of the spiritual investments that you desire to make during your life, you can make a church or other nonprofit a partial beneficiary of your life insurance policy. Your contributions are simply delayed until the death benefit is paid. With the exception of your premiums, however, you incur no cost during your lifetime.

Ownership of the policy is an important consideration. You can retain ownership of the policy and designate a part or all of the proceeds to go to a church, ministry, charity, or foundation. If you maintain ownership of your policy, you will not receive any immediate tax benefits from making a nonprofit a beneficiary of your policy, but there can be future estate tax benefits.

For instance, if you have a $100,000 life insurance policy, you could make your church or other nonprofit a partial beneficiary. You could allocate a percentage — say 10 percent of the proceeds — to your church. When the death benefit is paid, your church will receive $10,000.

If you have policies that for various reasons you don't need anymore, you can transfer ownership of your policy to your church or chosen nonprofit by gifting it to them. This may result in a deduction in your taxable income equal to the present or replacement value of the policy. You also can deduct the annual premiums as an annual charitable contribution. If this appeals to you, you should know that if the transfer occurs within three years of your death, the value of the policy is included in your taxable estate.

Retirement Plans

The Internal Revenue Service considers qualified retirement plans such as an IRA, 401(k), 403(b), Keogh, pension, SEP, and profit-sharing plans to be a part of your taxable estate. Charitable contributions from retirement plans are fully deductible from your estate as charitable gifts. Therefore, you may want to consider a charitable contribution from your retirement plan as part of your estate planning. With these kinds of retirement plans, you usually can change your beneficiary designation or distribution at any time. Just ask for a Change of Beneficiary form and indicate the amount or percentage you would like to go to charity.

Your Estate

Basically, your estate is everything you own at the time of your death. According to Ron Blue, with respect to estate planning, "We can say three things: We will die; we will take nothing with us; we probably will die at a time other than what we would like.
These realities create many practical planning problems!"[17] Notwithstanding, advice from proper professionals can help reduce these problems. If you don't plan for your estate distribution, the government will.

A good estate plan includes your will, insurance, beneficiary designations, appropriate record keeping, and numerous other factors. Part of being a good steward is ensuring that you have properly planned your estate distribution. As discussed in the Support Trust chapter, there are many reasons for proper estate planning that are not financial ones.

> **Part of being a good steward is ensuring that you have properly planned your estate distribution.**

Your Will

A will provides for the distribution of your assets upon death. It's never to early to have a will. About 30 percent of Americans die before they retire. Moreover, about 70 percent die without a will. It is said that the average person spends 40 years accumulating wealth, 20 years preserving it, and less than 6 hours planning for its disbursement.

As part of your Stewardship Trust, you should consult with an attorney and prepare a will. Every state has its own laws as to what constitutes a valid and legal will. If you just write out your wishes and leave it at that, you run a serious risk of having your will declared invalid. Your will is the primary instrument by which you can confidently know that the "at death" objectives of your Stewardship Trust will be fulfilled as you planned.

Financial Trusts

Trusts can give you control over what will happen to your assets after your death. Certain trusts allow you to remove assets from your taxable estate. Each trust becomes a separate entity that usually pays taxes on income and capital gains tax generated by those assets. Trust assets can grow outside of your taxable estate and avoid estate taxes when distributed to your heirs, church, ministries, or other beneficiaries.

You can integrate your financial trust into your Stewardship Trust planning. In this way, your financial trust can be used to provide for your family and also as a tool to help you accomplish a variety of goals such as spiritual investment management, and giving assets and money back to the work of the Lord.

A trust is not for everyone. Nor is one single trust the perfect planning tool for everyone. You should consult a professional for more information about the types of trusts that may work best for your specific situation and needs.

In short, you can fund your spiritual portfolio during your life and after in many creative ways. The good works you set in motion will have eternal benefits, and you will reap eternal rewards from your spiritual investments.

IN SUMMARY

Financial decisions are spiritual decisions. The Bible teaches us that financial blessings come from the Lord, that they are the Lord's, and that we are merely stewards of those blessings on behalf of the Lord. We shouldn't view giving as a deduction from our financial net worth. Instead, we should view giving as a multiplier of our heavenly treasures. The purpose of a Stewardship Trust is to set our sights on heavenly currency instead of earthly currency; to concentrate on building a spiritual portfolio more than a financial portfolio, and to see our finances from an eternal perspective instead of only from a temporary viewpoint.

If we are not good stewards of worldly wealth, we will not be entrusted with heavenly riches. A Stewardship Trust can create an important aspect of the heritage you establish for your family and the spiritual legacy you leave behind. It is a fundamental part of living with eternity in mind.

Recommended Resources

Alcorn, Randy. *Money, Possessions and Eternity*. Wheaton, IL: Tyndale House, Publishers, 1989.
Alcorn, Randy. *The Treasure Principle: Discovering the Secret of Joyful Giving*: Multnomah Publishers, 2001.

Blue, Ron, and Jodie Berndt. Generous Living: Zondervan Publishing House, 1997.
Blue, Ron, and Charles R. Swindoll. *Master Your Money*. Nashville, TN: Thomas Nelson 1991.
Busby, Dan. *The Zondervan 2002 Nonprofit Organization Tax and Financial Guide*: Zondervan Publishing House, 2001.
MacArthur, John. *Whose Money Is It Anyway?* Waco, TX: Word Publishing, 2000.
MacDonald, William. *True Discipleship*. Kansas City: Walterick Publishers, 1975.
Patterson, Ben. *The Grand Essentials*. Waco, TX: Word Publishing, 1987.

Websites
www.aafrc.org
www.ministrywatch.com
www.thegoodsteward.com
www.ecfa.com
www.emptytomb.org
www.estateattorney.com
www.independentsector.org
www.masterbuilder.org
www.philanthropicservice.com
www.philanthropy.com
www.acga-web.org

ENDNOTES:

1. Randy Alcorn, *Money, Possessions and Eternity* (Wheaton, IL: Tenderly House Publishers, 1989), p. 172.
2. In *The Grand Essentials*, by Ben Patterson (Waco, TX: Word Publishing, 1987), p. 17.
3. Randy Alcorn, *Money, Possessions and Eternity* (Wheaton, IL: Tenderly House Publishers, 1989), p. 172.
4. Randy Alcorn, *Money, Possessions and Eternity* (Wheaton, IL: Tenderly House Publishers, 1989), p.15.
5. John MacArthur, Jr., *Whose Money is it Anyway?* (Nashville, TN: Word Publishing, 2000), p. 3.
6. Randy Alcorn, *Money, Possessions and Eternity* (Wheaton, IL: Tenderly House Publishers, 1989), p.17.

7. Randy Alcorn, *Money, Possessions and Eternity* (Wheaton, IL: Tenderly House Publishers, 1989), p. 65.
8. *The State of Church Giving Through 1998*, Empty Tomb, www.emptytomb.org
9. *The State of Church Giving Through 1998*, Empty Tomb, www.emptytomb.org
10. *The State of Church Giving Through 1998*, Empty Tomb, www.emptytomb.org
11. According to the 2002 edition of the *Yearbook of American and Canadian Churches*, published by the National Council of Churches.
12. This allegory was derived in part from a tape entitled *Beauty and the Beast Financial Fairy Tales* Part 4, "Giving Means Subtracting," Woodman Valley Chapel, by Matt Heard.
13. William MacDonald, *True Discipleship* (Kansas City, KS: Walterick Publishers, 1975), p. 97.
14. Jimmy Hodges Ministries International, www.jhmi.ws
15. George Barna, *How To Increase Giving Through Your Church* (Ventura, CA: Regal Books, 1997), p. 50.
16. George Barna, *How To Increase Giving Through Your Church* (Ventura, CA: Regal Books, 1997), p. 33.
17. Ron Blue, *Master Your Money* (Nashville, TN: Thomas Nelson, 1991), p. 183.

Part Two

Developing and Implementing

Spiritual Trusts

SPIRITUAL TRUSTS

The Spiritual Trust System

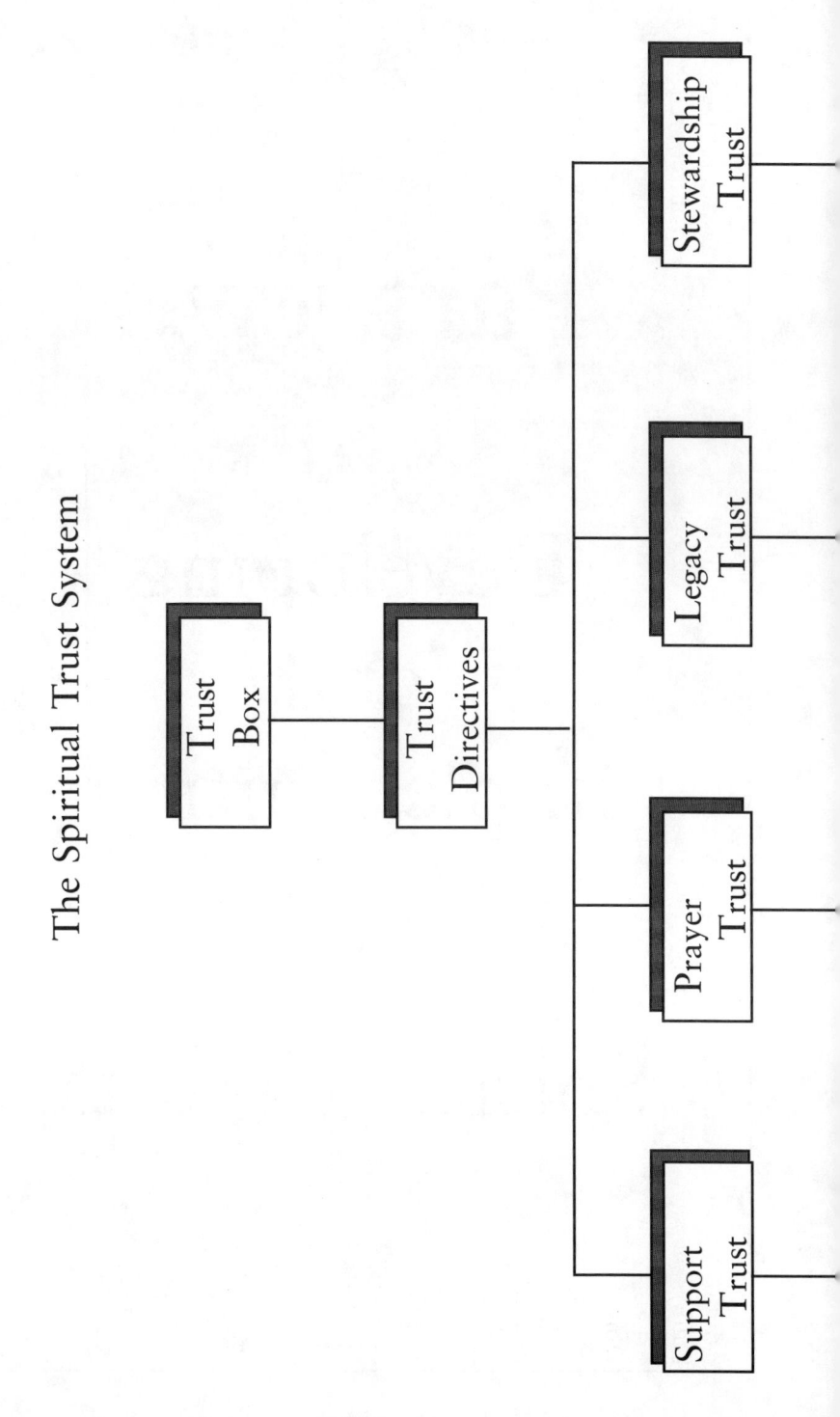

- Trust Box
  - Trust Directives
    - Support Trust
    - Prayer Trust
    - Legacy Trust
    - Stewardship Trust

Branch 1:
- Goodbye messages
- Eulogy messages
- Byeulogy messages
- Obituary
- Video montage
- Defend your death
- Funeral Support
- FaithMessages
- LifeMessages
- Benchmark support
- Monthly
- Birthdays
- Holidays
- Graduations
- Weddings
- Birth

Branch 2:
- Support prayers
- Protection prayers
- Salvation prayers
- Blessing prayers
- All good things prayers
- Prompting prayers
- Prayer requests
- Prayer reminders

Branch 3:
- Life Story
- Chronological
- Essence
- Spiritual
- Life Tribute
- FaithMessages
- LifeMessages
- Generational witnessing
- Benchmark Deliveries
- Monthly
- Birthdays
- Holidays
- Graduations
- Weddings
- Birth
- Legacy Journal

Branch 4:
- Spiritual Investments
- Your church
- Missions
- Bibles
- Churches
- Education
- Media
- Evangelists
- Other causes
- Paths of invesment
- Spiritual mutual funds
- Funding Spiritual investments

Recipient(s)

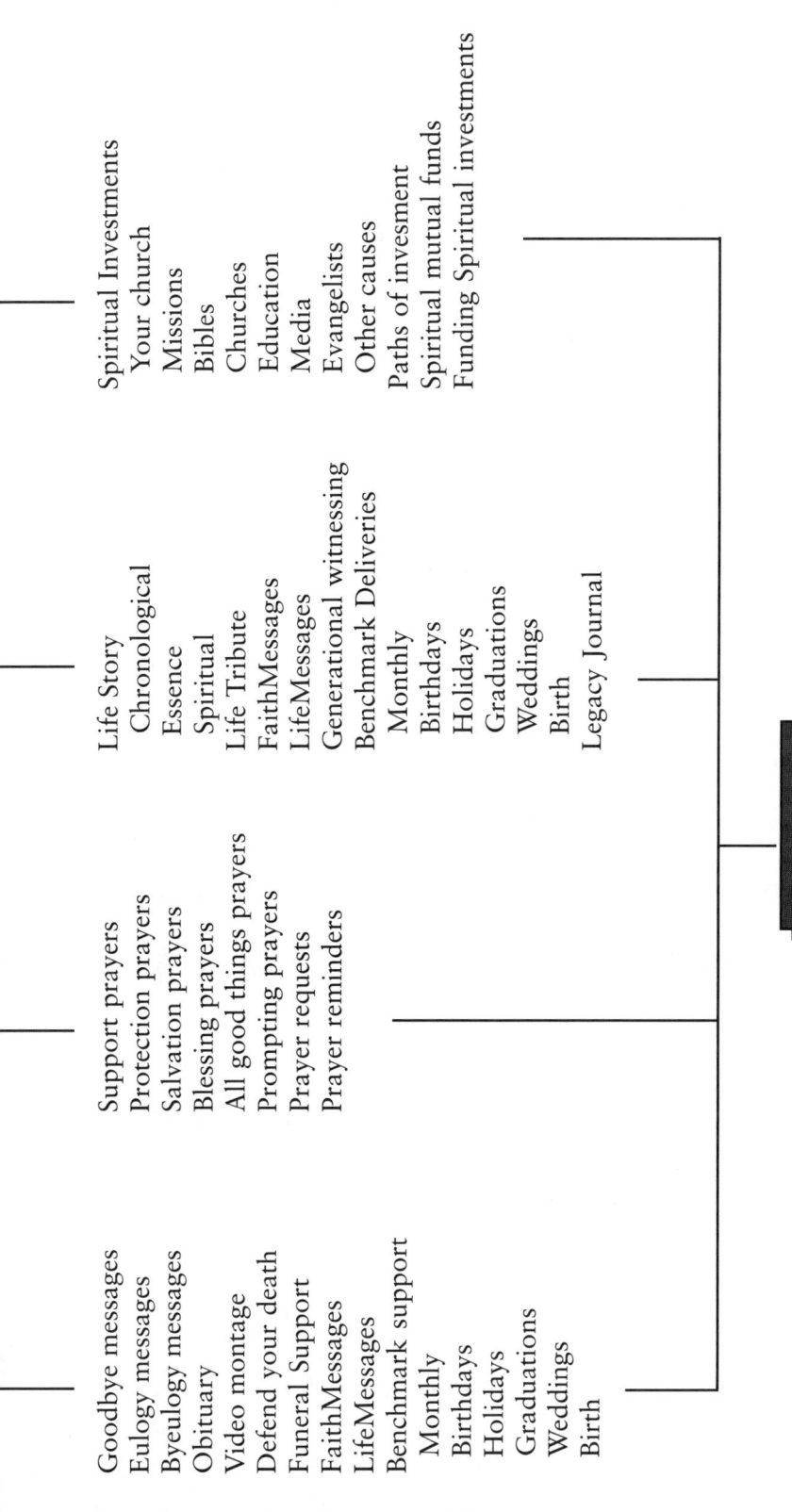

See next page for explanation of this chart.

163

EXPLANATION OF CHART

At the top of the chart, is a Trust box. It represents where your Trusts will be kept. You can choose from several options. I use, and will refer to, a Trust box because it is designed specifically to keep all components of your Spiritual Trusts and your most important and valuable documents safe. A Trust box can take the form of a portable safe, safety deposit box, etc.

Under the Trust Box in the illustration, you will find your Trust Directives. This is the form you create for the person who is going to be the executor of your Trusts (if you choose to use an executor). A sample form for your Trust Directives is in Appendix A. Your Trust Directives will contain all of your instructions and other information regarding the implementation and delivery of your Spiritual Trusts. The Trust Directives should be on the very top or in the very front of your Trust box, depending on how you have organized its contents.

Branching down from the Trust Directives are the four kinds of Spiritual Trusts. Under each Trust are the main components of that Trust, although you may mix and match Trust components as you like. For example, you may decide to have one general "Family Trust" and have components of each Trust combined into one single Trust. Or, you may decide to have only a Support Trust.

On the chart, all of the Trusts branch down to your recipients. This is where your Trust is actually delivered to your chosen recipients in accordance to your Trust Directives.

Part II

Developing and Implementing Your Spiritual Trusts

Part II of this book explains in detail how to develop and implement your own Spiritual Trust System. This is a four-step process:

- **Step 1, Selection:** Select which Spiritual Trusts you want to create and the recipients for whom you will create them. You have substantial flexibility. You may choose one or more Trusts as described in this book in their entirety, choose just one component of a Trust, or you may choose to take components of different Trusts and combine them into one Trust. Likewise, you may choose one or many recipients of your Trusts or Trust components. Chapter 7 covers this selection process.

- **Step 2, Creation:** Create your Trusts with as little as a pen and paper or with as much as your voice and video recordings. Chapter 8 addresses how to use a pen and paper, a computer, photographs, a voice recorder, and a video recorder, independently and in combination, to create compelling Spiritual Trusts.

Spiritual Trusts

- **Step 3, Storage:** Store your Spiritual Trusts so you are *sure* they will outlive you and get into the hands of your intended recipients when, where, and how you choose, no matter how long that may be. Chapter 9 reviews the most reliable methods to preserve and archive your Trusts and provides you with assurance and confidence in the sustainability of the Spiritual Trusts you create.

- **Step 4, Delivery:** Provide for the delivery of your Spiritual Trusts in your Trust Directives form. Chapter 10 will equip you with the information you need to prepare your Trust Directives and to intelligently select an executor of your Spiritual Trusts. You will be armed with contingency plans to assure that your Trust Directives will be implemented as you desire in the future.

Following these four steps will help you to create effective Spiritual Trusts that will impact the future lives of your recipients. Depending on the kinds of Trust you are developing and how far into the future you want to store and deliver them, you may utilize just some or all of the information in Part II. Consequently, as you read Part II, don't get bogged down in details that may not pertain to your goals or objectives. Concentrate on the Trust components you identify for yourself and your loved ones and the procedures to create, store and deliver them as you wish.

SIX

The Four-Step Process

Good intentions alone are not enough to influence the spiritual lives of your children, grandchildren, and others in the future. A Spiritual Trust is a call to action. Establishing a Spiritual Trust takes love, faith, and time. Love is the motivator. Faith gives you the persistence to see it through based on your eternal perspective. Your commitment of time ensures completion of what you started. Following the four-step process will get you there with relative ease, enjoyment, and great personal satisfaction.

Take a moment right now to imagine the impact on your recipients when they receive a Trust component from you. Play out in your mind what their reactions will be, and their first expressions after receiving the messages from you. Close your eyes and visualize the benefits your Spiritual Trust will provide to them. Think of the spiritual and emotional impact on their lives! Reflect on what your Spiritual Trust will mean to them. Recognize what it would have meant to you if you had received a Spiritual Trust.

A STEP AT A TIME

Establishing Spiritual Trusts might sound like a huge project to you, but you don't have to do them all, nor do you have to do them all at once. Some people decide what Spiritual Trust components they want to implement and finish them in hours, days or weeks. More complex Trust components may take months or longer. Some components, such as a Legacy Journal, might remain a work in progress for the rest of your life. Move at your pace, but move.

To paraphrase Laurence Peter of the Peter Principle: When faced with an important task, the competent person simply begins. I could throw dozens of motivational clichés at you, such as "a long journey starts with a single step" (sorry — I couldn't help myself), but if you are moved to develop a Spiritual Trust, you will need to begin.

Remember the "Noah rule": Predicting rain doesn't count, building arks does. As you begin, however, remember that Noah built his ark one plank at a time. Building your Spiritual Trusts becomes easier if you take it one step at a time, one day at a time.

> "The best thing about the future is that it only comes one day at a time." — Abraham Lincoln

THE PLAN

Before you start to develop a Spiritual Trust, you do need to make a commitment of time. Try to commit to a certain amount of time instead of focusing on a certain number of pages or other goal. If you invest the time, the substance will come soon enough.

The unique Spiritual Trust System you develop will depend on your personal goals, objectives, and situation. If you want to create more than one Trust or Trust component, a rule of thumb is to have one Trust component substantially completed before you begin creating additional Trust components. Notwithstanding, you have endless flexibility to customize your Spiritual Trust System and to progress at your own pace.

> **The unique Spiritual Trust System you develop will depend on your personal goals, objectives, and situation.**

The length and complexity of your Spiritual Trusts should relate to the information you want to communicate and the goals you want to achieve. On the one hand, I know people who have created each type of Trust, and each Trust had enough documents, video and audio messages, and so on to fill its own individual Trust

The Four Step Process

box. On the other hand, I know people who have prepared components of each Trust that all fit into one three-ring binder, or that just wrote a series of letters to their children or grand children.

Whatever the case, developing a Spiritual Trust follows these basic steps:

Selection

Your Recipients
Your Components

Creation

Outline
Draft
Revise
Compose
Finalize
Using Media Tools

Storage

Archiving
Storing

Delivery

Trust Directives
Delivery Options
Executors
Contingency Plans
Funding

As you go through this four-step process, you will begin to experience a deep sense of accomplishment from knowing that you will be able to have a positive influence on your loved ones long after your life on earth is over. This process will also have immediate and positive benefits on your life. This is another benefit from living with eternity in mind.

IN SUMMARY

The unique Spiritual Trust System you develop will depend on your personal goals, objectives, and situation. In general, a Spiritual Trust follows the four steps of: (1) selection, (2) creation, (3) storage, and (4) delivery. Attending to each of these steps will help to ensure that your Trusts will be delivered as you intend them to be. The subsequent chapters in Part II address each of these steps.

SEVEN

Step 1: Selection

The first step in the process of developing one or more Spiritual Trusts is to decide who the recipients will be and what kinds of Trusts or Trust components you want them to have. Having read Part I, you may know exactly what Trust you want to start with and the person or persons you want to receive each Trust, or you may have so many ideas and questions in mind that you don't know where to start.

If you're in the latter category, ask yourself:

- Would I like to provide *spiritual* support to my love ones through a Support Trust?
- Do I want to arrange for *prayer* support and protection for my loved ones through a Prayer Trust?
- Am I interested in leaving a *spiritual legacy and heritage* to my descendants through a Legacy Trust?
- Is it my desire to supplement financial blessings with spiritual ones through a Stewardship Trust?

Any question to which you answer "yes" will give you a good indication of the task in front of you. Then ask yourself: What is the main thing I want to accomplish through my Spiritual Trusts? What did the Lord lay on my heart when I was reading Part I? That will give you a good indication of where to start.

Selecting your Trusts and recipients is an intellectual, emotional, and spiritual exercise. Often, the selection of a certain Trust or component is directly related to the impact you desire for a specific recipient. You may have difficulty separating the two steps — selecting the person or persons you want to receive your Trusts, and then selecting which components you want to include. If the answers to these two questions come to you all at once, that's fine. For purposes of this discussion, however, I separate these two decisions, addressing the recipients first.

The selection of your Trusts and recipients is an intellectual, emotional, and spiritual process.

YOUR RECIPIENTS

Before you begin to create a Spiritual Trust, you should have a good idea of who your recipient or recipients will be. There are many possibilities. The Trust may be for your daughter — or for your great, great granddaughter. You could create one Trust and have messages in that Trust sent to a dozen people, or you could create multiple Trusts all for one recipient.

A good way to start this selection process is to ask God to impress upon you the person or persons He would like you to name as a recipient or recipients. Besides your family, He might lay it upon your heart to send a message to your neighbor, a co-worker, or your pastor. Who knows how God will lead you. But if you let Him lead and you follow His direction, He will bless your efforts.

For your Stewardship Trust you may think of categories of recipients such as orphans, the unsaved, youth, etc. For the other three Spiritual Trusts you will likely be directing your Trust components to people you know or to your future descendents.

*S*tep *O*ne: *S*election

A good way to begin is to make a list. Some possibilities are:

Parents	Children
Grandchildren	Great-grandchildren
Grandparents	Great grandparents
Future descendants	Siblings
Aunts and uncles	Cousins
Close friends	Friends of the family
Guardians	Godparents
Godchildren	In-laws
Associates	Co-workers
Mentors	Teachers
Students	Neighbors
Pastors	Sunday school teachers
Church members	Ministries you support
Heroes of yours	Classmates from the past
Roommates from the past	Prayer partners
Nephews and nieces	People you have influenced
People who have influenced you	People you admire
People you've been praying for	People you have been witnessing to

In reading this book, did someone in particular come to mind as a potential recipient of your Trusts? If so, that's a good place to start. As you progress with your evaluation of recipients, keep in mind that even after you have created various Trusts and Trust components, you can add or delete recipients as you desire.

YOUR COMPONENTS

As you select your recipients, you should be thinking about what Trusts and components you want to give them. For instance, if you feel led to create a Support Trust, do you want to send goodbye messages to your loved ones? Do you want to create your own eulogy? Or, do you want to ensure that your loved ones receive continuing prayers through a Prayer Trust. If a Legacy Trust appeals to you, do you want to do a story of your life? Do you want to create a Legacy Journal? Do you want to send FaithMessages to your children and grandchildren at certain times in the future? If you are concerned about your stewardship, do you want to start spiritually investing in your spiritual portfolio? Think and pray about your goals and objectives for your Spiritual Trusts.

In selecting your Trusts and Trust components, you are really deciding how you want to touch others. Here is an outline of Trust components and concepts covered in Part I from which you can choose:

Support Trust (Chapter 2)

Goodbye Messages
Eulogy Messages
Byeulogy Messages
Video Montage
Messages Defending Your Death
Funeral or Memorial Arrangement Support
Legal and Financial Arrangement Support
Designation of Personal Momentos and Heirlooms
FaithMessages
LifeMessages
Benchmark Support Messages
    Monthly
    First Wedding Anniversary After Death
    One-Year Anniversary of Death
    Birthdays
    Holidays
Mentors and Advisors

Prayer Trust (Chapter 3)

Spiritual and Emotional Comfort and Strength
Protection
Salvation
Blessings
All Good Things
Prompting Prayers
Initial Prayer Support Request Letters
Reminder Prayer Request Letters

Legacy Trust (Chapter 4)

LifeStory
    Chronological LifeStory
    Essence LifeStory
    Spiritual LifeStory
LifeStory for Your Living Parents and Grandparents
LifeTributes
FaithMessages
LifeMessages
Benchmark Messages
    Milestone Birthday Messages
    Time-Warping Birthday Messages
    Generational Birthday Messages
    Sequential Birthday Messages
    Graduations
    Weddings
Legacy Journals
    Audio Journals
    Written Journals
    Computerized Journals
    Video Journals
Generational Witnessing

Stewardship Trust (Chapter 5)

Investing in Your Church
Investing in a Ministry
Investing in Charities and Foundations
Spiritual Mutual Funds
Funding Spiritual Investments During Life
Funding Spiritual Investments at Death

    Think about these Trusts and their components as they relate to your recipients and to your goals and objectives for *your* Spiritual Trust System. If you want to create a number of Trusts and components, prioritize the list and start at the top.

In selecting your Trusts and Trust components, you are really deciding on how you want to touch others.

Once you have selected your Spiritual Trust components and Trust recipients, before you do anything else, you should fill out the Work in Progress form. A sample of this form is in Appendix B. It is a simple form that will provide the following information:

1. The location or possible locations of your work in progress;
2. The Trust components you are working on;
3. The intended recipients of those Trust components; and
4. When and how the recipients are to receive those Trust components.

If you do not do at least this much, your work in progress (no matter how far along) may not be found, or its discovery could be delayed for weeks, months, or even years after you want your Trust components to be delivered. A lot of unpredictable things can happen immediately after the death of a loved one, and you can avoid some of these pitfalls by completing your Work in Progress form early and placing a copy of it with your important papers and with at least one family member or other friend.

When you have completed each Trust component, you will fill out a Trust Directives form, which will provide additional details on the storage and delivery of the component. This subject is covered in Chapter 10.

IN SUMMARY

In developing one or more Spiritual Trusts, The first step is to decide who the recipients will be and what kinds of Trusts or Trust components you want them to have. Selecting your Trusts and recipients is an intellectual, emotional, and spiritual exercise.

With your recipients in mind, you can begin to think about what Trusts and components you want to create for them. Review the components of a Support Trust, Prayer Trust, Legacy Trust, and Stewardship Trust and evaluate what Trusts and components you want to do. Then prioritize your list and begin at the top.

EIGHT

Step 2: Creation

No matter how old you are, you have a dynamic message to send to the future. Moreover, everyone, young and old, can learn a lot about themselves through the introspective adventure of creating Spiritual Trusts for others. This is an exhilarating process that can enlighten, educate, and motivate.

No matter how old you are, you have a powerful message to send to the future.

THE CREATION PROCESS

The creation process involves the following five tasks, but Spiritual Trust creation is an art, not a science, and you should proceed in the style that fits you best:

1. Outline
2. Draft
3. Revise
4. Compose
5. Finalize

Outline

Some people are able to sit down and crank out a component of a Spiritual Trust with ease and clarity on the first try. Most of us, however, aren't that adept, particularly at first. To clarify what we want to include in any Trust component, outlining the content will help.

An outline for your Spiritual Trust is essentially a checklist of topics and key details that you want to cover. Creating and following an outline rather than simply writing or speaking will keep your message on track and focused. It also will help ensure that you cover everything you want to cover.

Before you create an outline, brainstorm all the areas you want to cover and write down the topics. Try to relax and just start writing. Once you have a list of topics, you can begin putting your thoughts into a more organized form.

You can organize your topics by grouping them logically into subjects, then determine the order in which you want to cover those subjects. After you have your subjects organized and sequenced, you can proceed to fill in the key points for each topic. Outlines are thoughts, not sentences. The details will be developed in the next task.

> **Outlines are thoughts, not sentences.**

Some outlines are necessarily more detailed than others. For example, your LifeStory outline likely will be much more detailed than your eulogy message outline. No matter how brief it is, however, you should develop an outline for every Trust component you create.

Once you have created the outline, review it to see if you forgot a topic or accompanying details. Then set it aside for at least a day or two before you look at it again in order to look at it from a fresh perspective. You can revise your outline as you see fit at any point in the process. It is a living document and your outline will continue to guide the creative process.

Draft

A draft extends the details of your outline into a narrative form. Most people have difficulty going directly from an outline to a finished piece, and the draft is an interim stage that helps get you to the

Step Two: Creation

final product. Depending on the Trust component you are creating, it might take you minutes, hours, days, or even weeks to develop a draft with which you are satisfied.

> A draft extends the details of your outline into a narrative form.

When you're creating your draft, keep in mind that you are creating just that — a draft. You don't have to concern yourself too much with how it sounds or flows, or worry about grammar, style, or technique. You just take the subjects and topics in your outline and begin fleshing them out in whatever order is the easiest for you, allowing your heart and spirit to flow into your draft. You will have plenty of time to revise and edit your draft later. Right now, all you have to be concerned with is creating a thorough first draft.

The first sentence or the first paragraph is often the hardest. Don't agonize over this. You might want to start with the easiest part of the outline first and work backward from there. You can save the hardest parts for last, then piece your draft together in the order of your outline. As you develop your draft, feel free to alter and revise your outline; it is not set in stone.

Furthermore, your drafts can be as long or as short as needed. There isn't any minimum or maximum length. If you feel in your heart that you have said what you want to say, you don't have to ramble on for the sole purpose of adding length to a Trust component. Actually, unnecessary length tends to detract from your message.

Keep your recipient in mind as you are developing your draft. What topics will have the most interest to your recipient? What is the best approach to take for this particular person?

If you come to a specific topic with which you are having difficulty, try these three things:

1. Stand up for a while as you are thinking about the topic. Standing up stimulates the blood flow to your brain. Your heartbeat actually increases by about 10 beats per minute. Take a walk, if you can, and think about the topic as you enjoy some exercise.

2. Come back to the draft later rather than sitting there, banging your head against the wall, trying to pound the right words out of your head. If you are meant to say it, the words will come to you at the right time.
3. Evaluate whether you really want to address the topic. If not, simply exclude it.

Revise

After you have finished the first draft, take the draft and outline, lay them out side by side, and compare them. Is everything there that you wanted to include to fulfill your original purpose in creating this Trust component? If not, is it because you decided to delete some of your outlined topics or details, or do you have some more work to do?

If you have covered everything you want, read and reread your draft. Does it convey what you want it to? Is it in a logical order? If not, revise your outline and draft accordingly.

If you are doing a written Trust component (rather than video or audio), this is a good time to check for spelling and grammar and to pay attention to possible word redundancy. Do not repeat certain words or phrases so much that they become a distraction.

When you are satisfied with your draft, wait a few days, then reevaluate it. If you are still satisfied, move to the next task. If not, revise it again.

Compose

Whether you are writing, typing, or recording your Trust, you should compose your Trust in the same sequence as your outline and draft. If you keep your outline and your draft handy, you can refer to them as necessary.

You don't have to try to write or record everything in one session. It's often a good idea to do the longer Trust components at more than one time. Each break could be for a few minutes or a few days, depending on the complexity of the Trust component and your schedule. A quick review of your draft will indicate logical places for you to take one or more breaks.

When you are composing a Trust, keep in mind that this is *your* Trust, so it should sound like you. A Trust is an extension of yourself, so the words and mannerisms should be yours, using your normal conversational language. Write the way you talk and talk the way you normally express yourself. You don't have to be eloquent to positively impact your recipient. Be yourself. Be natural. Be real.

A Trust is an extension of yourself, so the words and mannerisms should be yours.

If you have a good sense of humor, let it show. If you are videotaping, dress as you would in a similar setting and situation. If you are making the video in segments, you might want to change your type of clothes, reflecting the season or weather at the time.

In written messages, you should make an effort to use correct spelling and proper grammar. Although your family and descendants won't mock you if you misspell a word or violate a grammatical rule, poor grammar and misspelled words can detract from your message.

If you're uncomfortable with your writing abilities, you might consider having someone else help you. Most friends or family members will feel honored to help you. You also could engage the assistance of a Spiritual Trust System consultant. The main thing is to make sure that the final product reflects *you*, not your assistant. Your recipients will want to hear and see the real you, not a ghost writer.

Last, but not least, be honest. You must not state "facts" in the way you wish they had happened. If you can't tell things as they are or were, you should avoid that topic in your Trust.

Finalize

After you have composed your Trust component, take a few days or even weeks to clear your head. Then, depending on the Trust tools you're using, read what you wrote, listen to what you said, or watch what you taped. Take notes if you want to. Watch, listen, or read it from the recipient's perspective. Is your general impression favorable? Do you want to add or delete some things?

The Trust media tools (discussed below) allow you to make necessary changes. You can edit videotapes and audiotapes. You can revise typed or written messages. If you follow the outline and draft process described above, you should not have to edit your final Trust significantly. Over the years, of course, you might want to go back to a given Trust component and make changes. I encourage you to evaluate your Spiritual Trust System at least every few years and make any desired changes or additions.

Finalizing your Trust will take some paperwork. At this stage, you will enter in your Trust Directives the necessary information. This includes *what* the Trust component is, *who* the recipient is, *when* the recipient is to receive it, and *how* the recipient is to receive it. Completing your Trust Directives is an important task in the creation process. Trust Directives are covered in full detail in Chapter 10, and in Appendix A.

Ongoing Entries

Some Trust components, such as Legacy Journals, are designed to be works in progress. You might continue working on several Trust components throughout your life. Therefore, you will have to make sure that the "Work In Progress" form (see sample in Appendix B) addresses these projects. You also should leave word with close family members and friends about work in progress so if something happens to you unexpectedly, the work you have developed thus far will be utilized and not overlooked.

TRUST MEDIA TOOLS

To create your Trust components, you will use one or more of the following media tools:

- Video
- Audio
- Written or typed words
- Photographs and images

Each medium has its own strengths and weaknesses. You might find that one media tool fits your style and objectives for a certain Trust component and another media tool better fits a different Trust component. Most people who do several Trust components make use of more than one media tool. Their Trusts become a multimedia collection. This lends variety to Trusts and allows the strengths of each media tool to be matched with the objectives of each Trust component.

Following is a review of the media tools that you will want to consider for the Trust components you have in mind, along with some information and tips that will help you use these tools effectively. You may find that you have to spend some time with a media tool to become proficient in using it. Video, for example, can pose quite a challenge if you have never used this medium before. With a little work, however, you can become comfortable with any of these media tools.

Video

Although you may not want to use video for every aspect of your Trusts, video is the most compelling medium for many Trust components. Video usually is far more memorable than any other format because your recipients can see you, hear you, and observe your nonverbal communication.

If you are going to use video, you will need a video camcorder. Several types of video formats are available today. The most common are VHS, Beta, Hi8, and digital video. Digital video is the newest video format, and I recommend it if you have not already invested in a camcorder. Once you have a camcorder, you need to know how to use it.

There's a big difference between the quality of most home videos and those done by professionals. Fortunately, for Trust components, you will not *need* a professional videographer, although you may *want* one for some aspects. If you follow the basic video rules and tips given below, spend some time with the recommended reference guides, and practice a little, the quality of your video will be adequate for most Trust components. The recording conditions for most video segments are static. Usually, you will not be moving around; you will just be in one place giving your messages. Consequently, you will not have to contend with changing lighting environments, background movement, and other factors that can make video more challenging.

If you want to video-record certain Trust components but you are uncomfortable doing it yourself, consider asking a friend or family member to help you. Most people know someone who is proficient with a camcorder. If you explain the general nature of your video needs, the person you ask probably will be willing to help and even might be thankful that you asked! Who knows — the experience of helping you might even encourage your videographer to create a Spiritual Trust of his or her own.

If you are unable to secure the assistance of a friend or family member, or if the nature of your Trust component makes it inappropriate for someone who knows you to assist, or if you want a professional look to your Trust component, professional videographers are available for hire in just about every city and town. Look in the phone book under "videographer" or "video productions." We also maintain a list of videographers on our website at www.spiritualtrusts.com/videographers.

Many people who do a LifeStory on themselves or a LifeTribute on another person want to enlist the help of a professional videographer for at least part of the project. In addition to video-recording you giving the messages you want to send, these professionals can insert pictures about the people or places you discuss in the video. Moreover, they can insert home video clips you want to include. Professionals can help you prepare a LifeStory or a LifeTribute that will be enjoyed for generations. But, again, please don't think you need a professional to have a quality production. Your recipients will not be offended because you recorded your video instead of hiring a professional to do it. They will welcome your messages and will be much more interested in the substance of what you have to say than how "professionally" it is presented.

If you're interested in improving your video skills, you may want to go online to www.videomaker.com and purchase one of the instructional videos designed for amateurs who want to improve their video skills. Also, books are available online and in bookstores to help you master your camcorder.

Recording Your Own Video

If you are going to record your own video, here are some tips:

- Relax. Get as comfortable as you can in front of the camcorder and just be yourself. Don't let the camera intimidate you. If you feel uncomfortable at first, practice talking to the camera without actually recording until you do get comfortable.

- Set a picture next to the camera of the person who will receive this Trust component. The picture can help keep you focused and motivated.

Step Two: Creation

- Look into the lens of the camera as often as possible. This makes it appear that you are looking at the viewer. Don't watch yourself on the pop-out LCD monitor screen.

- Dress comfortably. Blues and pastels generally work the best visually on a television screen. Avoid patterns such as narrow lines and Herringbone, as they tend to "sizzle" on video. Also stay away from solid blacks and whites, which look bland, and bright reds, which "smear."

- Make sure you are in a quiet environment, as the microphone picks up background noises that you may not hear until you play back the tape. Be aware of household sounds inherent in your home, such as those made by ceiling fans, heaters, air-conditioners, dishwashers, clothes washers and dryers, and so forth. You have to really listen to detect sounds such as these, as they tend to blend into the environment, but they are significantly distracting to the listener if they are captured on video. Also, turn off your phone ringer before taping, and shut windows and doors to help eliminate outdoor sounds.

- Be conscious of other people in the room or house. They can cause unwanted noise by talking, laughing, coughing, clearing their throat, walking around, opening and closing doors, or running water.

- Sit in a comfortable location, and have anyone else in the video do the same. The best shots usually are from the belly button up to the top of your head. You don't want to get the entire person in the viewer or — the other extreme — have a close-up of a "talking head" either.

- Make sure the background is not too "busy." Keep the background simple so the person being recorded and those who will view it will not be distracted.

- When you take breaks or have other stops in recording, consider moving the camera slightly, perhaps from one side to the other side. A variety of camera angles tends to make the video more viewer-friendly.

- Look through the viewer before starting, to evaluate lighting conditions. You can eliminate shadows by using available lamps and natural light so lighting is uniform throughout the viewing area.

- When you start video-recording in a new location, check the volume level early on to ensure that you are clearly recording all the words spoken. Most cameras allow for use of a microphone. You can get small lapel microphones that work well. If you do use a lapel microphone, hide the cord as much as you can by running it under your shirt, blouse, sweater, or whatever clothing you are wearing.

- Have tissues handy. It's easy and natural to get emotional when you're videoing your messages, and you shouldn't feel that you have to edit it out.

- Keep a glass of water nearby. Your mouth will tend to become dry as you talk to the camera.

- Keep the battery charged, and have extra tapes available so you never miss an opportunity or moment of inspiration.

- Use your remote control, if you have one, to start and stop recording. If you don't have one, hit "record" and walk over to your position. At the end, walk away and hit "stop." You can edit out these parts later if you choose.

Although video is perhaps the most impressive media tool, it can be cumbersome to use. Equipment set-up and tear-down can be time-consuming and frustrating. For this reason, I have seen people enthusiastically begin video Trust components only to have their entries decrease in frequency until they cease altogether. If you find that video recording is not working for you, consider switching to a different media tool, but don't stop.

One way to minimize the inconvenience of video-recording is to leave your equipment set up near the place you usually record. I usually store my video recorder on its tripod and keep the tripod at the proper height for typical recording. When I want to record an entry, I walk down to my basement, set the tripod in the proper location, hit the "power" button and "record" button, and start talking. Not every entry will be spontaneous, but if your equipment is set up and ready to record, you will do it more often.

When you have the opportunity, record in places other than your standard location. If your video Trust component is more than an hour long, you will increase viewer interest by recording yourself in more than one location. If you work outside of the home and your work is an important factor in the messages you are recording, how about taking your audience to work with you one day? You can show your recipients firsthand where you worked while you talk about what work was like for you. Other locations could include places that are important to you such as the home you grew up in, the high school you attended, and any other places that fit your message. You also might want to insert video from a vacation or a reunion. The more creative you are, the more fun and interesting it will be for your recipients to watch.

The more creative you are, the more fun and interesting it will be for your recipients to watch.

Although you likely will be the "star" of your video Trust components, it is fun to get your kids or grandkids and spouse involved when you can. They typically are your Trust recipients, so they can "connect" by being a part of your messages. Couples often jointly record video messages and other Trust components — a wonderful way to create Trust components as you learn more about each other.

If you ever start to think that your video entries are getting to be too cumbersome, go back and watch your video privately, from your recipients' perspective. This usually will give you ample motivation to continue.

After creating a segment or a message, watch the tape again after a couple of weeks. This will help you view the video more objectively. If it is to your satisfaction, make at least one copy, label the original, and clearly indicate that it is the "master copy." Place the master into your Trust box or other safe location. Label the copies as such, and store them separately.

An all too common (but preventable) tragedy is for video recordings to be destroyed or degraded to the point of being unwatchable. Therefore, you *must* take measures to preserve your video messages and memories for future generations. Chapter 10 discusses how to properly preserve your video recordings and how to transfer them to digital formats.

Audio

Audio recordings often are more candid and revealing than written works or even video because they are so easy to use and, therefore, more spontaneous. Further, you can use your voice recorder in places where you cannot video-record, write or type. You can keep a recorder in your car, on your desk, or anywhere you routinely spend time. Actually, you can take a recorder with you almost everywhere you go.

Voice recorders offer freedom and convenience so you can use them practically any time, any place. Recording while you're in the car commuting to work will turn your drive time into something that is productive for your Trust — and will make your commute time seem to fly by. Business trips offer another opportunity for you to spend some time talking into your recorder. In one evening in your hotel room, you could complete a number of messages. Although you probably can't record on an airplane because of background noise, you can use that time to jot down points to be recorded in your hotel.

> **Voice recorders offer the freedom and convenience for you to use them practically any time, any place.**

As with camcorders, you can use a voice recorder to capture conversations with your children or grandchildren. This offers an irreplaceable opportunity to record the tone and pitch of their voices that will be changing as they grow and mature. You can record them singing songs, reciting scripture, and talking about what is important to them at that time. Over the years, without much effort, I have recorded more than a hundred hours for several different Trusts. About a third of that time I have recorded my children singing, talking, and answering probing questions that I put to them. They delight in these recording sessions because children love to hear themselves talking (at least mine do).

Although your audio entries can be transcribed if you want to turn them into written messages, one thing is almost guaranteed: After you pass away, your children and grandchildren will love hearing your voice. Whether in a video or audio recording, a gift your children and grandchildren will always cherish is the gift of your voice.

Step Two: Creation

A gift your children will always cherish is the gift of your voice.

If you're going to use audio recordings in your Trusts, you must have a reliable voice recorder. You have three basic choices: mini-cassette, standard cassette, and digital voice recorders.

1. *Mini-cassette recorder.* The mini-cassette's major advantage is its small size. These recorders are small and easy to carry. Personally, however, I have had many more mechanical problems with this kind of recorder than the other two.

2. *Standard cassette recorder.* Although the standard cassette recorder is a little bigger, it seems to hold up better against wear and tear than its mini counterpart — especially if you are prone to dropping it now and again as I am. Standard cassette recorders use the same cassettes that can be played in the cassette players typically installed in cars and stereo systems. They also may have a longer recording time, which means fewer tapes to contend with.

3. *Digital voice recorder.* Digital voice recorders usually are the smallest of the three and do not have any tape for you to contend with. Your voice is recorded digitally and stored on a small device within the recorder itself. Digital voice recorders are not expensive and typically have better quality. With most digital voice recorders, your recordings can be downloaded directly into your computer. Fast-forwarding and rewinding are instant, as is erasing an entry. If you are going to buy a voice recorder and are computer-literate, a digital voice recorder may be the best buy.

Here are some tips for audio-recording your messages on any of the three types of recorders:

- Make sure you have spare batteries with you. Portable audio recorders run on batteries, and if your batteries run down while you're recording a message, you want to be able to get the recorder running quickly so you don't lose your train of thought or inspiration.

- For the same reason, carry extra tapes.

- Experiment with how far away from the microphone you speak. Generally, your mouth should be about 6 inches from the microphone.

- Periodically review your recording to confirm recording quality and voice volume.

- Keep a glass of water nearby. Typically, the mouth becomes dry when talking for an extended period.

- Make sure you're in a quiet environment, as the recorder will pick up background noises that you might not hear until playback. The same tips given for video recordings apply here.

- Be conscious of other people in the room or house. They can introduce unwanted noise into the recording — talking, laughing, coughing, clearing the throat, walking around, opening and closing doors, or running water. If you're recording in a car, keep the windows closed to prevent as much "road noise" as possible.

- Have a picture of the person who will receive this Trust component with you. Looking at the picture can help keep you focused and motivated.

- Especially with digital voice recorders, practice recording test messages (testing 1,2,3) and play back to hear your voice level. Many people err on the side of talking too loudly, and this can result in your voice sounding distorted during playback. The microphones on voice recorders are highly sensitive, so you don't have to raise your voice. Talk normally.

An all too common (but preventable) tragedy is for audio recordings to be destroyed or degraded to the point that they cannot be listened to. Certain things *must* be done to preserve your audio messages and memories for future generations to hear. These are explained in detail in Chapter 10.

Written or Typed Words

The use of written or typed words is the most traditional way to create Spiritual Trusts. Whether Trust components are handwritten or typed, many people are simply more comfortable with this format than with the others. Short messages, in particular, lend themselves to the written word, as do Legacy Journals.

<u>Handwritten Trust Components</u>

For many people, handwritten documents have more sentimental value than other forms, and those who handwrite Trust components may find it more convenient and enjoyable than typing on a keyboard. Regardless, handwritten messages have been around for ages and likely will remain a valued Trust component.

I encourage you to handwrite at least some of your Trust components, even if it is just the short messages. Birthday messages, cards, notes — all of these short messages lend themselves to being handwritten. Longer Trust components, such as Legacy Journals, require more effort. If you are willing to put in the time to create a legible document, though, a handwritten journal is a priceless gift to the person receiving it.

> **A handwritten journal is a priceless gift to the person receiving it.**

You can create the longer, handwritten Trust components — Legacy Journals, LifeStories, LifeTributes — in a number of styles, including folders, spiral-bound notebooks, formal journal books, and three-ring binders. Whatever you choose to use, please pay particular attention to the information in Chapter 10 regarding the type of paper to use, storage tips, and the like so your document will hold up over time.

The longer handwritten Trust components can be of either of two general styles:

1. *Professional style.* These nicely handwritten pages are consistent in the color and weight of the paper and in the ink color used. Most of these documents are created using formal journal books marketed for this purpose.

2. *Instant inspiration style.* These Trust pages are written on all kinds of papers of various colors and with various colors of ink. The authors use whatever paper and pen are available when they are inspired to jot down an entry. I have seen Trust entries recorded on napkins, with the napkin (inserted into a plastic sleeve) inserted in a folder or notebook just like any other page. Sometimes people use the instant inspiration style at first, then later rewrite their entries in a more formal and consistent way.

Either style, or the many variations, is acceptable and will be appreciated by your recipients. Use whatever style reflects your personality and will be the most likely to hold your interest in adding to your Trust over time.

Use whatever style reflects your personality and will be the most likely to hold your interest in adding to your Trust over time.

Following are some tips for making handwritten entries:

- Use a pen instead of a pencil. Pencil lead can rub off over time.

- Keep paper (folder, notebook, journal) and a pen handy on the nightstand next to your bed, in your vehicle, at work, or wherever you tend to make entries. When you get an inspiration or a thought, you will want to write it down as quickly as possible.

- Write the date at the top of each entry.

- Keep a dictionary and a thesaurus handy.

*S*tep *T*wo: *C*reation

- Try to keep misspelled words to a minimum.

- Write as legibly as you can. You don't want to have your recipients struggle to read what you have to say.

Typed Entries

If you're one of the millions of people using a computer daily or weekly, you likely will find this method preferable to handwriting. Because typewriters are rare today, I will assume that the person typing the Trust component will be using a computer, a keyboard, and associated word-processing software.

When you create a computer-generated Trust component, you can do a lot more than just type words. You can easily integrate e-mails, pictures, images, articles, and even video and audio clips. Thus, your computer-generated Trust can be a multimedia production.

Your computer-generated Trust can be a multimedia production.

Although some might consider a computerized Trust component to be less personal than a handwritten one, that attitude is changing. Previous generations did not grow up using computers. For the current generation, however, computers are a normal part of life. The next generation will not be able to envision life without computers, just like the current generation cannot imagine society without television or radio. In short, the next generation probably won't think of a computerized Trust component as impersonal at all. This format likely will be the most comfortable for them to read, and they also will be able to copy, print, and reprint your entries.

In creating Trust components on a computer, some tips to follow include:

- Establish a folder in your computer that is dedicated to your Trusts, and regularly back it up onto disks. Ideally, you should keep two back up disks in separate locations. The disks, not your computer file, should be considered as your Trust components.

Spiritual Trusts

- Clearly label your disks with Trust component and date.

- Type the date of each entry into the document itself.

- Don't save other files on the same disks on which your Trust components are saved.

- As you're typing your entry, periodically hit "Save" instead of waiting until you are finished.

- Take advantage of your word processor's spellchecker and grammar checker, but don't rely on these features exclusively. Keep your dictionary handy.

Images and Photographs

People have saved photographs ever since the camera was invented. Most of us have saved pictures and other images throughout our lives, resulting at times in a large collection. Some people keep their photos well-organized in attractive scrapbooks with stylish covers, "theme" pages, and other features. Other people utilize the shoebox storage style — they just try to keep most of their pictures in one place and *might* even organize their shoeboxes by year or decade. Still others keep slides in boxes in a closet collecting dust because the projector is broken or only one member of the family knows how to operate it.

With the digital age upon us, more and more people are taking pictures with a digital camera, but that doesn't necessarily mean that the storage of the pictures has improved that much. Most of these digital pictures don't get printed at all; they stay stored on a computer or disk until they are deleted on purpose or by accident. The digital photos that are printed out often meet the same fate as their traditional counterparts — a scrapbook or a shoebox.

The point I want to make is that, notwithstanding the importance to us of our pictures, we too frequently fail to take adequate care of them. Storage methods are discussed in detail in Chapter 10. I bring up the subject here with the hope that when you are creating Trust components with photographs and other images, you will keep in mind how to best preserve these treasures for the future.

Using Pictures and Other Images

Most people who create Spiritual Trusts want to integrate pictures from scrapbooks, photo albums, and so forth into their Trusts. Pictures and other images can be used in a variety of ways including:

Each picture adds a significant touch to your Trust component.

1. Insert actual pictures directly in your Trust components. Simply take the original or a copy of a picture and insert it in any Trust component such as a Legacy Journal or a birthday message. A picture is worth a thousand words, as the saying goes, so each picture adds a significant touch to your Trust component.

2. Insert digital images in your digital or video Trust components. If you have a video or electronic Trust component, such as a LifeStory or LifeTribute on DVD or a computerized Legacy Journal, you can insert digital images of your pictures. If you don't already have a digital image of the picture, you can have it scanned and insert the image.

3. Make a scrapbook or photo album as an attachment to your Trust component. If you want to include many pictures, consider attaching to the Trust a scrapbook you have already created. You could attach it to a specific Trust component, or you might create a specific scrapbook as a Trust component. For instance, if you are creating a chronological LifeStory, you might want to make a scrapbook laying out the pictures of your life in chronological order and include it as an attachment to your LifeStory.

4. Include a photo CD as an attachment to your Trust component. You could copy specific photographs onto a CD ROM or a DVD ROM and include them as an attachment to a Trust component.

5. Create a video montage. Although the video montage was introduced in the context of Support Trusts (Chapter 2), this type of multimedia product can be used in other Trusts as well. A video montage is a short "movie" of your life or an aspect of your life. You place your pictures on VHS tape or DVD and play them on a television. In essence, you create a video scrapbook of your pictures with sound. You can add music or narrate the pictures. In this way, your recipient will watch your pictures like a movie and hear your words as you describe the meaning, significance, background, or other particulars of each picture. Most video studios will prepare these productions, or you can visit our website at www.spiritualtrusts.com/videomontage for more information and resources.

6. *Make a digital LifeAlbum*™. A LifeAlbum is an interactive digital version of a scrapbook or photo album on a CD ROM. Because it is in a digital format, it offers many benefits that scrapbooks cannot. A LifeAlbum stores your pictures and allows you to record narrations of each photo. You can include video clips as well. This allows you to view your pictures and video clips side by side on the same format. Moreover, each picture and video clip has a date, title, and key words. Thus, you and your recipients can search through your pictures and video clips by name, date, or key words.

LifeAlbums can be created for a specific event such as a wedding, reunion, or vacation, or they can be used to capture and organize certain time periods and events in your family history. For instance, I made a LifeAlbum of all the pictures, certificates, special drawings, and report cards from my daughter's first year in grade school. She narrated all of these so, when they are reviewed, we can *hear* her describe each item in her own special little voice. I also included excerpts of audio and video recordings I made of her during this year.

In this way, I have preserved the wonderful memories of this period of her life in one interactive format. At the end of each year, I create another LifeAlbum. This will result in a priceless chronicle of her life that we enjoy now and her own kids will be able to enjoy in the future.

I also use LifeAlbums to chronicle my annual Legacy Journal. Each year, I insert my typed entries, selected photographs, and video clips that I recorded as journal entries, and store it on one format. This gives me a way to consolidate the various kinds of journal entries onto a single format. The end result is that it makes viewing more organized, enjoyable, and simplified for my recipients. For more information on digital LifeAlbums see our web page at www.spiritualtrusts.com/lifealbums.

CREATING YOUR LIFESTORY

Because a LifeStory is usually more complex than most other Trust components, the "how-to" for a LifeStory deserves a little more attention here. As you recall from Chapter 4, the LifeStory could take three different paths — chronological, essence, or spiritual — or some combination of these.

> **The LifeStory is usually more complex than most other Trust components.**

First, you will have to decide how to address the three areas (chronological, essence, spiritual). If you combine them, you will use a chronological LifeStory form as the backbone and insert segments on the essence and spiritual aspects at appropriate points in your life. If you decide later that the story doesn't flow the way you would like, you can change the method to fit the material you have developed. Flexibility is the key.

Your LifeStory will not be boring, because your children and descendants want to know about you. But it will be even more interesting if you always keep in mind these two questions:

"Who is this for?"
"What is the purpose of covering a certain area?"

This will help you decide what you want to include, how you want to say it, and what you may want to exclude.

In addressing spiritual issues, some things are constant and some things change over time. Your descendants listening to your LifeStory 150 years from now will be living in a culture that will be very different from yours in some ways. In your LifeStory, therefore, you should share the Gospel in ways that those who receive it in the future will be likely to understand and respect. This doesn't mean watering down your faith but, rather, keeping it relevant to the basic life issues that will always be with us.

Visual Aids

Visual aids can really bring your story to life. Items of sentimental value or special meaning help people relate to memories. They also evoke a sense of nostalgia. You can incorporate physical items from your past in your LifeStory in various ways, as discussed above:

- Include the item itself.
- Include a picture of the item.
- Scan the item into a digital image and insert the image into your LifeStory.

Think of visual aids as special gifts to your loved ones. Telling the stories behind these images is a good way to communicate your LifeStory with those who will receive it in the future. Visual aids that tend to have sentimental value include:

Photos	Videotapes
Scrapbooks	Films
Slides	Family Bible
Newspaper clippings	Souvenirs
Letters and postcards	Report cards
Lockets of hair	Jewelry
Historical documents	Pressed flowers
Trophies and awards	Certificates
Maps	Plane ticket stubs
Love letters	Theatre programs
Concert ticket stubs	Awards

Going through your pictures and other items of sentimental value can be a lot of fun. You should take all the time you need to select the items that are best suited to the topics and stories you want to cover.

Dealing With Painful Memories

Delving into the past is interesting and even exciting for most people. It usually spawns deeper insight and enhances personal growth. Sometimes, however, a journey into the past evokes painful memories — memories you have forgotten or wish you had forgotten. For instance, it can stir up memories of sexual abuse, addictions, immorality, humiliation, abandonment, or the death of a person close to you, causing pain and heartache. Like a reopened wound, these memories can divert attention from the mission of continuing your LifeStory.

Although you can benefit from examining issues such as these in your life, you don't have to tell *everything* in your LifeStory. You have a right to privacy, and some things are better left in the past. Even if you have forgiven those who have hurt you, the resulting pain and grief can take a long time to heal.

In some cases, though, communicating about painful memories can be therapeutic. If you decide to do this, you may or may not wish to include these things in your LifeStory. One solution is to address the experience in your LifeStory but to generalize the facts and emphasize the feelings. You should think carefully about each such situation, pray, and possibly seek appropriate guidance from a counselor, your pastor, or others you trust and respect. Many people have one or more troubling issues from their past. Although revisiting painful experiences takes time, it can prove valuable.

> Although revisiting painful experiences takes time, it can prove valuable.

Outlining Your Life Chapters

When you're ready to create your LifeStory, you might begin a simple outline by dividing your chronological, essence, and spiritual LifeStories into chapters, like the contents of a book. Chronological chapters will be the easiest. Chapters for essence and spiritual LifeStories will take more thought.

Develop your detailed outline one chapter at a time, listing the topics and stories you want to include and the associated facts, feelings, and other details. In your outline, make notes referring to the pictures and other visual aids you want to accompany each topic or story. To help you in this process of outlining your LifeStory, I have included dozens of questions on numerous topics that you may want to cover. You can find these questions in Appendix C. When I started my LifeStory, I found it easier to work backward through my life. I created a table of contents of the chapters I wanted to cover and then completed the detailed outlines of each chapter in reverse order.

However you proceed, if you follow the creation process covered in the beginning of this chapter, you will have an organized LifeStory that flows well and is easy to follow.

IN SUMMARY

The creation step is probably the most fun of the four steps in the Spiritual Trust development process. As you create each Trust or Trust component, you will have a real sense of accomplishment and will be highly motivated to continue. Although your recipients will receive many benefits from your efforts, there are at least an equal share of benefits you will receive from the personal reflection and articulation of the important aspects of your life.

The creation step is a developmental process of outlining, drafting, revising, composing, and finalizing. In creating your Trust, you can avail yourself of one or more of the following media tools: video, audio, written or typed words, and photographs and other images. Choose media tools that fit the information you want to convey and that you are comfortable using.

NINE

Step 3: Storage

After you have taken the time and effort to create your Trusts, you will want to know with a high level of confidence that they will be preserved safely for delivery to your chosen recipients. If your Trusts are destroyed, misplaced, damaged, or lost, they will not be delivered to your recipients as intended. If you will be delivering Trust components to your recipients shortly after you create them, storage concerns will not be as vital as if you are planning to have your Trust components delivered years, decades, and even generations from now. Regardless, it is prudent to store your components, at a minimum, in a format that will survive long into the future, even if you are delivering them to the recipients shortly after you create them. This way, your recipients will be able to retain and enjoy your Trust components well into their future.

To ensure that your Spiritual Trusts will survive with sufficient quality and integrity well into the future, you must do two things:

1. Archive the Trust, and
2. Store the Trust is an appropriate container and location.

ARCHIVING THE TRUST

For the purpose of storing Spiritual Trusts, the term *archive* means to preserve Trust components in a way that will ensure their safety, quality, and longevity until they are delivered to the recipients decades and generations from now. The best way to archive your Trusts will depend, to a large extent, on what kind of media you use and the formats on which those media are stored.

Will your Trusts include handwritten or typed messages, audio or video recordings, photos, letters? Will your Trusts include other kinds of memorabilia such as diaries and journals, legal and financial records, birth announcements, obituaries, artwork and artistic creations, essays, report cards, portraits, birth and death certificates, marriage licenses, drawings, original poetry, business documents?

If you're like most people, you likely will be using a variety of media formats in your Spiritual Trusts. Many people want to pass along memories that were recorded in the past. For instance, in your LifeStory, you might include an old 16mm film of your grandparents, an audiocassette of your parents telling family stories, and a VHS videotape of your wedding. This variety of media formats can present formidable preservation challenges.

Even if you were to take all of your tapes and store them in an archival container inside Ft. Knox, they still would not be safe. In fact, your children and grandchildren likely would never get to see and hear these collected memories because this format of recordable media degenerates over a surprisingly short time. All magnetic tape formats, such as VHS, Hi8, Beta, and audiocassette tapes have an average life expectancy of about 15 years. After that, and in many cases before, the tape quality will degrade substantially to the point of being unplayable. Moreover, every time these tapes are played, they lose some of their integrity.

Does this surprise you? It does most people. You see, it is not good enough to record and save the Trust components and memories that you cherish. You have to store them in a *format* that will last long enough so your Trust recipients can benefit from them according to your intent. The formats on which you choose to *create* your Spiritual Trusts are important, of course, but in the long run the most important concern is the kind of format on which they are stored while awaiting delivery.

Digital Preservation

For our purposes in this book, *digital preservation* is the act of protecting, through proper methods and handling, your Trust components and memories in the optimal digital formats and storage locations. This will help to ensure that your Trust components and tangible memories will survive and maintain their current quality for future generations.

Currently, the best way to protect your Trusts for the long term is to transfer the content onto a digital format such as a CD (compact disk) or variations of a DVD (digital video disk). When I speak of transferring your Trust components and memories onto a digital format, I am *not* talking about transferring them onto the mini DV tape that is used on digital camcorders. This is still a magnetic tape and, therefore, still susceptible to all of the dangers to which other magnetic tapes are subjected. "Digital" refers to a disk, not a tape.

> *Digital preservation* is the act of protecting, through proper methods and handling, your Trust components and memories in the optimal digital formats and storage locations.

DVDs are rapidly growing in popularity. DVD players are the fastest growing consumer electronic commodity ever. DVD disks are replacing VHS tapes just as CDs have made audiocassette tapes nearly obsolete. If you don't already own a DVD player, you should contemplate purchasing one, as digital preservation has many advantages. The quality is far superior to VHS players, and so many DVD players are being sold that the prices are quite reasonable.

Basic information on digital preservation is presented here, but digital technologies are advancing at such a rapid rate that it would be fruitless to go into detail in this book. A free "Going Digital" booklet, that we update regularly, with resources, information, and tips for converting (and storing) your video, audio, photographs, and documents into a variety of digital formats, can be downloaded from www.spiritualtrusts.com/goingdigital.

If you don't understand what the digital world is about, the information in our "Going Digital" booklet will help you learn about it. With this information, you can transfer your Trusts and memories into a digital format yourself. Alternatively, companies in every city will do this for you. In short, you can digitally preserve your own material or find someone to do it for you. If you want to preserve your Trusts and other tangible memories, you should pursue one of these options.

Digital Basics

Digital information is created by burning tiny "pits" into the surface of a disk using a laser. It is not an analog format like the videotape or audiotape. Instead, digital recordings use binary signals (ones and zeros). In general, you can create as many copies as you want, and they will be truly identical to the original.

Digital disks such as CDs and DVDs have projected life expectancies ranging from 30 to 100+ years, making them the clear choice for preserving your Spiritual Trusts and memories for generations to come. Someday, digital technology will be surpassed by newer technologies, but having your Trusts and memories preserved in a digital format will enable them to survive long enough to be transferred with no loss of image quality into whatever new formats come along.

Transferring Video and Audio Components Onto DVD

The best method for archiving your videotape and audiotape Spiritual Trust components and other video and audio memories is to transfer them onto a DVD or CD ROM. A DVD can store your video in a digital format that can be played repeatedly without damaging the disk. Moreover, making DVD copies doesn't result in any loss of video resolution or quality. Each copy, in essence, becomes another original. Each regular DVD holds approximately two hours of video. A CD ROM provides similar digital benefits for audible recordings.

You can do a straight transfer of your videotapes onto DVDs, or you can customize each DVD with a title page, a chapter list that serves as a table of contents, and a customized photo or label on the face of the DVD itself. You can purchase equipment to do this yourself or you can have it done for you.

See www.spiritualtrusts.com/digitaltransfers for more information on DVD and CD transfers.

Other Preservation Tips

Even though "going digital" is superior to other preservation methods in regard to the safety and longevity of your Spiritual Trusts and other tangible memories, a good percentage of people have "sworn off" the digital age and will not transfer their Trusts or other memories into a digital format. If you are in this group and are unwilling to change your position, you should do *all* of the following:

1. Have your Spiritual Trusts delivered in the short term as opposed to the long term.
2. Make several copies of your Trusts and keep them stored in various locations.
3. Follow the preservation tips below for video, audio, photos, and paper.
4. Ask your recipients to transfer the Spiritual Trusts *they* receive from you onto a digital format as soon as they can.

Your non-digital Trust components and other tangible memories are under assault whether they are on videotape, audiotape, paper, or photographs. And I'm not just talking about loss, mishandling, theft, water damage, and fire. Some of the primary dangers are far less obvious. Let's look at these dangers to your tangible memories.

Videotapes and Audiotapes

All your tapes, including VHS, Beta, Hi8, audiotapes, and even digital video cassettes, record onto a magnetic tape. The research findings and overall opinions vary as to whether your videotapes and audiotapes can survive 10 to 30 years before they degrade to the point of being useless. This, however, takes into account that your tapes are being stored in ideal environmental conditions.

According to an internal study by Sony in Japan, if you keep your tapes at a constant temperature range of 59 to 64 degrees and a relative humidity level of 40 to 60 percent, you can expect your tapes to last about 15 years without significant degradation. Not many people, however, store their tapes in such a controlled environment. The average life expectancy of your VHS tapes and other modern tape formulations varies, but *I* wouldn't comfortably count on more than a decade. Consequently, the memories contained on magnetic tapes recorded more than 10 years ago are in serious jeopardy of being lost forever.[1]

Among the many factors that can destroy or damage your tapes in a much shorter timeframe are heat and humidity extremes and fluctuations, fire, water, electromagnetic fields, tape-eating machines, mishandling, and accidental record-overs. If your tapes survive these threats, they still cannot survive their eventual demise from chemical causes. Without getting into the complicated details, the disintegration of your tapes' chemical components —the plastic base film, binder polymers, back-coating materials, and lubricants — is inevitable. It's just a matter of time before your videotapes and audiotapes, and all the memories recorded on them, will become so degraded that they will be lost forever. It is not a question of *if*; it's is a matter of *when*.

Of all the videotape and audiotape formats, the one with the shortest life expectancy is the VHS tape — and that's the most popular video format in the United States. Nearly every home has a VCR, and many have two or three. VHS tapes were designed for easy recording, over and over again. They do that well. But they were *not* designed to preserve a memory so you could view it again decades later with acceptable quality. Needless to say, I don't recommend using VHS tapes for your Trust component masters.

If you follow the digital archiving guidelines in this chapter, you can make VHS *copies* from your digital master. If you are unable to digitally transfer your Spiritual Trust video components or other video or audio memories within a year of their creation, following the tips below will prolong the life of your recordings. This will not preserve them (nothing will) for the long term, more than a decade or so, but can preserve the quality for the short term until they can be transferred to a digital format.

- Break off the "record" tab on the outside of your cassette if it is a master. This will prevent inadvertent record-overs.

- Don't play your master tapes. Make copies and view or listen to the copies.

- If you are shipping tapes, make sure you have copies and pack them in an insulated package to reduce temperature and humidity fluctuations during shipping. I recommend shipping them overnight or at the beginning of the week to minimize potential exposure to extreme heat or cold.

Step Three: Storage

- Use bubble-wrap when shipping, and ship the tapes standing vertically, not laying flat.

- Store your tapes in a cool, dry environment to minimize temperature and humidity variations.

- Tapes should never be exposed to temperatures lower than 32 degrees or higher than 70 degrees Fahrenheit.

- An alternative to storing tapes in a humidity-controlled environment is to seal each tape individually in two quick-seal plastic bags. I like freezer bags best. Before sealing a tape in the bag, expose it to a very dry environment for a few days to remove moisture in the tape that would be harmful if trapped in the bag. Remove the tape from its container before conditioning it. If possible, insert a container of silica gel with the tape to help further reduce moisture. Use a couple of rubber bands to hold the bag securely to the tape; this also will make the tape label easier to read.

- Don't store tapes on radiators, windowsills, television sets, electronic equipment, or machinery. Keep them away from speakers and magnets.

- Store tapes on end (like books); they should not be stored laying flat.

- Keep tapes rewound to the very beginning. Properly wound tapes can survive greater variations in temperature and humidity.

- Rewind and fast-forward the tapes once each year for ventilation.

- Properly maintain and regularly clean any machines in which you will play or record tapes. Dirty tape heads can ruin a tape by distributing debris across the surface of the tape and scratching it. Improperly aligned tape heads can tear and stretch the tape.

- Make sure your player is working properly before you put your master or original tape into it.

In general, magnetic tape should receive the same kind of care that you would give to a valuable book or an important photograph. Handle the tapes with care, keep them clean, and use common sense.

Photographs and Slides

If properly cared for, photographs and slides have a much longer life span than video and audio recordings, but they are susceptible to the same general threats already mentioned plus threats from elements that damage the paper on which photographs are placed (see the discussion on paper documents, below). Almost everyone has old family photos that have faded substantially from these threats. Thus, having a digital backup makes good sense. The best way to preserve copies of your pictures is to make a digital copy on a digital format such as a CD ROM, a digital LifeAlbum (discussed in the previous chapter under photographs) or a DVD video montage. The best digital format for you to use will depend on the quantity of your pictures and the way you want to view and interact with them (organization, voice narration, music, and so on).

Photographs can be digitally copied by scanning them into your computer or (less desirable) by taking a digital picture of the photograph. Once you have made one digital copy, it is easy to make additional copies by electronically transferring them to other CDs. Each digital copy then will be just as good as the original copy.

Although many people are switching to digital cameras, people who use digital cameras often store their digital images on their computer. Computers are not 100 percent reliable, so your files can be lost or deleted for many reasons, including lightning strikes, power outages, hardware or software malfunctions, viruses, and human error. Therefore, you should be sure your photos are backed up on a CD.

Scrapbooks and Photo Albums

Storing photographs in photo albums and scrapbooks is a common way for people to organize and preserve their pictures.

A neighbor of mine has spent literally thousands of hours through the years developing impressive Creative Memories scrapbooks. She has created theme pages for every kind of memory, cropped photos, and decorated the pages for special and sentimental effects. Her family and guests enjoy looking at these albums. As valuable as these scrapbooks are, however, they are still susceptible to the usual threats — fire, water damage, theft, natural disasters, and the like.

Moreover, just going out and buying scrapbooks and photo albums and putting your photographs in them does not mean they will be completely protected. If you don't take care in selecting the plastic sleeves and the paper on which your photos are placed, some commercially available scrapbooks can damage your photos. You should be sure to use photo-safe albums and supplies.

If you are unable to digitally copy your photographs and other images, the following tips will prolong the life of your photographs.

- Store your photographs in photo-safe, quality albums, scrapbooks and boxes. Make sure the paper is pH-balanced and acid- and lignin-free. The bindings should allow pages to lie flat so that they do not bend the photos.

- Use photograph album paper that is white or off-white to prevent the colors from bleeding.

- Secure photographs on album pages with pH-balanced paper or plastic mounts that have a chemically stable photo-safe adhesive. *Never use commercial adhesives,* which are acidic and will discolor photographs.

- Make copies, and keep them in different locations.

- Store any scrapbooks and photo albums in an upright position to prevent photos from rubbing against each other.

- Do not crop Polaroid prints or originals, as the paper can peel.

- Do not write in ink on the picture, as the ink can bleed through over time.

- Use UV-filtered Plexiglas or glass in picture frames. Framed photographs tend to fade faster than those in scrapbooks because they are exposed to light.

- Store your photographs in an environment that has a temperature of about 65 degrees with about 45 percent relative humidity.

- Make sure that any paper touching the photograph on the back side is acid-free. If you aren't sure, spray the backing and photo mat with an archiving spray such as Archival Mist®.

Paper and Other Documents

Paper documents are susceptible to damage from all of the general threats mentioned already such as fire, water, loss, theft, mishandling, and rapid fluctuations in relative humidity. Another major cause of damage to paper is exposure to high levels of light, which leads to fading and discoloration as a result of heating.

Ultraviolet (UV) radiation, which is emitted by the sun and fluorescent bulbs, is particularly damaging to paper items. UV is the invisible high-energy portion of the light spectrum. UV filtering for windows and picture frames is commercially available and can significantly reduce the damaging effects of UV light.

Visible light also can damage documents. Colored inks are particularly susceptible to damage from light and should be displayed in areas that are free from bright light sources.

Many other common elements can also cause damage. Insecticides can cause fading and discoloration of paper, leather, or parchment. Many books, diaries, programs, news clippings, and scrapbooks are silently burning because of the acid content in the paper. Countless documents are ruined by adhesive tape and rubber cement. These and other threats warrant your taking action to protect your documents for the future.

Paper documents such as handwritten letters, certificates, awards, keepsake projects, journals, and books should be scanned onto a digital format such as a CD or a DVD ROM to best preserve them. They are subject to the same hazards as photographs. Some books and other documents that use high-quality paper and ink can last for centuries, but digital copies are still a good idea.

If you are unable to digitally copy documents used in your Spiritual Trusts, the following suggestions can prolong their life.

- Store paper materials in dark, cool, relatively dry locations. Aim for 35 percent relative humidity and below 72 degrees Fahrenheit. Avoid light, heat and dampness. A steady temperature and relative humidity are preferable to variable environmental conditions.

- Do not banish your papers to attics or basements as these areas typically have wide fluctuations in temperature, humidity, mold, mildew, and bugs, all of which can damage or destroy your documents.

- Use pencils when working with your collection to avoid possible disfigurement from inks.

- Avoid adhesives such as tape, mucilage, rubber cement, and spray mount. Many adhesives will turn the paper yellow and brittle over the years.

- Photocopy documents on acid-free paper. Newspaper clippings and faxes are endangered species.

- Store paper items flat rather than folded, which can result in creases and tears.

- Store paper materials and place fragile, rare, and frequently used items in acid-free alkaline folders, polyester film sleeves, or alkaline mats. Alkaline paper or board provides a desirable neutralizing effect on acidity.

Before storing documents, carefully remove paperclips, staples, and rubber bands. If you must keep pages fastened together, use plastic or stainless steel paperclips.

Film

Film, both 8mm and 16mm, has a longer life expectancy than magnetic tape, but still is susceptible to the dangers of fire, water, theft, loss, natural disasters, and mishandling. Many memories from the 1930s to the 1970s were recorded on film. The few memories that were captured of my childhood were recorded on film, and all of the "video" memories of my parents' youth and grandparents' life during the World War II era were on film. Recently, I took dozens of my grandparents' reels of film and transferred them to a DVD for them and the rest of the family. Unfortunately, many segments were ruined before I did this, and vital pieces of my family history were lost forever.

The Image Permanence Institute explains that as film degrades, it gradually shrinks. This causes the film to become brittle and generates acetic acid, which evaporates into the air, producing a sharp vinegar odor. This form of chemical deterioration from poor storage conditions has been called the "vinegar syndrome." The Institute further states that the facts of life for acetate film preservation are that at room temperature and moderate relative humidity, film will begin to seriously degrade in about fifty years. Film stored under poor conditions may become degraded within a few decades.[2]

Many companies can transfer your film onto a DVD. In film transfers, you should find a company that does straight film-to-DVD transfers instead of projecting the film onto a screen and video-recording it. We list several companies that offer this service on our website at www.spiritualtrusts.com/digitaltransfers.

For film that you cannot digitally transfer now due to a lack of time or other reason, preservation suggestions include:

- Store film in a clean, cool, dry environment. The greatest damage is caused by rapid fluctuations in relative humidity.
- Avoid exposing your film to intense light, which can cause it to fade and discolor.
- Prevent contamination of film by dirt, dust, fingerprints, cigarette smoke and ash, and airborne pollutants.
- Keep food or drinks away from your collection.

This knowledge will help you preserve the memories that have been created already and will show you how to create Spiritual Trust components that your recipients will enjoy and cherish for generations.

Making Copies

Making copies is *essential* to preserving your Spiritual Trusts and can be considered a part of your archiving objectives because the existence of multiple copies enhances the likelihood that your Trust

Step Three: Storage

components will be available for future delivery to their recipients. It simply is too easy for the original or one copy to be lost, damaged or destroyed in a fire or other calamity. Make digital copies when possible. Whether or not the copies are digital, I suggest that you make at least *two* copies of each Trust component. This is one of the easiest and best ways to assure that your Trust components and memories will make it to the future. You should keep the originals and each copy in separate locations.

Having multiple copies will make it easier for your executor and family to find and fulfill your Spiritual Trust Directives.

STORE THE TRUST IN AN APPROPRIATE CONTAINER AND LOCATION

Storing your Trusts in an appropriate container and location are both important to the long-term storage of your Trusts. Usually, the originals are kept in a Trust box or safety deposit box and the copies are retained in other locations. Keeping your Trust documents in several locations is good insurance for your Trusts.

> Keeping your Trust documents in several locations is good insurance for your Trusts.

Using a Trust Box

The container that holds your Spiritual Trusts may determine whether or not they make it to your recipients. If you do not store your Trusts in a safety deposit box, you should use a "Trust box" with the following characteristics.

- It should be large enough to hold all of your Trusts and their components, unless you use multiple boxes for multiple Trusts.

- It should be fireproof or have a high fire-resistance rating.

- It should use either a key or a combination lock.

Small safes, portable safes, and fire-rated cabinets and file boxes make excellent Trust boxes. See www.spiritualtrusts/trustbox.com for information on Trust box options you might consider. Safety

SPIRITUAL TRUSTS

deposit boxes are addressed below under the storage location section because an important part of the benefits of a safety deposit box is not just the characteristics of the box itself, but the location of the box within a vault.

SELECTING APPROPRIATE STORAGE LOCATIONS

Where to store your Trusts is an important decision, and one that depends somewhat on the formats you use for your Trusts. If your Trusts contain mostly CDs and DVDs, for example, you have more flexibility in where you can safely store them because CDs and DVDs are less susceptible to damage by the environmental factors noted previously. If you have a lot of original photographs, magnetic media (VHS, etc.), and paper documents, however, you will have to be more careful in determining where to store your Trusts. As a general rule, you should store your Trusts in places that environmentally preserve the materials and that are safe and convenient.

Locations to consider include your home, your executor's home, a friend's home, a family member's home, a safety deposit box, and a trust company vault. Your Trusts should be stored in at *least* two locations. I recommend that you keep the originals of your Spiritual Trusts in a trust company vault or safety deposit box, and store one copy in a Trust box in your home and another copy in one of the other locations listed above, preferably with your executor. Although this may seem like "overkill," I do not want anyone's Spiritual Trusts to be lost, misplaced, damaged or destroyed. They are far too important. If you have multiple Trusts and multiple executors, you don't have to provide a Trust box for each one, although this is preferable. It certainly will increase your peace of mind.

So that your Trust components are readily identifiable, you should not store them with other items. For example, you should not keep your video Trust components stored with the rest of your videos, or your computerized Trust components with the rest of your computer disks. By keeping the components of your Trusts together, all of your Trust components will be easy to locate.

Safety Deposit Box

A safety deposit box is a secure means of storing your Spiritual Trusts, but there are some things you need to know about. If you choose to use a safety deposit box, you should make your spouse, executor, or

Step Three: Storage

another trusted individual co-owner of the box.

A co-owner can retrieve the contents after your death without having to go through a host of legal steps. If you have Trust components stored in a safety deposit box that you want delivered immediately or soon after your death, someone else must be a co-owner; otherwise, access to the box could take weeks or longer.

One way to handle this is to request that upon your death, your executor transfer the contents of your safety deposit box into a safety box that is in his or her name. If this appeals to you, you will need to make your executor a co-owner of your box.

To arrange to have your Spiritual Trusts stored in a safety deposit box for an extended period *after* your death, you will have to provide for long-term payments of the annual fee. This can get a little tricky. Usually you cannot go to your bank and prepay your safety deposit box fees for a period of years. Regulations keep banks from being able to accept payments for more than a year at a time.

The easiest way to arrange for future rental payments is to leave your Spiritual Trust executor sufficient funds to cover the annual costs and make the executor the co-owner of the box. I go into this in the discussion of providing funds to your Trust in Chapter 10. If this is not practicable for you, however, there are other methods to ensure that your box rental will continue to be paid after your death.

One method involves estimating the future fees and depositing an appropriate amount to cover those payments into a jointly owned savings or money market account that will remain open after your death. Ask your bank to project what the total cost will be for the number of years you want covered following your death. Make sure that estimated annual fee increases and inflation are taken into account, and add 10 percent to that amount for a cushion. Deposit this amount into the account and establish an automatic transfer payment program so that at the end of each 12-month rental term, the funds for the following year are automatically debited from this account for payment of you safety deposit box. During your life, deposit the annual rental fee into your savings or money market account so you will have the full amount needed for the term you want set aside and ready at death.

Alternatively, your could have your safety deposit box rental paid out of a custodial account through a trust company (discussed in Chapter 10). There are other ways to ensure the payments on your safety deposit box will continue to be paid after your death.

Consult with your bank to evaluate other options. Additionally, you should ask your bank whether it has any other policies or regulations you may need to follow to store your Spiritual Trust in one of its safety deposit boxes for years after your death.

Trust Institutions

Trust companies and Trust departments of banks have vaults that virtually guarantee the safety of your Spiritual Trust components from most dangers including fire, water, loss, theft, natural disasters or mishandling. For long-term storage of your Trust components, this is my personal choice because it eliminates so many potential risks.

Because using a trust institution for storage is so closely related to how your Trusts will be delivered, I have put this information in Chapter 10, under "Trust Institutions."

IN SUMMARY

Preserving your Trusts into the future requires careful measures and knowledge. The two things you need to do are to archive the Trusts and store the Trusts in an appropriate container and location. The term *archive* here means to preserve Trust components in a way that will ensure their safety, quality, and longevity until they are delivered to the recipients decades and generations from now.

Currently, the best way to protect your Trusts for the long term is to transfer the content onto a digital format such as a CD or a DVD, which have projected life expectancies ranging from 30 to 100+ years. This contrasts to VHS tapes, for example, which have a life span of as little as 10 years. This longevity makes the digital format the clear choice for preserving your Spiritual Trusts and memories for generations to come.

Among the many factors that can destroy or damage your audiotapes and videotapes in a much shorter time are heat and humidity extremes and fluctuations, fire, water, electromagnetic fields, tape-eating machines, mishandling, and accidental record-overs. If your tapes survive these threats, they still cannot survive their eventual death from chemical causes.

Non-digital Trust components and other tangible memories are under assault whether they are on videotape, audiotape, paper, film or photographs. If properly cared for, photographs and slides have a much longer life span than video and audio recordings, but they are susceptible to the same general threats.

This chapter offers many practical suggestions for preserving these media and your Spiritual Trusts in the best possible way for the future. Things you can do to ensure your Spiritual Trusts will last well into the future are to make copies, store the originals and copies in various locations, and use appropriate containers that will protect and preserve your Trusts. Storage of your original Trust components in a safety deposit box or a trust institution vault will provide the optimum protection.

If you follow the guidelines contained in this chapter, your Trust components will last for many generations, or for as long as your Trust Directives provide for their delivery.

Recommended Resources

I have found helpful information for a number of preservation topics in the following websites:

AFI (American Film Institute) www.afi.com
ANSI (American National Standards Institute) www.asni.org
ASTM (American Society for Testing Materials) www.astm.org
Council on Library and Information Resources www.clir.org
ISO (International Standards Organization) www.iso.org
Library of Congress www.lcweb.loc.gov
NARA (National Archives and Records Administration) www.nara.gov
NISO (National Information Standards Organization) www.niso.org
SAA (Society of American Archivists) www.archivists.org

Some additional web pages that you might find interesting are:

www.dvddemystified.com/dvdfaq.html DVD Demystified FAQ. This site is the best Q & A I have read about the details and specifics of DVDs.

http://www.clir.org/pubs/reports/pub54/4life_expectancy.html
Talks about the life expectancy of magnetic media and similar information.

http://www.clir.org/pubs/reports/pub54/index.html
Presents a report about magnetic tape storage and handling.

http://www.vidipax.com/articles/care.html

Tells how to care for your original videotapes.

http://www.vidipax.com/links.html
Offers many links to resources and periodicals for magnetic tape preservation.

http://www.lionlmb.org/quad/format.html#2in
Gives detailed information on videotape formats.

http://creativememories.com
An excellent site for preservation ideas and products for your photographs.

http://www.rit.edu/~661www1/
Image Permanence Institute — shares research on the preservation of visual and audio materials.

http://www.cd-info.com
Good informational site about CDs and DVDs.

http://www.sonicraft.com
Good site for information on analog transfers and preservation.

http://www.idc.com/
Provides data on various aspects of information technology.

http://www.ebrain.org
Provides market research for the consumer electronics industry.

Endnotes

1. Article in *Video Magazine*, "Magnetic Tape Deterioration: Tidal Wave at Our Shores," by Jim Linder, February 1996.
2. http://www.rit.edu/~661www1/sub_pages/page9a.htm

TEN

Step 4: Delivery

Delivery of the Trust is the final stage of the Spiritual Trust System. You can use many methods to confidently arrange for the delivery of your Trusts at the appropriate time. Individual circumstances dictate the best methods of Trust delivery. Here, I will describe several ways by which to ensure that your Trusts will get into the hands of your chosen recipients. Like the Creation step, however, you may think of other ways that better suit your specific needs.

YOUR TRUST DIRECTIVES

The first step in arranging for the delivery of your Trusts is to complete your own Trust Directives form. This is recommended for all of the delivery options you will be considering. Each type of Spiritual Trust you develop could have separate Trust Directives. Depending on the scope and breadth of your Spiritual Trusts, however, you may elect to use only one Trust Directives form for all of your Trusts.

Your Trust Directives form is an overview and reference guide for your family or Trust executor that clearly conveys your wishes and directives concerning delivery and implementation of the Spiritual Trusts you have created. Your Trust Directives include information and instructions on what Trusts and Trust components you have developed, *what* their purpose is, *where* you have stored them, *who* your recipients are, and *when*, *where*, and *how* your recipients are to receive their Trust components.

Your Trust Directives form is an overview and reference guide for your family or Trust executor that clearly conveys your wishes and directives concerning delivery and implementation of the Spiritual Trusts you have created.

A sample form for your Trust Directives is provided in Appendix A. You also can print a blank Trust Directives form from our website or download it at www.spritualtrust.com/trustdirectives.

You should keep one copy of your Trust Directives form with your Trusts. If you have an original and two copies of your Trusts, as recommended, you should have three copies of your Trust Directives, so each set of your Spiritual Trusts has a copy of your Trust Directives. I also recommend you keep a copy of the Trust Directives form without the Trust components with your will and other important documents. Your Trust executor should also have a copy.

THE DELIVERY OPTIONS

The four basic kinds of delivery options are:

1. Surprise!
2. Pre delivery or Personal Delivery
3. In-house
4. Executor

Option 1: Surprise!

If you pass away and no one knows that you have created a Spiritual Trust, your recipients will be quite surprised to receive a Trust component — *if* they do receive it at all. Because of the uncertainty, this is the least desirable delivery method. I suggested it first only in the hope that you will *not* use this method!

Don't just expect that someone will find your Trusts after you die and appropriately deliver them.

One circumstance that results in more surprise deliveries than any other is the death of a person who is still in the process of creating a Spiritual Trust component. Because delivery is the last in the four-step development and implementation process, some people do not address that part until they have done everything else.

To avoid this situation, fill out your Work in Progress form (a sample of which is in Appendix B) before you begin to create a Spiritual Trust.

Option 2: Pre Delivery or Personal Delivery

Where appropriate and possible, personally giving your Trusts to your chosen recipients can be rewarding. This does not work for all Trusts or for all recipients. Some Trust components are not appropriate for pre delivery. In general, personal delivery of Legacy Trust and Stewardship Trust components may be appropriate, whereas personal delivery of Support Trust and Prayer Trust components tends to be less appropriate. Moreover, some of your recipients may not even be born yet — ruling out personal delivery. Notwithstanding, when personal delivery can be used, it is the most reliable and least complicated delivery method.

If you do a LifeStory as part of your Legacy Trust, I highly recommend that you consider giving it to your family during your lifetime. It opens a door of opportunity for further dialogue about the substance of your life and your Spiritual Trusts. Your recipients will be able to ask you to expand on their specific areas of interest. They may understand in a new way that they are not going to have you around forever. Usually, the personal delivery of a Spiritual Trust component brings the giver and recipient closer together in some unexpected way. It also could encourage recipients to start thinking about the legacy *they* are living and will be leaving. This is a bold reminder that their actions will affect the actions of others. Recipients of Spiritual Trusts often are motivated to create their own Spiritual Trusts, wanting to affect their family in the same way they were affected.

You can personally deliver Spiritual Trust components during your life in numerous ways. You could deliver your Trust as soon as you have finished creating it, or you could deliver it on a special occasion such as a birthday, wedding, anniversary, or other milestone. A Spiritual Trust component can make for the most unique and meaningful Christmas present your recipient could ever receive.

> **A Spiritual Trust component can make for the most unique and meaningful Christmas present your recipient could ever receive.**

Option 3: In-house

In-house delivery is literally that — you store your Trust in your house and your family knows where it is. When you die, a family member simply opens the Trust box or other container and retrieves your Trust.

This method is simple and reliable for some of your messages and Trust components. Especially if your family is involved in developing some of your Trust components, it is convenient to store them in your home and leave them there for in-house delivery. For example, my family members know that I'm creating a Legacy Trust, and they are active participants. They are not privy to everything I record or write, but they do have a general understanding of what I'm doing. I keep one copy of my Legacy Trust at my home in a Trust box (portable safe), and my entire family knows where it is. When it is my time to go to be with our Lord, they will know where my Trust is stored.

Option 4: Executor

With a monetary trust, a *trustee* oversees the directives and disbursements of your trust. With a will, an *executor* oversees the directives and disbursements from your estate. In a similar way, you can have your Spiritual Trusts implemented by a Spiritual Trust executor.

You can have one executor for all of your Trusts, or you may choose to have more than one. You should have a Trust Directives form for each executor. Even if you intend to deliver all of your

Step Four: Delivery

Trusts during your lifetime, you still should have a Trust Directives form with basic directions concerning who gets what. This will avoid confusion if you pass away before you have delivered all your Trusts.

If you use an executor, implementation of your Spiritual Trusts will depend upon your executor's following through with your Trust Directives. In accordance with the number and type of Spiritual Trusts you have developed and the method and timing of their delivery, the duties and obligations of your executor could be quite substantial. If you set up your Trusts so your executor has to give your family only one package upon your death, your executor's duties will be minimal. But if your executor will be sending your family and numerous other recipients your Trust components several times a year for a period of years, your executor's duties will be considerable. If your executor has a key role to play in implementing your Spiritual Trusts, the selection of an executor is a particularly important task.

Any executor you consider should have some key characteristics. I suggest that you focus on people you know who are mature, trustworthy, responsible, and — depending on the complexity of your directives — detail-oriented. You might want to have an executor who lives in proximity to your spouse and children. If so, you should take a closer look at those on your list who are more apt to move away to another city or state because of career, retirement, or other reason.

Some people can immediately think of several potential executors. Others, for a variety of reasons, might not know even one person with whom they would be comfortable as executor of their Trusts. Regardless of your situation, you do have options. The primary options for a Spiritual Trust executor are a trusted individual and a trust institution.

A Trusted Individual

A trusted individual is just that — someone you can count on to carry out the responsibilities of a Spiritual Trust executor. For many people, the most logical choice for an executor is their spouse, a sibling, or a son or daughter. A close family member could be an excellent choice for most of the Trusts you create, but a family

Spiritual Trusts

member may not be ideal as the executor for a Support Trust or a Prayer Trust. These Trusts are designed primarily to provide support to your grieving family, so it's usually best to have someone else serve as the executor of these Trusts. Therefore, you likely will want to select an executor who isn't a recipient of your Trust components to oversee your initial Trust deliveries, but you may want to keep the executor responsibilities for longer-term Trust components within your family.

Using a "buddy system" is effective for some people. In a buddy system, you and another person agree to be each other's executor. The buddy system can work with anyone you are close to, such as a spouse, best friend, or sibling. Obviously, each person should have a contingent executor because one of the buddies will die first, leaving the surviving buddy in need of an executor.

> **In a buddy system, you and another person agree to be each other's executor.**

Dividing the responsibilities for executing the directives of multiple Spiritual Trusts will keep you from putting all of your eggs in one basket, so to speak. It also will allow you to shift the various areas of responsibility to different people who are best able to serve in specific capacities.

For example, your best friend might be the executor of your Support Trust. He or she will carry out your initial wishes and post-death arrangements, deliver your messages, and the like. The executor of your Prayer Trust might be another friend, whom you consider to be a prayer partner. Finally, your spouse or a close family member could be the executor of your Legacy Trust and your Stewardship Trust.

Of course, there are many options. You should arrange the delivery of your Trusts according to your own unique circumstances and the people who fit the various Trust categories. The point is that you must have utmost confidence that the individual or individuals

*S*tep *F*our: *D*elivery

you select to be your executor will carry out the objectives in your Trust Directives form as you have specified with respect to the storage and delivery of your Trust components.

How To Ask a Trusted Individual To Be Your Executor

We have talked about the qualities you should seek in an executor of your Spiritual Trusts and suggest that you make a list of the people in your life who have these qualities. Then you can decide who you would most like to have as your primary and alternate executors. Now it is time to ask them if they will be your executors. This is an important step.

To help you do this, I have created an Executor Request Outline. This is a helpful guide that you can use as is or alter to fit your own situation.

Executor Request Outline

Explain to the Potential Executor:

1. *What* my purpose and intent for my Spiritual Trusts is:

Review the Spiritual Trust System. Lend him or her a copy of this book. Get him or her interested in the vision of your Spiritual Trusts and ensure that he or she understands and supports that vision.

2. *Why* I have created these Spiritual Trusts:

Explain the needs you want to meet and the benefits you expect as a result of your Spiritual Trusts.

3. Why I want *you* to help me:

Tell why you think he or she is a good choice to be an executor. Express the personal qualities that give you confidence in his or her ability to be an excellent executor of your Trust.

4. *How* I want you to help me:

Give a brief overview of your Trust Directives. Tell him or her you would like to go over the Trust Directives with him or her in detail if he or she agrees to be your executor.

5. What your *responsibilities* would be:

Explain the spiritual and physical responsibilities of the executor of your Trust.

Step Four: Delivery

6. **How I will make this as *easy* as possible for you:**

Explain how you have made this as simple and straight-forward as possible for him or her. Tell him or her how you have provided Trust Directives, a Trust box, safety deposit box, funds, and so on.

7. **My advance *gratitude*:**

Let them know how much it would mean to you if he or she accepts your request to be your Spiritual Trust executor. Sincerely convey your appreciation.

8. **The need to *pray* about this:**

Tell them you want him or her to be spiritually comfortable with this and have a firm commitment to your Trust and Trust Directives. Ask them to think about it and pray about it. You want a "yes" answer to be the result of thoughtful and prayerful consideration.

9. **The need to *meet* after you have prayed and thought about my request:**

Being an executor of a Spiritual Trust is a significant responsibility that must not be undertaken lightly. Encourage thought and prayer about your request because you want to have confidence that when they say "yes," your Trusts are in good hands and your Trust Directives will be carried out.

10. **My willingness to serve as an executor for *your* Spiritual Trusts should you create one:**

Tell them that you would be happy to do the same for them. Encourage them to create a Spiritual Trust and inform them of the buddy system.

I recommend that you address the above points in person and in writing. Leave your potential executor with a letter you have written addressing the above points. This emphasizes the importance to you of your request. If you are unable to meet in person, make your request by phone initially and tell him or her that you will follow up with a letter (or e-mail).

The person who agrees to be your executor must make this decision independently, free of arm-twisting. That is the only way for your executor to feel personally bound and committed to implement your Trust Directives, and it is the only way for you to have a high level of comfort that your Trust Directives will be implemented.

A Trust Institution

When most people think of a trust company or a bank and trust, they think of *financial* or *monetary* trusts. In this book, I use the term *trust institution* to refer to any trust company or bank and trust with a trust department that handles financial or monetary trusts. Although trust institutions specialize in setting up and administering monetary trusts, some of them also will help you store and implement your Spiritual Trusts. I caution you, however, that this can be complicated. Moreover, the scope of services that a trust institution can provide as a Spiritual Trust executor will be far more limited than those that a trusted person can provide. But if you are unable to use a trusted individual as an executor, or you want the added security of a trust institution, you should explore this method for all or part of your Spiritual Trusts.

Storing your Spiritual Trusts with a trust institution and using the trust institution as an executor (referred to as "trustee") is a safe and reliable way to have your Spiritual Trusts stored and implemented. Trust institutions are audited and regulated by state and federal governments. Your Spiritual Trusts will be kept safely in the institution's vault, and the government protects consumers if a trust institution is sold so the acquiring institution will be subject to the terms of the agreement you established initially.

Although most trust institutions deal only with monetary trusts, some will handle other tasks, such as Spiritual Trusts. These generally are referred to as "non-monetary trusts." Trust institutions that handle non-monetary trusts typically have different rules and fees for such trusts. You will need to inquire at various trust institutions about, first, whether they handle non-monetary trusts and, if so, how they would store and implement your Spiritual Trusts and what their fees are.

Look for a trust institution that is willing to be a "custodian" of your Spiritual Trusts. This means that the institution will store your non-monetary trust (your Spiritual Trust) in its vault and follow your directives about how to implement your Trusts after you die. When you speak with a trust officer, be patient, as the concept of a Spiritual Trust probably will be new to him or her. During your inquiries, I suggest that you use the term "non-monetary trust" so the trust officer will quickly understand what you are trying to accomplish. You also might have to modify your directives somewhat to fit the trust institution's rules and procedures.

If you elect to use a trust institution, you can designate numerous recipients to receive Spiritual Trusts from you through the institution. At the benchmarks you specify, your recipients would go to the institution with proof of reaching the benchmark and thereupon would receive their Trust components.

Alternatively, you could designate in your directives to the trust institution that your executor (trusted individual) will pick up your Trusts at death, or at any other time you have designated. Your executor then would fulfill his or her executor responsibilities in delivering your Trusts and implementing your directives.

This option provides a safe and secure method for storage, and it relieves your executor of those responsibilities. For example, for years after your death, your Spiritual Trust executor could go to the trust institution and receive a package containing all of the messages you want to have delivered that year. Your executor then would follow the directives you left with him or her and deliver your messages. This ensures that your Trust components will be *delivered* by a trusted individual but are *stored* by a trust institution. This option can provide peace of mind for you and your executor alike by lifting the burden from your individual executor of safely storing your Trusts for years to come.

Again using myself as an example, I will illustrate how I am using a trust institution for some of the Spiritual Trusts to be delivered to my children. After I talked with a trust officer and we agreed that the company could serve in the capacities I desired, I filled out a form explaining that my Spiritual Trust was divided into two parts. One part is to be given to my son when he turns 21 years old and the other part is to be given to my daughter when she turns 21. Both parts are in one Trust box that is stored in the trust institution's vault.

I have left word through my will, my family, other Trust components, and my Spiritual Trust executors that each of my children, upon turning 21, has a Spiritual Trust from me waiting to be picked up at the trust institution. I also have left current contacts and other personal information on my spouse and children so the trust institution can make a reasonable effort to contact them if that becomes necessary.

When my children turn 21, they will go to the trust institution and show their driver's license and birth certificate. After validating that they are my selected recipients, and also meet the age requirement (you may have a variety of different requirements), a trust officer will retrieve my child's Spiritual Trust from my Trust box located in the vault and give it to my child. My children will not have to pay anything. I have taken care of payment in advance.

Prepayment, however, can be tricky. Trust institutions typically charge one percent of the value of a monetary trust to serve as trustee. Most institutions also have a minimum annual fee, which can be substantial. The trust institution I use charges a minimum annual fee of $1,500 to maintain monetary trusts, but non-monetary trusts (Spiritual Trusts) typically cost much less. My trust institution charges me $400 annually (the minimum) to act as the custodian of my Spiritual Trusts and to follow the delivery directives in my Trust Directives. If I were to die tomorrow, my children would not turn 21 for several years. Now for the tricky part, prepayment of fees incurred *after* I die.

To ensure that the trust institution continues to store and deliver my Trusts years after my death, I have arranged for payment of the annual fees from now until my youngest child turns 21. Let's say that is ten years. Prepayment can be arranged in two ways: pay now or pay later. You can pay the fees now for the next 10 years, which would cost $4,000 (10 years x $400 per year). Or you can pay the annual fee each year during your life and have the balance paid in full at your death. This can be accomplished by making the trust institution a partial beneficiary of your life insurance policy.

Another way to handle payment is to establish a monetary trust at the same trust institution you select for your Spiritual Trusts. The trust institution can be directed, as part of your monetary trust, to pay the annual fees for storage and administration of your Spiritual Trusts. Some trust institutions will even store your Spiritual Trusts with no charge if you are using that institution as trustee of your monetary trusts. Again, I recommend having a long conversation with the trust officer about these possibilities before you select a trust institution as your executor.

Because trust institutions that offer custodial services for your Spiritual Trusts can be more difficult to locate and identify, we maintain a list of trust institutions we have identified and their contact information on our website at www.spiritualtrusts.com/trustinstitutions.

CONTINGENCY PLANS

We seem to need contingency plans for everything in life, probably because life is so uncertain. Contingency plans for your Spiritual Trusts are no exception. These contingency plans involve your executor and the recipients of your Spiritual Trusts.

Alternative Executors

If your executor is a trusted individual, what will happen to your Spiritual Trusts if he or she dies before fulfilling all of your directives? You won't know what will happen unless you plan for such a possibility. Therefore, you should have an alternative executor for each of your executors, if you have more than one, and select each alternate in the same way that you select your primary executors.

If you have more than one executor for your Spiritual Trusts, you should consider giving each of them a letter listing all of your executors and their contact information. If one of your executors no longer can fulfill his or her obligations, that person could contact your other executors and pass the torch to one of them. You could provide a list of your executors in a stated order of succession, such as:

1. Dustin — Support Trust
2. Michelle — Prayer Trust
3. Ben — Legacy Trust
4. Linda — Stewardship Trust

If something were to happen to someone on the list, those responsibilities could go up or down the list as you direct.

Or you might want to choose an alternative executor for each kind of Trust, such as:

1. Dustin — Support Trust   Alt. Sarah
2. Michelle — Prayer Trust   Alt. Josh
3. Ben — Legacy Trust   Alt. Hannah
4. Linda — Stewardship Trust Alt. John

The method you use should be one that best suits the needs of you and your executors. I also recommend that you establish a formal way for the various executors to maintain contact if they are not close friends or family members. This way, they will know if another executor passes away or becomes incapacitated, and they can take action to see that all of your Trust Directives are met.

Alternative Recipients

You also should advise your executors of your desires if, for any reason, an intended recipient cannot receive the Trust component you created for him or her. If an intended recipient dies, what do you want done with the Trust intended for that person? Do you want to have it delivered to someone else, or do you want your executor to destroy it?

Further, you should have a contingency plan if a recipient declines to receive a Trust component or message. Should your executor hold onto it for a designated time to see if your recipient changes their mind? Do you want your executor to give that Trust component to someone else? Or, do you want your executor to destroy it?

Your Trust Directives form should clearly state your contingency plans so there is no question as to your wishes if any of these circumstances occurs.

FUNDING FOR YOUR EXECUTOR(S)

If any Trust component will require your executor to purchase something or make financial payments of any kind, you should arrange for your executor to receive the necessary funds. The executor might incur expenses for purchases he or she is to make for recipients (such

Step Four: Delivery

as flowers for an anniversary) as well as for mailings, safety deposit box rentals, and so on. You should not put a financial burden on your executor. Instead, provide the funds for your executor to carry out all of their responsibilities.

Let me start by identifying two ways you should *not* use to leave money for your executor. Do not leave your executor a check from your personal checking account because your account could be closed upon your death. Do not use money orders or cashier's checks because most banks have short expiration dates for such funds.

Fortunately, there are a number of easy ways to provide necessary funding to your Spiritual Trust executor. You could make a specific bequest in your will of an appropriate amount. If your executor is a family member, or other person who will be receiving a bequest from you anyway, this is a simple way to handle the funding. I recommend you specifically state what portion of the bequest is to be used for implementing your Trust Directives. Other options include:

Life Insurance

You can easily add your Spiritual Trust executor as a designated beneficiary of your life insurance policy for the amount needed to carry out your Trust Directives. Just ask your insurance agent to provide you with a "Change of Beneficiary" form and make your executor the beneficiary of an amount appropriate to cover the requests you have made through your Trust Directives.

Bank Options

Your bank has several options from which you can choose in getting funds to your executor after you die. For example, you can set up a savings, checking, or money market account in your name only. Then you deposit the funds needed for your executor to accomplish the directives you have requested. Next fill out a "Payable on Death" form, provided by your bank, indicating that your Spiritual Trust executor (use his or her name) is to receive the entire amount of this account upon your death.

After you die, your executor will go to the bank and show his or her driver's license and a copy of your death certificate. The bank then will close the account and liquidate the funds to your executor. A visit with your banker will be helpful to learn about all the methods available for you to transfer funds to your executor upon your death.

Cash

I do not recommend that you provide your executor with cash unless your death is expected and the amount is not substantial. In such situations, you could leave the cash in a sealed envelope to be given to your executor upon your death. A good way to discretely conceal cash is to put it in a cardboard envelope such as is used by FedEx and the US Postal Office.

IN SUMMARY

Attending to all the details of delivery will ensure that the Spiritual Trusts you have so carefully developed will be implemented in the way you intend. Although it marks the culmination of the process, many aspects can be instituted from the very beginning.

The Trust Directives form is an overview and reference guide for your family or Trust executor that clearly conveys your wishes and directives concerning delivery and implementation of the Spiritual Trusts you have created. You should keep your Trust Directives form with the original and copies of your Trust components, and keep another copy with your will and other important documents.

There are a number of ways to deliver your Trust components and you should evaluate these to determine the best way considering your objectives, your Trust recipients, and your executor. The selection of your Spiritual Trust executor or executors is particularly important to the assured delivery of your Trusts. It is also important to provide your executor(s) with any funding that will be required to carry out your Trust Directives and there are several methods to do this.

We seem to need contingency plans for everything in life, and Spiritual Trusts are no exception. You should designate alternative executors in the event someone you have named becomes unavailable. You also should advise your executors of your desires if, for any reason, an intended recipient cannot or will not receive the Trust component you created for him or her.

APPENDIX A

Trust Directives

This appendix includes the recommended information to ensure that your Spiritual Trusts will be delivered and implemented according to your wishes. The standard Trust Directive forms do not fit within the space confines of this book so I have listed much of the information from these forms in a text format. You can go to our website at www.spiritualtrusts.com and either print or download the Trust Directive forms for free. They also can be found in any Spiritual Trust workbook.

The information that should be included in your Trust Directives is segmented into the following categories:

- Cover sheet
- Executor letter
- Directives
- Monetary issues
- Executor information
- Recipient information
- Personal information

Depending on the complexity of your Spiritual Trusts, you may only need to include a portion of this information or you may need to elaborate even more. I recommend that you prepare one Trust Directives form for each of your Spiritual Trust executors.

It is much easier on your executor, if he or she has a copy before your death of the Trust Directives for which they will be responsible. This way, upon your death, they can act quickly if certain Directives require them to do so. In addition, when possible, before your death they should also have the Trust components they are to deliver, or assured access to them. For example, if originals of your Trust components are in a safety deposit box or a trust institution vault, access for your executor upon your death should be pre-arranged.

If possible, seal your Trust components in envelopes or boxes that are clearly labeled with the contents and the name of the recipients or executor (e.g. "Support Trust for my family"). You may note on the outside that it should remain unopened until delivery to the recipient.

Cover Sheet

This is simply a cover sheet that identifies your Trust Directives package. You may label it for a Spiritual Trust or for an individual Trust component. For example, this is what I use as a cover sheet for one of my Trusts:

TRUST DIRECTIVES

FOR MY

SUPPORT TRUST

Created by:

Darin Manis

This package contains my Trust Directives for the delivery and implementation of the Support Trust components I have created. The information contained in my Trust Directives is confidential and is intended only for my Support Trust executor and alternate executor.

Support Trust executor: Skip Smith
Alternate Trust executor: Tammy Werner

Appendix A

Executor Letter

This is a letter to your executor providing an overview of the objectives of the Trust Directives he or she will be delivering or implementing. You should review this with your executor while you are alive and also cover it thoroughly in this letter. This also gives you the opportunity to express your appreciation for all they are doing for you, and provides a place to write a special message to them. This is also the place you want to include any other details or instructions that do not necessarily fit within the confines of your Trust Directives.

An example to get you started might be something as simple as this:

Dear David,

It is hard to express how grateful I am that you have agreed to be my Support Trust executor. I know I have placed a serious responsibility on you and I appreciate your commitment to execute my directives and last wishes contained within this package.

I know my family is going through emotions right now that make me shudder. Thank you for being there for my family during this time.

I do want you to know how much I have appreciated our friendship. I hope God continues to bless you and your family in extraordinary ways...

Directives

This is where you give the details for the delivery or implementation of your Spiritual Trusts and Trust components. Take each Spiritual Trust or Trust component individually and give at least the following information. For this section, I have included sample answers to make this easier to picture.

Support Trust and Legacy Trust Directives

The following two examples work for most Support Trust and Legacy Trust components:

- **Trust component:** Byeulogy message.
- **Executor:** Skip Smith.
- **Alternate executor:** Mark Brown.
- **Recipient:** Amy Jones (sister).
- **Event or delivery date:** At my funeral service.
- **Delivery instructions:** Discretely give to her before the services begin.
- **Format of component:** It is a written letter in a sealed envelope.
- **Location of component:** In the portable safe in my bedroom closet—the combination is 9-4-3.
- **Identification of component:** It is a sealed white envelop marked "Amy—Byeulogy message."
- **Contingency instructions:** If Amy cannot attend the funeral for any reason, please deliver in person. If that is not possible, then send to her by FedEx. If Amy is no longer living, then please give to Amy's daughter, Ella.
- **Additional instructions:** Skip should notify Mark when delivery is complete.
- **Expenses:** Possible FedEx shipping costs.

Or another example could be:

Appendix A

- **Trust component:** FaithMessage.
- **Executor:** Mark White.
- **Alternate executor:** Jason Cooper.
- **Recipient:** Dillon Welch (oldest son).
- **Event or delivery date:** On his 21st birthday which will be November 9, 2007.
- **Delivery instructions:** Hand deliver.
- **Format of component:** DVD with attached letter.
- **Location of component:** One copy is with Mark (primary executor) and the other copy is with Jason (alternate executor).
- **Identification of component:** It is in a sealed manila envelop marked "For Dillon, Happy 21st Birthday my son, from Dad."
- **Contingency instructions:** If this cannot be hand delivered, please FedEx it to him. If he is no longer living give to my other son, Dustin.
- **Additional instructions:** If Dillon is going through serious life difficulties, gets in any kind of legal trouble or has to receive counseling for any reason, please deliver this early.
- **Expenses:** Possible FedEx shipping costs.

Repeat as necessary.

Prayer Trust Directives

Prayer Trust and Stewardship Trust components are handled a bit differently. Let's take your Prayer Trust Directives first. Your Prayer Trust components will be divided primarily in one of two ways. First, you might be sending directives to a prayer partner. These directives can be given to them during your lifetime, after your death, or both.

- **Prayer partner:** Wanda Moore.
- **Prayer recipient:** Lauren (daughter).
- **Prayer requests:** Spiritual comfort, protection and growth.
- **Timing or benchmark:** Please remember to pray for Lauren often. Specifically pray for her spiritual and emotional support and comfort during the first month or so after my death. Continue to pray that she is protected from doubt and fear. Please pray for her purity of heart on her 18th birthday, which is July 17, 2010.
- **Special requests:** Please get others you know to pray for Lauren. I pray that you will make Lauren a part of your daily prayer life. Adopt her as one of your prayer children that you take care of daily through lifting her up to the Lord.

The other kind of Prayer Trust components would involve your executor sending a prayer request or a prayer reminder to selected people.

- **Executor:** Bandi Christman.
- **Alternate executor:** Carla Grizzell.
- **Prayer beneficiary:** My family.
- **Prayer request:** General well being, spiritual support and protection, blessings.
- **Recipients of requests:** Rick Powers, Cindy Palmer, Dennis Willard, Dustin Morris, Michelle Simms, Travis Haggard, Jordan Johnston, and Amanda Webb.
- **Event or delivery date:** 1 month after my death and again 6 months after.
- **Delivery instructions:** By mail.
- **Format of component:** Letters.
- **Location of component:** Both executors (primary and alternate) have copies.

Appendix A

- **Identification of component:** The letters to be sent out on the 1 month benchmark are all together within the larger manila envelop that is titled "One month prayer request letters." The letters to be sent out on the 6 month benchmark are also all together within a larger manila envelope titled "Six month prayer request letters."
- **Special instructions:** All the letters are stamped and addressed. Please make sure that I have enough postage to cover any postal rate increases. If any letters are returned to you because the address is no longer current, please take measures to find their current address and re-send the letter. My wife or pastor will know how to locate everyone on this list.
- **Contingency instructions:** If it is more appropriate to hand deliver some of these letters, you have my blessing. If any of these recipients have passed away, their letters may be destroyed.

Stewardship Trust Directives

Here is an example of how you can formalize your Stewardship Trust Directives during and after your life. You may wish to use this basic idea, but format it differently with different stewardship goals.

Date:

As long as I shall live and be of sound mind, I will be the Executor of this Stewardship Trust. At the time of my death or incapacity, I hereby appoint Robert Smith, my brother, to be the Executor of this Stewardship Trust.

Gifts from income:

During my lifetime I solemnly vow to tithe ___ percent of my income (before taxes) to my church, _____;

Because the Lord has blessed me with resources, I solemnly vow to give an additional ___ percent of my income to the work of the Lord through:

[List church, ministry, charity, foundation and the amounts and terms of the gifts.]

Gifts from net worth other than income:

Although the exact beneficiaries may change over time, I have prayerfully considered the work of the Lord to which I should contribute and have identified the following areas as those to which my spiritual investments will be focused:

[List church, ministry, charity, foundation and the amounts and terms of the gifts.]

Gifts after death:

Upon my death I...
    Options:
        Have left a bequest in my will for $___ to _____
        Have left a portion of my life insurance, $____, to ____
        Have established a Trust to _____.

Appendix A

Some of your Stewardship Trust Directives should be included in legal documents such as your will and/or financial trusts. Do not simply create Stewardship Trust Directives and think that is all that is needed to allocate finances or assets to the work of the Lord *after* your death. There are legal steps that must be taken to ensure that your last wishes with respect to financial matters are carried out, whether or not they are a part of your Stewardship Trust Directives.

These Directives, however, can serve as a guideline for you to use within your overall estate planning. You can take these directives to your lawyer, CPA, or financial planner and ask them how to make your Stewardship Trust Directives legally enforceable.

Your Stewardship Trust, like your other Trusts, will be highly individualized, but the above information should give you a good start.

SPIRITUAL TRUSTS

Monetary Issues

This is where you advise your executors of funding needs and how you have provided for these expenses. You do not want to burden your executor financially. The least you can do is to make sure that they have available funds, even if the amounts seem insignificant, so that they are not spending their money on your Directives.

Provide each of your Spiritual Trust executors with the following information that will apply to the Trusts for which they will serve as executor:

- *Identify expenses for all Trust Directives*

- *If your executor will receive funds from your estate through a bequest in a will or in a financial trust, provide:*
  ~The amount:
  ~The name and contact information of the executor of your will and/or trustee of your financial trust:
  ~How your Spiritual Trust executor will receive these funds:

- *If your executor will receive funds through any bank account that you have set up for this purpose, provide:*
  ~Name of the bank:
  ~Address:
  ~Phone number:
  ~Bank contact person:
  ~Applicable account numbers:
  ~Is your executor the "Payable upon Death" beneficiary of your account?
  ~Will your executor be required to provide their driver's license and a copy of your death certificate?
  ~Is anything else necessary for them to liquidate the account?
  ~What is the approximate balance of this account?

- *If your executor is a partial beneficiary of a life insurance policy, provide:*
    - ~Amount:
    - ~Insurance company and policy number:
    - ~Agents name and contact information:

- *If your executor will receive cash, provide:*
    - ~Amount:
    - ~Location:
    - ~Point of contact:
    - ~Is the cash in a package or envelope addressed to them?
    - ~Who else knows your executor is supposed to receive this cash?

Executor Information

You will want to make a master list of all of your executors and alternate executors. The more you have, the more important documenting this information becomes. I suggest a master list be given to all of your executors and alternate executors so that they will be able to contact each other if necessary (if they do not know each other) and even hold each other accountable.

This list can also be given to your family and other recipients. Executors are only human and may accidentally forget a certain delivery date. If your recipient is expecting a message for their 21st birthday, but hasn't received it after their birthday, they should be able to contact your executor and retrieve their message. If this happens, it likely will only happen once, but you still should address the possibility.

Your executor information varies depending on the type of Spiritual Trust executor you are using for a particular Spiritual Trust (trusted individual or trust institution):

Trusted Individual

You will want to list the following information for each executor and alternate executor:

- Name:
- Address:
- Home phone number:
- Place of employment:
- Work phone number:
- Cell phone number:
- Email address:
- Executor of which Trust components: (list)
- Identify any components the executor already has in his or her possession:

Trust Institution

- Name of institution:
- Address:
- Contact person or officer:
- Secondary contact person:
- Phone number:

- Account number:
- List each trust component the Trust Institution is in possession of:
- List each recipient of each Trust component:
- Is the Trust released to an executor or directly to the recipient?
    - ~Name of executor:
    - ~Name of alternate executor:
    - ~Name of Recipient(s) with authorization to retrieve Trust:
    - ~Name of any alternate recipient:
- Have you set any requirements that must be met before Trust can be released? (specific birthday, graduations, marriage, etc.)
    - ~If so, list such requirements for each Trust component and/or recipient
- Will any form of identification or other proof need to be presented?
    - ~If so, list what will need to be presented:
- What are the delivery or pick up instructions?
- How long is the term of storage?
- Have all fees been prepaid?
- Is the Trust account officer to be notified for any reason? (change of address, birthday, death, etc.)

SPIRITUAL TRUSTS

Recipient Information

- Name:
- Address:
- Home phone number:
- Place of employment:
- Work phone number:
- Cell phone number:
- Date of birth:
- Place of birth:
- Social security number:
- Email address:
- Contact information of other people who would know how to reach the recipient if the recipient were to move:
- Trust components recipient is to receive:
- Date or event on which each Trust component is to be delivered:
- Is recipient aware that he or she will receive this Trust component?
    ~If they are not aware, are there any conditions under which recipient may be made aware of the Trust component before delivery?
- Are there any conditions that may occur upon which you would want the Trust component delivered earlier or later than the original schedule?
- Are there any conditions that may occur upon which you would not want the Trust component delivered?
    ~If so, what is executor to do with the Trust component?

Repeat for each recipient.

Appendix A

Your Personal Information

The following information may benefit your Spiritual Trust Executor and anyone else who will be responsible for handling the details of your estate such as the executor of your will.

Provide the following relevant information to your Trust executor. Such information may be necessary for them to execute certain directives or it may help them with other after-death duties that you may request of them.

General Information:
- Full name:
- Address:
- Home phone number:
- Social security number:
- Date of birth:
- Place of birth:
- Current place of employment and contact person:

Financial and legal information:
- Location of my financial records and will:
- My financial planner's name and contact information:
- My CPA or accountant's name and contact information:
- My lawyer's name and contact information:
- My life insurance agent's name and contact information:

Account information—for each account, list institution, account or policy number, and contact person:
- Checking:
- Saving:
- Life insurance policy:
- Other insurance policies:
- Safety deposit box:
- Money market accounts:
- IRA:
- Retirement funds:
- Brokerage accounts:
- Other accounts:

These sample Trust Directives should give you a good start on *your* Directives. If you need further assistance, please go to our website or one of our Spiritual Trust workbooks.

APPENDIX B

Work In Progress Form

WORK IN PROGRESS FORM
(With example answers)

Trust Type	Trust Component	Format	Location of Trust	Recipient(s)	Special Instructions
Support	Eulogy	Video	Mini DV tape kept in camera or desk in study	Those at funeral service	Play at funeral service
Legacy	LifeStory	Handwritten	Desk in study, spiral notebook bottom right drawer	Family	Make copies available to any family member that wants one
Legacy	FaithMessage	Audio	Desk in study, tapes are in addressed envelopes	Son & daughter	My wife should give to them on the birthdays I write on envelopes
Legacy	Journal	Handwritten	Table by bed in top drawer	Family	Make copies and give to my spouse/children
Prayer	Support prayers	Handwritten	Table by bed in top drawer	Family	Give any prayer requests I have completed to Joe, my prayer partner

© 2002, FaithMessages. License granted to purchasers of *Spiritual Trusts* to reproduce and use this form for personal use.

APPENDIX C

Life Questions and Thoughts

This appendix will be helpful for you in creating many of the Trust components discussed in this book. Depending on what Trust component you are creating, you may consider using this appendix extensively, or maybe not at all.

For LifeStories and LifeTributes, you will find many questions, statements and memory joggers to help you convey your life, or the life of another, to the future.

For Legacy Journals, picking one (or a few) of these topics to discuss each day, week, or month, is a fun way to share your life through an ongoing effort of love.

For LifeMessages and FaithMessages, you might find these topics useful in giving additional ideas of things you want to discuss with your loved ones in the future through the messages you send them.

Do not feel you have to answer every question here for any Trust component you are working on. This list is merely an assortment of questions that may or may not relate to you. The following questions and topic headings are just a *sampling* of the hundreds of questions and "memory joggers" that are offered in our workbooks.

TIPS FOR JOGGING YOUR MEMORY

- Pull out and reflect on your family photos, historical photos, or painting of the time.
- Refer to any journals, letters, yearbooks, or newspapers saved through the years.
- Make lists about yourself and family members: favorite foods, sayings, pastimes, songs, etc.
- Try and create a family tree: including where they were born, maiden names, or death information.
- Talk about the past with people who were there.
- Write time capsule descriptions of yourself or others.
- Read a book or see a film set in the same era.
- Close your eyes and imagine your favorite place. What do you see, smell, taste, and feel?
- Listen to old records, tapes, or CDs with familiar songs on them.

Appendix A

- Reflect on any heirlooms that have been passed on to you.
- Visit the house or town that you grew up in.
- Review any trophies, ribbons, or certificates that you have received through the years.

GUIDELINES

When thinking about what you want to share, consider these helpful guidelines that you may or may not want to consider:

1. Does it teach a valuable lesson?
2. Does it reveal why you are a certain way today?
3. Did it change your outlook on life?
4. Does it reveal aspects of your essence?
5. Does it provide meaningful insight into a particular period of your life?
6. Does it evoke strong feelings or emotions in you even today?
7. Are you compelled to make sure it is never forgotten?
8. Is it interesting?
9. Do you have pictures, video, or other items that you can include with the story?

LIFE ESSENCE STATEMENTS

Completing most of the following statements and then explaining why you completed each statement in the way you did (when applicable) will richly convey your essence as a person. After completing this exercise, you likely will come up with more topics of your own and will be well on your way to capturing the real you for future generations to know. Feel free to expand on any statement and, of course, add any others you wish.

1. My favorite memory is…
2. My favorite hobby is…
3. My biggest hero is…
4. The favorite time in my life was…
5. If I could, this is what I would do over…
6. If I could change one thing about me, it would be…
7. My three main political beliefs are…
8. Three major turning points in my life were…
9. My biggest crisis as a child was…
10. If I were guaranteed one wish, it would be…
12. My favorite successes are…

Spiritual Trusts

13. My biggest disappointment in life is...
14. My strongest characteristics or traits are...
15. The most costly lesson I learned was...
16. My greatest hope is...
17. My three funniest memories are...
18. The importance of honesty is...
19. The most courageous thing I ever did was...
20. My earliest vision of my future was...
21. I believe my purpose in life is to...
22. I get emotional about...
23. I get angry when...
24. I grimace at the thought of...
25. Some of the most teachable moments I had were...
26. Words I would use to describe my inner self when looking in the mirror are...
27. The three non-relatives who have most influenced me are...
28. My favorite list — color, food, places, people, songs, books, movie — is...
29. When a homeless person asks me for some spare change, I...
30. The event I regret the most is...
31. The saddest event of my life was...
32. My secret joy is...
33. I tend to handle conflict by...
34. I would describe my sense of humor as...
35. One of the most important milestones in my life is...
36. The three wisest decisions I ever made were...
37. Three times I have cried were...
38. My weakest character traits are...
39. My three biggest fears are...
40. My three proudest moments were...
41. I define faith as...
42. I define honesty as...
43. I define integrity as...
44. I define character as...
45. My current vision of my life is to...
46. I have been blessed because...
47. Three of the standards I live by are...
48. My dream is to...
49. My three biggest life goals are to...
50. I want to be remembered for...

Appendix C

Some questions to consider that help convey your essence as a person are:

LIFE ESSENCE QUESTIONS

- How is your life different today from how you thought it would be?
- What is the best part of being the age you are today? What has surprised you about this time in your life?
- Talk about your friends. Which friendships do you cherish the most at this point in your life and why?
- What things do you enjoy doing now that you haven't in the past?
- What is one thing you couldn't live without?
- Who from your past would you like to see again, and what would you want to do together?
- What are the social and political issues that most concerned you when you were younger? What are your concerns today?
- What is one thing you would like to do before you die and why?
- What dreams do you feel you left behind? Which of your dreams did you follow?
- What feels unfinished that you would like to resolve?
- In what ways would you say life today is more satisfying than in the days when your parents were your age? In what ways is it less satisfying?
- Tell of something you learned the "hard way."
- When was a time when you felt unconditional love?
- What and who have been the greatest influences on your life and in what ways?
- Describe a lost opportunity in your life.
- What is your greatest talent and what have you done with it? What talent do you feel you have that you have never developed?
- What do you think are the most crucial changes that need to be made in society?
- How do you see the world 50 years from now? What are your concerns for the future?
- What do you feel matters most in life? What did your parents tell you mattered most?

SPIRITUAL ESSENCE STATEMENTS

Completing most of the following statements and then explaining why you completed each statement in the way you did (when applicable) will richly convey your spiritual essence. After completing this exercise, you likely will come up with more topics of your own and will be well on your way to capturing the real you for future generations to know. Feel free to expand on any statement and of course add any others you wish.

1. I know God is real because...
2. I know Jesus loves me because...
3. I became a Christian because...
4. I most often pray for...
5. My favorite Old Testament story is...
6. My favorite Old Testament book is...
7. I know the Holy Spirit lives in me because...
8. I value Christian fellowship because...
9. I believe the Bible is the word of God because...
10. My spiritual gifts are...
11. My biggest temptations are...
12. My definition of spiritual maturity is...
13. Spiritual maturity has taught me that...
14. I fear the Lord because...
15. My favorite benefits of Christianity are...
16. I got saved when I was...
17. I pray when...
18. Christianity is sometimes difficult because...
19. I have been persecuted for my beliefs when...
20. My favorite worship song is...
21. My perception of heaven is...
22. Faith is my foundation because...
23. I know Jesus is the son of God because...
24. I know I am saved because...
25. My three favorite scriptures are...
26. My favorite New Testament story is...
27. My favorite New Testament book is...
28. I maintain intimacy with God by...
29. My favorite way to worship is...
30. I view grace as...
31. My perception of hell is...
32. I view Satan as...

Appendix C

33. My view of stewardship is...
34. God has blessed me by...
35. I am most thankful to God for...
36. I have seen answered prayer in my life when...
37. A witnessing experience I would like to share is...
38. Some of the biggest mistakes I have made in my faith are...
39. The ways I enjoy worshiping God are...
40. I am most curious about which of God's many mysteries...

Some questions to consider that help convey your spiritual essence are:

FAITH QUESTIONS

- Were you born into a particularly religious family?
- What were the traditions that you remember as a child? Did you follow your family's religious tradition throughout your life?
- Who was the most influential person in your spiritual development?
- Was there a point in your life when you doubted your faith? Describe.
- What have the difficult times in your life taught you about your faith?
- What do you believe will happen to you and your family after death?
- Is there a particular time in your life when your faith helped you?
- Have you ever had a prayer, dream, or wish answered?
- What traditions have been passed down that remind you of who you are and where you come from? What are your hopes for the continuation of these traditions by future generations?
- What resistance and challenges have you experienced from your children toward your religion? What would you say to your children if they chose another faith?
- Describe and affirm the spiritual growth you have seen in each of your children's lives.
- What would you like to say to other people you care about who have turned away from their faith?
- What has helped you and your family grow spiritually strong?

- Who in your life has been your spiritual mentor?
- What are the benefits of leading a spiritual life?

BEGINNINGS

- Reflect on the who, what, when, and where of your birth.
- Do you know how you got your name? Explain. What does this mean to you?
- Describe your earliest memories as a child?
- What items have you kept from childhood? What meaning do these items carry?
- Who other than your parents were involved in taking care of you?

FAMILY CONNECTIONS

- Mother's name? Father's name? Grandmothers' names? Grandfathers' names? Did you have nicknames for your family members? What were they?
- Describe the circumstances that brought your parents to the place where you grew-up.
- Describe the kind of work your father did for a living? Your mom? Your grandparents? How has this shaped your own work ethic?
- What is your most vivid memory of a family vacation or outing?
- What did your family do on holidays?
- Can you remember any special stories your parents or grandparents told? Which stories would you like to pass on to your children?
- What was your parents' relationship like?
- How would you explain your role in your immediate family?
- Is there a family heirloom that is very important to you? Why?

EARLY HOME & ENVIRONMENT

- Describe your childhood home: smells, colors, sounds, decorations, temperature, building style.
- Describe your bedroom. Why was it special?
- Did you have a favorite season of the year as a child and what did you enjoy doing at this time?
- What did your family do for entertainment?
- If you could, what would you change about the house you grewup in?

CHILDHOOD

- Did you have a best friend? What did you do for fun?
- What poems, sayings, nursery rhymes, or bedtime stories do you remember?
- Did you collect anything? Bugs, baseball cards, marbles, dolls, stuffed animals?
- What or who scared you when you were a child?
- Did you ever have to move when you were a child? What was that like for you?
- Would you like to have raised your kids in a neighborhood like the one you grew up in? Why? Why not?
- Did you go to camp? What kind of camp was it and what do you remember feeling and seeing while you were there?

GRADE SCHOOL

- What do you remember of your earliest days of grade school? How did you feel about going to school? What did you like about school? What did you dislike?
- Did you have a favorite teacher? What made them special?
- Did you attend private or public school? What was it like?
- What was your favorite subject?
- What kind of clothes did you and your schoolmates wear?
- How did you get to school? What was that experience like for you?
- Did you have any friends who you have kept in touch with since grade school?
- What is the most embarrassing thing that ever happened to you while at school?

HIGH SCHOOL

- How did you feel when it was time for you to go to high school? Did you have to switch schools?
- What school activities were you involved in? What did this mean to you?
- Do you own a class ring, remembrance book, or annual? What does it mean to you?
- What teachers do you remember? Why?
- Were you ever honored at school? Varsity letter? Homecoming court? Valedictorian? Do you remember the students who were? Did you receive any scholarships? What did all of that mean to you at the time?
- What were your favorite subjects? Why? What were the most difficult classes for you? Why?
- Describe a dance, basketball game, class trip, concert, etc. that stands out in your mind.
- What did you discover about yourself during your high school years.
- Have you ever attended a high school reunion? Why? Why not? What was it like?
- If you today could have one conversation with yourself when you were a high school student, what would you say?

COLLEGE

- What motivated you to attend college? How did your family feel about your decision?
- How did you choose which school to attend?
- How was your education funded? Did you have to work while you were going to college?
- What were your images of college life? What was the reality for you?
- What was your living situation? Did you live in a dorm or a room off campus? Who was your roommate? Did you get along?
- What was your major? Why did you pick it? Did you ever change your major?

Appendix C

- Have you stayed in touch with anyone you met at college? Did you visit each other over the years? How have you kept in touch?
- Did you change much at college? How? Did your family and friends notice? What did they say to you?
- What is your biggest regret from your college days?
- If you could go back, what one thing would you do differently?
- Did you attend any kind of graduate school? Tell about that decision and experience.

MILITARY CAREER

- Give your name, rank, and serial number.
- Were you drafted or did you enlist? What feeling were you having when you actually signed on? Did you ever have second thoughts?
- What was the name of your company? Did it have a nickname? Did it have a mascot?
- What were your expectations of the military when you signed on? What was the reality for you?
- Where were you stationed? Describe what it was like.

CAREERS

- What was your very first job? Your first real job?
- Do you feel your career was right for you? What would have been your dream career? What kept you from that?
- Did you ever run your own business? How did it start? Was it rewarding or difficult?
- Were you ever the boss? Would you have wanted to be?
- Did you have a mentor? What was that relationship like?
- Were you a mentor? When did you realize that there was someone looking up to you as a professional person in your chosen career?
- Were you proud when people asked you what you did, or would you rather have been able to say something else?
- What was your most significant learning experience in your professional life?

ROMANCE AND RELATIONSHIPS

- Do you remember your first kiss? Who was it with and what was it like?
- Were you always attracted to the same type of person?
- Who was your first crush? How did that person make you feel?
- Who was your first love? Did you think it was going to last? Who broke whose heart?
- Did you know on the first day you met your spouse, that he or she was the one? How did you know? Did he or she know it too?
- What was it like when you took your intended to meet your family? What was it like when you met their family?
- Describe your wedding. Your outfit. The bridal party. The church or hall. The reception.
- How were you feeling throughout the ceremony? Who performed the ceremony?
- How do you get along with your in-laws? What did your parents have to say about your intended?
- What song do you consider the most romantic? Do you remember the songs played at your wedding?
- Describe a gift that your spouse gave you that has great importance to you.
- In your years of marriage, what have you learned about your spouse that you didn't know on your wedding day?

PARENTHOOD

- How did you pick out your children's names?
- What pet name did you use for your children when they were babies? Did you keep using them, even when the children grew older?
- What was your children's favorite bedtime story or poem? Can you still recite any of it?
- How did you discipline your kids? Was this hard for you to do? Would you discipline them the same way if you had it to do over?
- Which of your children needed the most discipline? Why, do you think?

Appendix C

- Where did your kids play? What did they play?
- What was your biggest fear when your children were out of your sight?
- What were the teenage years like for you?
- What was it like when they were learning how to drive? Who took them to practice and where did they go?
- What was the scariest moment in parenting? The toughest? The moment that made you most proud?
- Can you remember one memorable thing that each one of your children said?
- What was the best part of being a parent? The worst?
- What was the transition like when you went from being someone's child to being someone's parent? How long did it take you to really get used to the idea?

GRANDPARENTHOOD

- Where were you when your child told you that you were going to be a grandparent? What were your first thoughts and words?
- Were you able to go to the hospital to see the new baby? What did you think the first minute the nurse brought the baby to the room?
- What do your grandchildren call you?
- Do your grandchildren ever come spend the night with you? How do you spend those evenings?
- Do your grandchildren look like your own children did as babies? Do you ever miss the days when you had babies of your own?
- Do you remember any memorable gifts you've given them over the years? Do you know what they did with the gifts?
- Have you taught your grandchildren any games or hobbies or skills? What does this mean to you?
- What do you call your grandchildren? Do you have nicknames for them?
- Can you see your face anywhere in your grandchild's face?
- Can you recall one especially memorable thing each of your grandchildren has said?
- What are your hopes and dreams for your grandchildren?
- What one thing would you like to be sure they remember and value?

- What do you want them to remember about you?
- What is the best part of being a grandparent? The worst?

ABOUT YOUR SPOUSE

- Describe your first kiss.
- Did you know on the first day you met your spouse, that this would be your life's partner? How did you know? Did he or she know it too?
- Describe your courtship.
- What was it like when you took your intended to meet your family? What was the first impression? What was it like when you met their family?
- Describe the day you got engaged.
- Did you pick out wedding rings together? What was that like?
- Was planning the wedding stressful? Explain.
- Was there anything unusual in your wedding vows? How were you feeling throughout the ceremony?
- Did anything go wrong during the ceremony or celebration afterward?
- Where did you go on your honeymoon?
- What did you like best about your spouse when you were dating? And today?
- What were the best times and the hardest times in your marriage? What got you through these difficult times?
- Describe a gift that your spouse gave you that has special meaning.
- What's been the secret to your success as a couple?
- Describe the first time you said, "I love you."
- Share some of your happiest memories of your life together.
- What about your spouse led you to fall in love with them? What unique qualities and talents do you admire in your spouse?

REFLECTIONS ON THE PAST

- What was your favorite year? What was your favorite age? Why?
- Describe the hardest thing that you ever had to do in your life.
- When in your life were you the most fulfilled?
- Describe the angriest you've ever been? What did you do about it?
- Have you had a struggle being able to afford the things you want and need? Have you ever felt wealthy?
- When do you first remember feeling like an adult? Were you pleased or shocked by the feeling?
- What was your favorite fad over the last so many years?
- Did you have definite life goals? Did you achieve them? Are you still working on them? Any new ones?
- Did you have a year of living dangerously? Describe.
- Summarize where your family has been, and where it looks like it's going.
- Is there anything in your life you would have done completely different? Describe.
- What regrets do you have about a road not taken or an opportunity missed?
- If you could look into the future, would you? Why or why not?
- What haven't you had enough of in your life? Time? Money? Love?
- Was there one moment in your life that changed everything for you?
- Have you ever been in the right place at the right time? What happened?

EULOGY AND BYEULOGY

- What words would others use to describe you?
- If you could leave one piece of advice for your family and friends, what would it be?
- How would you describe your relationship with your family?
- What is the biggest lesson you've learned in life?

Spiritual Trusts

- What accomplishment are you most proud? What has your family accomplished that you are most proud of?
- Close your eyes and imagine all of the friends and family that have passed through your life. What would you like to say to them if they were in front of you now?
- If you could apologize to someone you had wronged, who would it be and what would you say?
- What do you feel matters most in life? Have you ever wished for a more meaningful life?
- What is it you worry most about after you are gone?
- What is the one thing you want people to remember about you when you are gone?

SENTIMENT AND EMOTIONAL SUPPORT

- Who are the people most important to you? Tell them why you care so much about them.
- Are there people to whom you would like to say things (diplomatically and without hurting them) that you've never said before?
- What are the great strengths of the people around you? Acknowledge them for the important contributions they made to your life.
- Is there anything you wish to request of a particular person after you are gone?
- Are there people you need to forgive or from whom you would like to receive forgiveness?
- What would you like to say to your children if you knew you wouldn't be there to watch them grow up?
- How have each of the people you care about impacted your life?
- Can you give your spouse permission to marry again after you are gone?

Glossary of Terms

These are definitions of terms as used in the context of this book. You will note that some of these terms are new and unique to the Spiritual Trust System.

Alternate executor
Someone who can perform the duties of your Spiritual Trust executor if the primary executor becomes unable or unwilling to serve in that capacity.

Archiving
The act of preserving documents, including Spiritual Trust System components and other memories, so that they will be available in acceptable quality and integrity in the future.

Autobiography
The biography or LifeStory of a person that is written by the same person.

Benchmark deliveries
Future milestones, dates, or events in which any Trust component is to be delivered. These include birthdays, graduations, weddings, the birth of children, holidays and other similar events. These kinds of deliveries give you the opportunity to be involved in significant events your family and loved ones will experience even though you may no longer be there in person.

Bereavement
A process of mourning and suffering following the death of a loved one.

Bequeath
To leave to another through a will.

Biography
The history of a person's life.

Birthday messages
Messages you create to be delivered on the recipients' future birthdays, even if you have already passed away.

Byeulogy
The act of a person who has died that speaks well of, or praises the living. Usually given to the recipients at or near the time of the funeral service.

CD ROM
A Compact Disk, which is a digital medium on a small disk containing data that can be read on a computer.

Charity
An organization to which contributions may be partially deductible from gross income due to its status as a qualified charitable organization under the Internal Revenue Code.

Chronological LifeStory
A LifeStory that relates the major events of your life from birth to the present. It is an historical account, but does not have to cover every chapter of you life.

Direct support
Messages or other support *you* provide directly to your family or loved ones after your death, even though the support will be delivered by your Spiritual Trust executor or other trusted messenger.

DVD
A Digital Video Disc (DVD) is a high-capacity optical disk that can store your video and other images in a digital format. A DVD can be played repeatedly without significant deterioration in resolution. Copies can be made on other DVDs that are identical to the original. DVDs can have interactive characteristics through use of graphics that allow the user to select a specific chapter from a menu screen.

Essence LifeStory
An Essence LifeStory explains what kind of a person you are emotionally, spiritually, intellectually and socially, and why you are that way. It focuses on the person behind the events of your life, thereby allowing those experiencing your LifeStory to connect with you as a person.

Glossary of Terms

Eulogy
To speak well of a person. The most common usage of this word is to speak well of, or praise, a person who has died at his or her funeral service.

Executor
The trusted person who implements your Spiritual Trusts after you have died. Similar to the "executor" appointed in your will to oversee the directives and disbursements from your estate. Your Spiritual Trust executor may be the same person as the executor appointed in your will, but does not need to be the same. Moreover, you may have multiple Spiritual Trust executors if you chose to have separate executors for each type of Spiritual Trust you establish.

FaithMessage
A FaithMessage is a message with a specific spiritual content or purpose to be delivered to a person or persons at a time of your choosing, including after your death. Although a FaithMessage can address a variety of issues, the underlying theme of a FaithMessage is about faith. A FaithMessage can be written, typed, audio or video. A FaithMessage can be used to support your family and loved ones after your death and it can be used to tell them more about you and your faith.

FaithMessages™
A company that provides education, training and materials on how to live a more spirit-filled life and how to give spiritual and emotional support to family and loved ones after your death through the Spiritual Trust™ System. Darin Manis, the author of this book, is the founder and CEO of FaithMessages.

Family fund
A fund into which each person in the family contributes to be used for the Lord's work. You can use your Family Fund to help pay a friend's doctor bills, fund missionaries, send a youth to camp, provide bibles, feed the hungry, etc. Your Family Fund helps to develop a family tradition of stewardship and a family heritage of giving back.

Financial trust
A legal arrangement through which something of value is owned by a person or entity for the benefit of another. Trusts can give you control over what happens to certain assets after your death. A financial trust may also be used to secure tax benefits.

Foundation
An organization or institution established by endowment, usually with provisions for future maintenance and support.

Generational birthday messages
An "interview" of your children on their birthdays to be delivered to *their* children when they reach that same age.

Generational witnessing
A type of FaithMessage prepared by you for future generations of your family wherein you witness to them and share your faith. With generational witnessing, you can water the spiritual seeds you have planted during your life, long after your death.

Goodbye messages
Usually a brief message to be delivered to your family and friends shortly after you die expressing your love and other sentiments. This message gives you an opportunity to say goodbye until you are able to see them again in heaven.

Going digital
The process of putting your pictures, video and other memories in a digital format so that they are preserved for the future.

Grief
The intense physical, emotional and spiritual suffering caused by the loss of a loved one.

Heritage
The memories and traditions about a person or family that are passed down through generations.

Indirect support
Support you arrange for your family or loved ones to be provided *by others*, such as your executor, friends, minister or other family members.

Intercessory prayer
To plead to God on behalf of another through earnest prayer.

Legacy Journal
Legacy Journals are a powerful way to leave your messages to your children and descendants. They are created on a daily, weekly or monthly basis and they focus more on topics upon which you want to communicate a particular message. A Legacy Journal's entries are always for the benefit of your family - they are messages to *them*.

LifeAlbum™
A digital version of a scrapbook or photo album on an interactive CD ROM. It offers many benefits that scrapbooks cannot. A Life Album not only stores your pictures, but it allows you to record your voice narrations of your photos as well. You can also include video clips, titles and key words. This allows you to view your pictures and video clips side by side on the same format.

LifeMessage
A LifeMessage is a message addressing an important issue of life to be delivered to a person or persons at a time of your choosing, including after your death. A LifeMessage can be written, typed, audio or video. A LifeMessage may be used to support your family and loved ones after your death and it may be used to tell them more about you.

LifeMessages®
A company that helps people create LifeMessages, LifeStories, LifeTributes and other similar products that enable them to capture the past, preserve the present, and influence the future. Darin Manis, the author of this book, is founder and CEO of LifeMessages®. Its web site may be found at www.lifemessages.com.

LifeStory
A compilation of stories and facts about the events and essence of your life. A LifeStory can be an easy stroll down memory lane, highlights from any chapter in your life, or a summary of your life experiences organized into broad themes such as spiritual journeys, personal callings, lessons learned or experiences worth sharing. There are three primary types of LifeStories: chronological, essence and spiritual. These three types can be, and often are woven together into the tapestry of your life.

LifeTribute
A LifeTribute preserves the memory of a loved one for future generations even though that person was unable to prepare their LifeStory during their lifetime. A LifeTribute can encompass the lives of a couple as well as an individual. A LifeTribute is an excellent way to preserve prized stories and memories about a lost love.

Media tools
The primary formats with which you will be creating your trusts such as video, audio, written words and photographs.

Mentor
A trusted counselor or advisor that you select to provide a supporting role in the life of a particular loved one after you have passed away.

Mourning
The expression of grief for the death of a loved one. A period of time for which the signs of grief are shown.

Omnipresent
Present in all places at all times.

POD- Payable on Death form
"Payable on Death" form that is provided by your bank. On this form, you may leave instructions that your executor receives the entire amount of the account upon your death.

Prayer Trust
Prayer Trusts are created by asking others to pray for specific requests that you have after you pass away. They are implemented by the prayer partners you select when the time for the requested prayer has come.

Recipient
A person who receives any Spiritual Trust component.

Sequential birthday messages
Birthday messages you prepare well in advance to be sent to your loved ones such as your children or grandchildren on their birthdays, even if you are not alive to deliver them yourself.

Glossary of Terms

Spiritual inheritance
You don't have to leave money or possessions to provide a valuable inheritance to your family and loved ones. Leave spiritual nuggets of wisdom and truth that far surpass the value of material wealth and possessions.

Spiritual investing
Giving a portion of your money and other resources, out of love and obedience, to the work of the Lord. Spiritually investing is more than giving, it is the creation of your spiritual portfolio through which you receive spiritual rewards and benefits.

Spiritual LifeStory
A LifeStory that focuses on your spiritual beliefs, ideologies, convictions, practices, and, most importantly, your witness. A Spiritual LifeStory reinforces values and creates a sense of family heritage and strengthens emotional and spiritual bonds. A Spiritual LifeStory can address subjects from the Christian perspective and plant deep and sturdy roots from which your family can grow and develop spiritually.

Spiritual mutual funds
The diversification of your spiritual investments into a variety of causes.

Spiritual philanthropist
Voluntary giving for the spiritual good of others. Spiritual philanthropy does not require any degree of financial wealth; it only requires a mindset to do good for others.

Spiritual portfolio
The heavenly portfolio you build up through your spiritual investing. It consists of heavenly rewards, crowns, treasure, promises and blessings. Although your financial portfolio can't go with you, your spiritual portfolio will be waiting for you.

Spiritual Trust™
Any one of the four Trusts addressed in this book: a Support Trust, Prayer Trust, Legacy Trust, or Stewardship Trust. A Spiritual Trust is an expression of your faith, love and spiritual responsibility that transcends your life on earth.

Spiritual Trust components
An application of a Spiritual Trust. For example, a Legacy Journal and LifeStory are components of a Legacy Trust. Each Spiritual Trust has many components.

Spiritual Trust™ System
The system outlined in this book for creating and implementing your Spiritual Trusts.

Spiritual Trust™ System consultant
Individuals trained to provide professional and efficient support through any and all aspects of the four-step creation and implementation process. You can use a consultant for the entire Trust you create or just for an aspect or Trust component on which you want some help.

Stewardship
Being entrusted with another's wealth or property and charged with the responsibility of managing it in the owner's best interest.

Stewardship Trust
A Stewardship Trust is a spiritual tool that involves managing the wealth and possessions you have been given by God. A Stewardship Trust is a spiritual application of your financial planning. A Stewardship Trust is the process of making certain financial arrangements during life that reap spiritual dividends during and after your life.

Support Trust
A Support Trust is a means for you to provide emotional and spiritual support for your family in the event of your death. You create your Trust, properly store it and, when you pass away, your chosen executor delivers the Trust contents according to your instructions.

Time-warping message
A message recorded on *your* birthday to be delivered on your *child's* birthday when they reach the *same* age — their parallel birthday!

Trust box
A fire-rated box, such as a portable safe or safety deposit box, in which your Trust Directives and Spiritual Trust components are stored pending delivery.

Trust Directives
A written guide created for your family or Spiritual Trust executors that clearly conveys your wishes and directives concerning the delivery or execution of the Spiritual Trusts you have created. A sample format for your Trust Directives is in Appendix A of this book.

Trust institution
Refers to any trust company or bank and trust with a trust department that handles financial or monetary trusts.

Video montage
A short (usually 3 to 20 minute) multimedia "movie" of a person's life or an event, experience, or part of that life. Includes pictures, short videos clips, background music and voiceovers to emphasize a theme or themes.

Video will
A video will is not a replacement for your written will. Rather, it is a way for you to explain decisions you have made in your estate distribution.

Will
A will provides for the distribution of your assets upon death.

Workbooks
Guidebooks that walk you step-by-step through the process from your initial vision to creation and application of your Spiritual Trusts. These books are filled with additional details, creative ideas, forms, and other resources.

INDEX

A

Advisors, 61
A Grace Disguised, 62
A Grief Observed, 31
Albums, 122–123, 208–210
Alcorn, Randy, 12, 129, 134
All good things, prayer for, 75
Alternative
    executors, 231–232, 234
    recipients, 232
American Association of Fund Raising Counsel (AAFRC), 145
American Bible Society, 146
American Council on Gift Annuities, 155
"Angels Watching Over Me," 72
Anger, in grieving, 20, 32
Anniversary benchmark
    of death, 45–46
    wedding, 45
Annuity plans, 155
Apostle Paul, 141
Appreciated securities, 153, 155
Archiving, 201, 216. *See also* Preservation
A Time to Grieve, 62
Audiocassettes / audiotapes, 202, 203, 205–206, 216
Audio journals, 118–119
Audio recording
    for albums and scrapbooks, 122
    for Legacy Trusts, 100, 105, 112, 113, 117
    for Spiritual Trusts, 188–193, 202, 203, 204
    for Support Trusts, 22, 44, 55, 57
Autobiography, 97, 100
    spiritual, 103

B

Bank. *See also* Trust institution
    funding of Trust through, 233–234
Benchmarks, 38, 41, 53, 55, 92, 108, 109–113, 116, 229
    anniversary, 45–46
    birthday, 46, 109
    Christmas, 46–47
    graduations, 114–115

holiday, 46
monthly, 42–44
prayer at, 86, 87
weddings, 115–116
Beneficiary(ies), 37
executor as, 233
of LifeStory, 102
Prayer Trust, 71–72, 75, 77, 78, 80, 83, 87
of Stewardship Trust, 156
trust institution as partial, 230
Bereavement, 14, 19, 49, 94. *See also* Grief and grieving
family resources for, 62–63
phase of grieving, 20, 38–40, 63, 108
prayer during, 72, 83–86
Bereavement Magazine, 63
Bible, 11, 14, 49, 98, 103
believers, 136
discussion of blessings, 134
financial discussion in, 132, 133, 140
legacy examples in, 6
ministries, 146
stewardship discussion in, 7, 158
translation ministries, 146
Birthday benchmark messages, 46, 109
generational, 112
handwritten, 191
milestone, 109–112
sequential, 112–114
Blessings
financial, 129–130, 132, 133, 137, 139, 158, 171
prayer for, 74–75, 86
spiritual, 171
Blue, Ron, 157
Bonds, strengthening, 111
Books. *See* Resources
Brainstorming, 178
Buddy system, 224
Busby, Dan, 152
Byeulogies, 5, 28–29, 30

C

Camcorder, 184, 188, 203
Campus Crusade for Christ, 147
Cassette recorder, standard, 189

Index

CD
    albums and scrapbooks on, 122
    example of graduation, 115
    photo, 195
    ROM, 195, 204, 208, 210
    for storing Spiritual Trusts, 203, 204, 214, 216
Centering Corporation, 63
Charities, 150, 151, 152, 155, 156
Charity Navigator, 150
Children, 70. *See also* Benchmarks; Birthday
    audio recordings with, 188
    involvement in video Trust components, 187
    Legacy Trust for, 95, 112, 117
    and loss/grieving, 15, 16, 40, 49
    messages to, 16, 42, 53-54, 55, 117
    supporting, 51–53, 61
    video for, 58, 112
Christ. *See* Jesus
Christian and Missionary Alliance, 145
Christian Broadcasting Network, 147
Christian Children's Fund, 148
Christians
    evangelical, 150
    number of, 136
Christian Service Charities, 150
Christmas benchmark, 46–47, 48, 222
I Chronicles 4:10, 75
Church
    as beneficiary of Stewardship Trust, 156
    financial needs of, 143, 144, 145, 148;149
    planting and building, 146–147
    as prayer partners, 79
    as recipients of Stewardship Trust, 7, 148
    role in initial phase of grieving, 81–82
2 Corinthians 5:10, 141
Chronological LifeStory, 100–101, 102
Comfort, 72
Compassion, 15, 40, 51
Compassion International, 148
Compose step of creating Spiritual Trust, 180–181, 200
Computer-generated Trust components, 193
Computerized journals, 120–121
Confessions of a Grieving Christian, 62
Consumption, 132–133
Contingency plans, 231–232, 234
Copies of Trust components, 212–213, 214, 217
2 Corinthians, 5:8, 25, 59

Council on Foundations, 150
Counseling, grief, 49
Creation step in developing Spiritual Trust, 165, 170, 177, 200
Crisis of faith, 5, 31–32

D

Death, 25
    dealing with, 12–14, 18
    discussing, 64
    and dying, 8–9, 12
    and funeral, 25
    and grieving, 20
    messages defending your, 31–34
    and Support Trust, 15

Death Through the Eyes of a Funeral Director, 36

Delivery
    in-house, 222
    options, 220–223, 234
    pre or personal, 221–222
    step in developing Spiritual Trust, 166, 170, 201, 234

Dennis, David, 55
Depreciated securities, 154
Descendants, 95, 102, 104, 125. *See also* Beneficiaries
    witnessing to, 123

Deuteronomy 6:6–7, 109
Deuteronomy 8:17,18, 129

Digital
    backups/copies, 208, 213
    basics, 204
    cameras, 208
    formats, 203–204, 216
    images, 194, 195, 198, 208
    LifeAlbum, 196
    preservation, 203–204, 208
    scrapbooks, 196
    video, 183, 205, 206
    voice recorder, 189, 190

Directive. *See* Trust Directives
Direct support messages, 48–49
Dobson, Dr. James, 150
Documents, storing, 213. *See also* Paper
Draft step in creating Spiritual Trust, 178–180, 200
DVD, 57, 107, 195, 204, 210, 212
    storing, 214, 216
    video montage, 208
DV tape, 203

E

Earll, Steven, 16, 40, 61
Ecclesiastes 3:1, 14, 39
Education, fundraising for, 147
Ellenberg, William, 35
Elliot, Jim, 129
Emotional support, 11, 12, 13, 53, 72
Emotions accompanying grief, 18–19
Empty Tomb, 148
Ephesians 1:3, 74
Essence LifeStory, 102–103
Estate
    planning, 156, 157
    taxes, 158
Eternal life / eternity
    Legacy Trusts and, 123, 125
    Stewardship Trusts and, 132, 142, 158
    Support Trusts and, 8, 11, 13, 14, 25, 27, 64, 73, 88
Eulogies, 5, 25–27, 28, 178
Evangelical Council for Financial Accountability (ECFA), 149–150
Evangelism, 145, 147, 150
Everyone Dies!, 35
Examples
    Bob's byeulogy, 30
    Carl's generational witnessing, 124
    David's audio journal, 118–119
    Dustin's appreciated securities, 153
    Evelyn's birthday messages, 113
    John and Susan
        anniversary benchmark, 46
        byeulogy message, 28–29
        Christmas benchmark, 47–48
        defending death message, 32–33
        eulogy video message, 26–27
        funeral arrangements, 34
        LifeMessage, 43–44
        memories, 59–60
        ongoing support, 53, 60
        Prayer Trust, 81–82, 83–86
        Support Trust, 16–17
        video Goodbye Message, 23–24
        wedding anniversary, 45
    Hunter's missions investment, 146
    Manis, Isham, 96–97
    Mary, 71, 74, 75
    Patricia, 104, 119–120

Rick and Deborah, 108–110
Sarah and Hannah, 114–115, 116
Executor(s)
    alternative, 231–232, 234
    characteristics of, 223–225
    duties/responsibilities of, 223, 229
    funding for, 232–234
    Prayer Trust, 78, 79, 81, 86, 87
    Legacy Trust, 115
    Request Outline, 226–227
    Spiritual Trust, 166, 213, 214–215, 219, 222–223, 224
    Support Trust, 12, 36, 45, 46, 62, 78
    trust institution as, 228

F

Faith, 3, 4, 6, 9, 14, 16, 17, 40, 41, 53, 54, 88, 92, 98, 118, 123, 132, 167
    crisis of, 5, 31–32
    prayer and, 70, 76, 87
FaithMessages, 41, 53, 96, 108, 115
    example, 119–120, 124–125
Family
    culture, 92
    development needs, 148
    Fund, 153
    heritage, 94, 103, 153
    history, 92, 94, 99, 104, 107
    involvement in your, 106
    LifeStory and, 102, 105
    messages from, 97
    photographs, 95
    prayer for, 78, 80, 81, 83, 85
    as prayer partners, 76, 77
    prayers of protection for, 73
    prayers of salvation for, 73–74
    relationships, 105
    stories, 92
    as Spiritual Trust executor, 224
    traditions, 92
    tree, 106
    video, 57
Family support, 64
    through direct support, 48–49
    through indirect messages, 50–51
    Legacy Trust and, 55
    Stewardship Trust and, 139

Family Traditions, 93–94
Fear, 17
Feed The Children, 148
Feelings accompanying grief, 18–19
Fellowship of Christian Athletes, 147
Film, preserving/storing, 202, 211–212, 216
Finalize step in creating Spiritual Trust, 181, 200
Financial
    arrangements, 36–37
    blessings, 132, 134, 158, 171
    needs of church, 143, 144
    planning, 127, 128
    portfolios, 7, 140, 151, 152
    resources, 137
    support/security, 12, 37, 155
    trusts, comparison with Spiritual Trusts, 4, 139
    views expressed in Bible, 130–132
Focus on the Family, 61, 148
Food For the Poor, 148
Foreign missions, 144–146
Foresight, 3
Formats, 214
    audiotape, 206
    digital, 203, 208, 216
    videotape, 206
Foundation Center, 150
Foundations, 150, 151
Four-step process, 167
Friends
    as prayer partners, 76, 77
    as Spiritual Trust executors, 224
Fundraising, 147
Funeral, 20, 22, 24, 25, 30, 81
    arrangements, 34–36
    messages, 25, 27, 28, 30

G

Genealogy (Patricia), 104
Generational
    birthday messages, 112
    witnessing, 6, 123–125
Generations, passing legacy to, 97–98, 99, 107
Gift, spiritual, 140
Giving, financial, 132, 136, 140, 141, 142–143, 145, 158
Goals, setting, 54–54

God, 70, 103
    anger at, 31, 32
    faith in, 31
Goodbye Messages, 22–25
Good Grief Resources, 63
Grace, 98, 103
    giving through, 142
Graduation messages, 114–115
Graham, Billy, 150
Grandchildren, 70
    audio recordings with, 188
    messages to, 53–54, 55, 112, 117
    video recordings with, 187
Grandparents, 54, 93, 94, 95, 97
    involvement in your LifeStory, 106
    LifeTribute to, 106–107
    of living, 105–106
    messages to grandchildren, 111
Grant, Amy, 72
Greed, 135. *See also* Materialism
Grief and grieving, 6, 11, 14, 19–21, 36, 39, 46, 49, 94
    bereavement phase of, 38, 41, 83–86
    of children, 40, 49, 51–53
    counseling, 49
    initial support phase of, 22, 78, 81, 83
    ongoing phase of, 53–61, 86–87
    phases of, 19–21, 22, 63
    prayer during, 72, 81, 83
    resources on, 62–63
    of spouse, 40
Guilt, 49

H

Habitat For Humanity, 148
Halverson, Richard, 130
Handwritten Trust components, 191–193, 202, 210
Healing, 21, 39, 59, 63
    prayers for, 51
Henry, Matthew, 11
Heritage, 93–94, 96, 99, 128, 139, 153, 158, 171
Hickey, Marilyn, 78
Hicks, Ralph, 35
History; family, 92, 94, 99, 104, 107
    personal, 98
Hoarding, 138
Holiday benchmark messages, 46

Index

Holtkamp, Sue, 32
Holy Spirit, 8
    Legacy Trusts and, 98, 103, 104, 123
    Prayer Trusts and, 74, 75, 76, 79, 87
    Steward Trusts and, 142, 143
Honesty, in LifeStory and Spiritual Trusts, 102, 181
Hope, 8, 115
Humanitarian ministries, 148
Humor, in Spiritual Trusts, 181

I

Illness, life-threatening, 13, 22
Image Permanence Institute, 212
Images. *See also* Photographs; Pictures
    digital, 208
    in Spiritual Trust, 194, 195–196, 198, 200
Indirect support, 50–51
Inheritance (spiritual), 97, 98, 104, 105, 123
In-house delivery of Spiritual Trust, 222
Initial phase of grieving, 20, 22, 38
    prayer support during, 78, 81–83
Insurance, life, 35, 37, 128, 155, 156, 157
Intercessors International, 78
International Bible Society, 146
International giving, 145
Internet, prayer requests on, 79
Investment, spiritual, 134–135, 141–142, 150, 151, 158
    options, 143, 144, 145, 148–149, 158

J

Jesus, 5, 8, 11, 14, 27, 34, 40, 59, 73, 74, 75, 98, 103, 111, 112, 144
    salvation message of, 123, 145
    teachings on money and wealth, 9, 130, 132–134, 142
Jimmy Hodges Ministries International, 145
John 14:26, 75
Journal, 49, 117, 121, 202, 210. *See also* Legacy Journals
    handwritten, 191
    and journaling, 120

K

Kramp, Erin, 53
Kushner, Harold S., 51

L

Legacy, 221. *See also* Legacy Trust.
  messages, 53, 97, 125
  spiritual, 97, 104, 158, 171
Legacy Journals, 108, 117–118, 168, 182
  audio, 118–119
  computerized, 120–121
  digital, 196
  pictures in, 195
  video, 121–122
  written, 119–120, 191
Legacy Trust, 1, 6, 53, 55, 58, 60, 91, 94, 97–98, 104, 108, 123, 125, 171
  components in, 175
  delivery of, 116, 221
  description of, 92
  executor of, 224
  moral need for, 93–94
  types of, 95–96
Legal and financial arrangements, 36–37
Letter, 54–55, 202
  to church after your death, 83
  goodbye, 22
  handwritten, 210
  in LifeTribute, 107
Lewis, C. S., 31, 56
L'Engle, Madeleine, 56
LifeAlbum, digital, 196, 208
Life insurance, 35, 37, 128, 155, 156, 157, 233
  trust institution as partial beneficiary of, 230
LifeMessages, 41, 43, 53, 96, 108
LifeStory, 55, 98–100, 184, 202, 221. *See also* LifeTributes, 106–107
  chronological, 100–101, 102, 195, 197, 199
  creating, 197–200
  digital images in, 195
  essence, 102–103, 197, 199
  handwritten, 191
  of living parents and grandparents, 105–106
  outline, 178, 199;
  spiritual, 103–105, 197, 199
  video, 105
LifeTributes, 106–107, 184, 191, 195
Lincoln, Abraham, 168
Listening, 50, 51
Living with the End in Mind, 53, 62
Loneliness, 20

Loss, 20, 51.
    coping with, 14–16, 18
    example of, 16–17.
Love, 3, 8, 18, 22, 98, 167
    Legacy Journal as message of, 117
Luke 16:19–31, 9

M

MacDonald, William, 138
Macro method, 78–79
Magnetic tapes, 203, 205–206, 208, 211, 214
Marriage. *See* Weddings
Matching funds, 149
Materialism, 132–133, 135
Matthew 18:19–20, 80
Media tools, 181, 182–183, 200, 202
Mementos and heirlooms, designation of, 37–38
Memorial
    arrangements, 34–36
    messages, 25
Memories, 46, 54, 55, 63, 97, 107, 202
    audio, 206
    fading, 56–58, 94
    on film, 211
    no more, 60
    painful, 198–199
    picture, 56
    video, 56, 206
    wrong, 59–60
Memory bank, 55–56, 57, 60
Men's ministries, 148
Mentors, 61
Mercy, 103
Mercy Corps, 148
Messages, 12, 16, 22, 24, 96, 108, 179. *See also* FaithMessages; LifeMessages
    audio, 6, 57, 188–191, 200
    benchmark, 41–48
    birthday, 46, 109, 109, 195
    byeulogy, 5, 28–30
    defending your death, 31–34
    delivering, 229
    eulogy, 25–27
    example of funeral, 26
    Goodbye, 22–25
    handwritten, 191–193, 202

holiday, 46–47
joint, 62
legacy, 53, 92, 97
Legacy Journal, 117
milestone birthday, 110
ongoing, 53, 54, 59
from parents, 97
prayer, 11, 54
of salvation, 124
time-warping, 111
typed, 191, 193–194, 200, 202
video, 6, 27, 57, 187, 200
written, 6, 57, 191, 200
Micro method, 77
Milestone birthday messages, 109–112
Mindset, spiritual, 8, 25, 87, 140
Mini-cassette recorder, 189
Minister
as prayer partner, 77
as resource, 62
Ministries, 145, 149–150, 151, 152
as beneficiaries of Stewardship Trust, 156
evangelical, 150
humanitarian, 148
as prayer partners, 78
providing Bibles as, 146
as recipient of Spiritual Trust, 7
Missions, 143, 149–150
foreign, 144–146
Money, 135–136, 137, 138. *See also* Financial
Monthly benchmarks, 42–44
Morals, 93, 98
Mortality, 11, 13, 17, 20, 27. *See also* Death
Mourning, 18, 25, 36, 49. *See also* Bereavement; Grief and grieving
Multimedia presentations, 30. *See also* Video montage
Mutual funds, spiritual, 151

N

National Center for Family Philanthropy, 150
Navigators, 148
"Noah rule," 168
Nonprofits, 152, 154, 156

O

Obituary, 35, 36, 202
Ongoing phase of grieving, 20, 53, 55, 60, 63

Index

    prayer support during, 86–87
Outline
    life chapters, 199–200
    for Spiritual Trust, 178, 179, 180

P

Paper documents, preserving and storing, 210–211, 214, 216
Parallel messages, 111
Parents, 94, 95
    involvement in your LifeStory, 106
    LifeStory of living, 105–106
    LifeTribute to, 106–107
    messages from, 54, 97
    in today's society, 93
Parables, about money, 9, 132, 138, 140
Patience, 50
Peace, Richard, 103, 104
Peter, Lawrence (Peter Principle), 168
I Peter 3:12, 76
I Peter 5:8, 73
Philanthropy, spiritual, 139–141
Photo
    albums, 122–123, 195, 208–210
    CDs, 195
Photographs, 194, 196, 200, 202, 203. *See also* Pictures, 194
    storing/preserving, 208–210, 214, 216–217
Physician Assisted Suicide: Not Worth Living, 61
Pictures, 56, 92, 95, 198. *See also* Photographs
    digital, 194, 196
    in LifeStory, 101, 105
    in LifeTribute, 107
    preserving, 208
    in Spiritual Trust, 194, 195–196
Portfolios
    financial, 7, 140, 142, 151, 152
    spiritual, 7, 140–141, 142, 143, 145, 151, 155
Prayer, 9, 11, 64, 69–70, 80, 85, 98, 132, 143
    answers to, 70, 71
    at benchmarks, 86–87
    beneficiaries, 87
    chains, 77, 79, 83, 86
    delivering, 221
    for family, 78, 80, 81, 83, 85, 86
    for healing, 51
    for ministries, 147
The Prayer of Jabez, 75

Prayer partners, 1, 6, 70, 72, 73, 76–77, 79–80
    on Internet, 79
    ministries as, 78; as Spiritual Trust executor, 224
Prayer Trust, 1, 6, 22, 53, 69–70, 73, 74, 76, 78, 79, 80, 81, 88, 171, 224
    beneficiaries of, 71–72, 75, 77, 83, 86
    components in, 174
Pre delivery option, 221–222
Prend, Ashley Davis, 21, 45
Preservation, 208–210, 216
    digital, 203–204, 205
    of paper documents, 210–211
    of video components, 206–208
Protection, 171
    prayers for, 72–73, 86
Proverbs 13:22, 97
Proverbs 15:22, 152
Psalms, 49, 98

R

Real estate donation, 154
Recipients, Trust, 164, 165–166, 167, 179, 181, 182, 187, 192, 200, 201, 202. *See also* Beneficiaries
    alternative, 232
    delivering Trusts to, 220–221, 230
    selecting, 171, 172–173, 176
    of video, 187.
Remarriage, 42, 44
Resources for family, 62–63
Retirement plans, 156
Revise step in creating Spiritual Trust, 180, 200
Romans 8:5, 8; 26–28, 76
Ronsvalle, John and Sylvia, 136

S

Sadness, 20
Safety deposit box, 213, 214–216, 217
Salvation, 123, 132, 145
    example of message, 124
    prayers for, 73–74
Samaritans Purse, 148
Satan, 31, 52, 53, 73, 87, 98, 133, 141
Scrapbooks, 122–123, 194, 195, 208–210
    digital, 196
    video, 196

Scriptures, 80, 95, 104. *See also* Bible
    teachings about money and giving, 130–132, 138–139, 142, 147
Securities
    appreciated, 153, 155
    depreciated, 154
Selection step in developing Spiritual Trust, 165, 170, 171
    components, 173–176
    recipients, 172–173
Self-exploration, 102
Sensitivity, 21, 50, 51, 64
Sequential birthday messages, 112–114
Share America, 150
Shock, in initial phase of grieving, 20, 22, 81
Sibling. *See* Family
Single parent, 62
Sittser, Gerald, 62
Slides, storing, 208, 217
Society, decline of, 93
Sony study, 205
Spending. *See* Financial
Spiritual
    crisis, 20
    gifts, 140
    health, 144
    heritage, 92, 128
    inheritance, 98
    journey, 4, 99, 104
    legacy, 95, 97, 104
    maturity, 76, 87, 98, 139
    mindset, 8–9, 25, 87, 140
    mutual funds, 151
    philanthropy, 139–140
    portfolios, 7, 25, 87, 140–141, 142, 143, 145, 151, 155, 158
    principles, 4
    stewardship, 133
    support, 11, 12–13, 22, 53, 53, 72, 86, 144, 171
    values, 92
Spiritual investments, 141–142
    giving through, 142–143
    options, 143–151
    funding at death, 155–158
    funding during your life, 153–155
Spirituality, stewardship and, 7
Spiritual LifeStory, 103–105
Spiritual Trusts, 8–9, 63, 164, 167, 168, 170, 171
    archiving, 201, 202, 216
    characteristics of, 3–4

chart, 162–163
components of, 4–5, 164, 166, 168, 172, 173–176, 205
compose step of creating, 180–181, 200
computer-generated, 193–194
creation step of, 177, 200
delivering, 219, 234
digital images in, 195
draft, 178–180, 200
executor, 81, 214–215, 222–223, 228, 234
finalization step in creating, 181–182, 200
handwritten, 191–193
images and photographs in, 194–196
outline, 178, 179, 180, 200
revision step in creating, 180, 200
storing, 201, 205, 214, 228
typed, 191, 193–194, 200
types of, 1, 4–5
written, 191, 200
Spiritual Trust System, 2, 3, 9, 11, 41, 58, 62, 77, 100, 128, 219
consultant, 181
evaluating, 182
as a four-step process, 165–166, 168, 169 (chart), 170
Spouse
assistance for, 61–62
involvement in video recordings, 187
phases of, 19–21, 22
remarriage of, 42, 44
support for grieving, 40
Support Trust for, 41, 63
video for, 58
Staudacher, Carol, 19, 20, 39, 43, 54, 62
Stewardship
church's, 149
and taxes, 152
Stewardship Trusts, 1, 7, 127–129, 133, 134, 137, 139, 140, 158
assets, 157–158
components in, 175
delivery of, 221
executor, 224
funding of, 151–152, 153, 15
need for, 129–130
options, 143–144
selecting recipients for, 172
Stock options, 154
Storage. *See also* Preservation
of audiotapes, 201–208, 216
of digital images, 208

fees, 231
of film, 211–212, 216
locations, 214–216
of paper documents, 210–211, 214
of photos and slides, 208–210, 214, 216–217
step in developing Spiritual Trust, 166, 170, 201, 213
of tapes, 207
in Trust box, 213–214
by trust institution, 229
of videotapes, 205–208, 216
Stories, family, 92, 93, 96, 100, 107. *See also* LifeStory; LifeTribute
Support
for children, 51–53
churches as, 144
direct, 48–49
emotional, 11, 12, 53
financial, 12, 37
indirect, 50–51
ongoing, 53, 55
prayer, 11, 80, 83, 171, 224
spiritual, 11, 12–13, 22, 53, 81, 171
timing of, 63
Support Trust, 1, 5, 11–12, 14, 15–16, 17, 18, 21, 62, 63, 64
components in, 174
delivering, 221, 224
selecting, 171

T

Tapes, magnetic, 203, 205, 208, 211, 214
Taxes
capital gains, 153, 154, 157–158
estate, 158
stewardship and, 152, 156
Time-warping messages, 111
I Timothy 2:1, 72
Tithing, 137, 142
Traditions, family, 92, 99, 103
Trust. *See also* individual Trusts
assets, 158
as characteristic of executor, 223–225
components, 55, 173–176, 178, 179, 180, 181, 182, 213, 219–220
financial/monetary, 157–158, 222, 228, 230, 231
non-monetary, 228–229, 230
recipients, 172–173, 176
Trust box, 164, 187, 213–214, 222

Trust Directives, 164, 166, 176, 182, 213, 217, 219–220, 222–223, 229, 230, 232, 233, 234, 236 (Appendix A)
Trustee, 222
Trust institution, 228, 231
    as partial beneficiary, 230
    vault, 214, 216, 217, 229, 230
Trust media tools, 182–183
Typed messages in Spiritual Trust components, 191, 193–194, 200, 202

U

Ultraviolet (UV) radiation, effects of, 210

V

Values, spiritual, 92, 103
VHS tapes, 26, 47–48, 183, 196, 202, 205, 206, 214, 216
Video montage, 305, 28–29, 30–31, 57, 122, 195–196
    DVD, 208
Video recording
    for albums and scrapbooks, 122–123
    of Legacy Trusts, 97, 100, 101, 112, 113, 117
    Rick and Deborah, 110
    of Support Trusts, 22, 27, 44, 55, 56–57, 181
    tips, 184–187
    of Trust components, 183–187, 200, 202
Video
    camcorder, 183
    clips, 196
    digital, 183, 203, 205
    journals, 121–122
    LifeStory, 105
    Life Tribute, 107
    preserving, 187
    scrapbook, 196
    Trust components, 195
    will, 38
Videographers, professional, 184
Videotapes, 205–206, 216
    transferring to DVD or CD ROM, 204
Visual aids, 198
Voice recorders, 189–191
Voice recording
    of albums and scrapbooks, 122
    for audio journal, 118, 119
    for funeral, 25–26

of memories, 105
for scrapbook, 122
of Spiritual Trust, 188–191

W

Wagner, Peter, 76
Wealth, 134, 136, 142, 158. *See also* Financial
Wedding
  anniversary, 45
  Legacy messages, 115
Weiss, Doug, 98, 99
Wesley, John, 60
Will, 37, 38, 128, 157, 222, 230
  video, 38
Wilhite, B. J., 70
Wilkinson, Bruce, 75
Witnessing, generational, 123–125
Wolfelt, Alan D., 18
Women of Faith, 148
Women's ministries, 148
World Vision, 148
Work in Progress, 182, 176, 182, 221
  example, 250 (Appendix B)
Written journals, 119–120
Written message
  eulogy as, 25
  LifeStory as, 100
  in Spiritual Trust, 181, 191, 200
Wycliffe Bible translation ministry, 146

Y

Youth, organizations for, 147
Youth for Christ, 147

Z

Zigler, Zig, 39, 62, 81
Zondervan 2002 Church and Nonprofit Organization Tax and Financial Guide, 152

ABOUT THE AUTHORS

Darin Manis is a businessman living in Colorado Springs with his wife and two children. Darin is the CEO of LifeMessages, Inc., which he started in 1999 because he perceived a need to help people preserve their family memories and pass down those memories to future generations through high-tech, yet high-touch, products and services. Shortly thereafter, Darin launched a separate division of LifeMessages, called FaithMessages. This division is focused on helping people capture the essence of their faith and pass it down through time. As part of his work for FaithMessages, Darin recognized the need for a book that would help people do this themselves and would also help people support their family and loved ones spiritually and emotionally after they die.

Dr. Milton "Skip" Smith is an attorney who helped Darin launch LifeMessages, Inc. Skip resigned as a Member of one of the largest law firms in Colorado to become the President of LifeMessages. Skip is a graduate of the U.S. Air Force Academy, the George Washington University Law School and the McGill University Institute of Air and Space Law, where he received a doctorate in Space law. He has written a book and many articles on a variety of high-tech subjects. Skip is married and has two children. He also lives in Colorado Springs.

Darin and Skip worked together over the last two years developing the Spiritual Trust System embodied in this book and refining the concepts. They have seen the powerful effect of this System on the lives of many people, including their own. They would enjoy learning about how this book has impacted the lives of its readers. Please feel free to contact them at: LifeMessages, Inc., 407 S. Tejon, Colorado Springs, CO 80903.